INSIDERS TALK

HOW TO *SUCCESSFULLY* LOBBY STATE LEGISLATURES

Over the Years—Legislative Experts' Reviews of Our Lobbying Book and Training Seminars

"Not only has Bob Guyer written THE BOOK on lobbying at the state level... his seminars are of exceptional value for novices and seasoned government affairs specialists alike. If you are looking for an exceptional 'one-stop-shop' for lobbying strategies and tactics, Mr. Guyer's book is the place to go."

—Ron Meyers, Esq.
Speaker pro tempore
Washington House of Representatives (former)

"Mr. Guyer is an excellent presenter and has a wealth of knowledge and experience to share with lobbyists. The two-day seminar is packed with an agenda filled with valuable information and exercises to enhance the skills of a novice or a practitioner. The information he provided was so generic it could be applied to any organization whether it be a union, corporation or nonprofit. When I brought my team we were able to design our strategy for the ensuing session. I can also add that his book is a must if you want to maximize your lobbyist skills by reminding you of the nuts and bolts of lobbying. I always use it as a reference guide."

—Bernal C. Baca, Ed.D.
Lobbyist
AFT Washington AFL-CIO (former)
Centro Latino (Seattle, current)

"While I am a lobbying veteran, the workshop and book provided me with a fresh perspective on advocacy. Mr. Guyer's clear structure and methodology for an effective lobbying campaign added to my own effectiveness with the legislature contributing to me being ranked one of the five best lobbyists in the state of Florida."

—Desinda Wood Carper
Senior Legislative Advocate
Florida League of Cities (former)
Chief Legislative Assistant
Florida State Rep. Sharon Pritchett (current)

INSIDERS TALK

HOW TO *SUCCESSFULLY* LOBBY STATE LEGISLATURES

Guide to State Legislative Lobbying, 4th Edition –
Revised, Updated, Expanded

ROBERT L. GUYER

LOBBY SCHOOL

Books by Robert L. Guyer

Guide to State Legislative Lobbying (2000-2007, 3 editions)

Insiders Talk Series of Best Practices Manuals:
Manual 1. *How to Get and Keep Your First Lobbying Job* (2020)
Manual 2. *Glossary of Legislative Concepts and Representative Terms* (2019)
Manual 3. *How to Successfully Lobby State Legislatures: Guide to State Legislative Lobbying, 4th edition*—Revised, Updated and Expanded (2020)
Manual 4. *Winning with Lobbyists*, Readers edition (2019)
Manual 5. *Winning with Lobbyists*, Professional edition (2019)
Manual 6. *Guide to Executive Branch Agency Rulemaking* (2021, with Chris Micheli)

INSIDERS TALK: HOW TO *SUCCESSFULLY* LOBBY STATE LEGISLATURES: Guide to State Legislative Lobbying, 4th Edition—Revised, Updated, Expanded

Copyright © 2020 Engineering THE LAW, Inc.
Published and Distributed by Engineering THE LAW, Inc.
www.lobbyschool.com

PRINT VERSION DATA
First Edition published 2000, Revised Edition published 2003, Third Edition published 2007. Requests for permission to make copies of any part of this book should be sent to:
Engineering THE LAW, Inc.
13714 N.W. 21 Lane
Gainesville, Florida 32606

Library of Congress Control Number: 2019907640
Main entry under title: Guide to State Legislative Lobbying
Print ISBN: 978-0-9677242-5-6
Ebook ISBN: 978-0-9677242-8-7

Book design by Sarah E. Holroyd (https://sleepingcatbooks.com)

This guide is dedicated to advancing a government of the people and for all the people by fostering the skills individuals and organizations need to influence their state legislatures.

LOBBY SCHOOL

LOBBYIST CAREER DEVELOPMENT PLAN

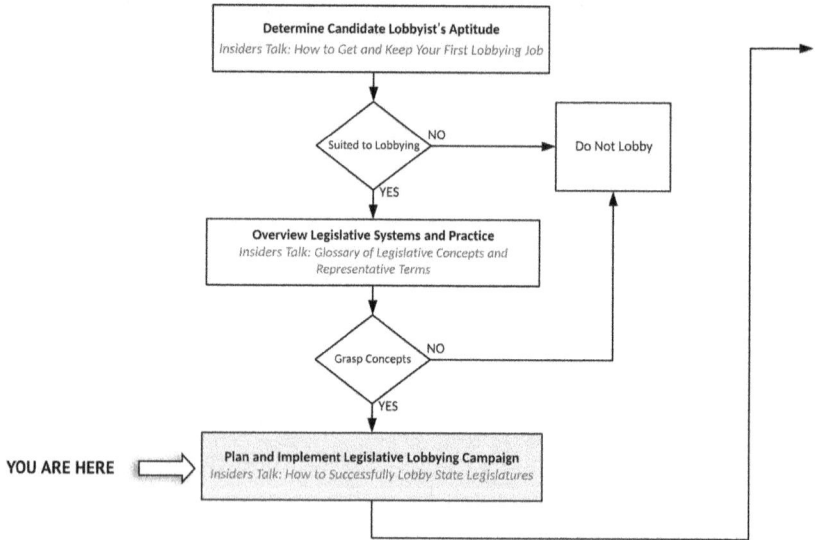

Determine Candidate Lobbyist's Aptitude
Insiders Talk: How to Get and Keep Your First Lobbying Job

Suited to Lobbying — NO → **Do Not Lobby**

YES

Overview Legislative Systems and Practice
Insiders Talk: Glossary of Legislative Concepts and Representative Terms

Grasp Concepts — NO →

YES

YOU ARE HERE ⇨ **Plan and Implement Legislative Lobbying Campaign**
Insiders Talk: How to Successfully Lobby State Legislatures

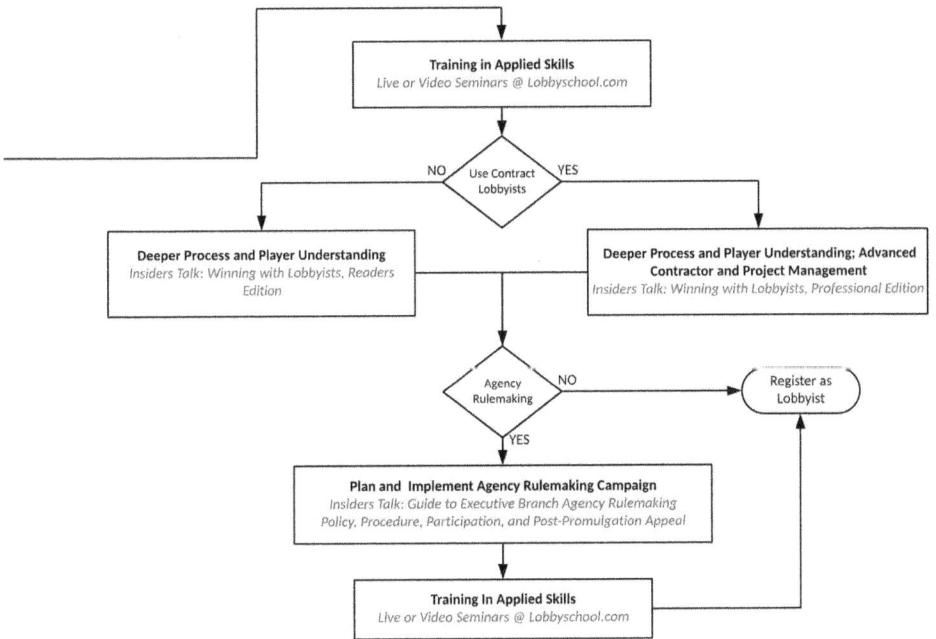

Training in Applied Skills
Live or Video Seminars @ Lobbyschool.com

NO   Use Contract Lobbyists   YES

Deeper Process and Player Understanding
Insiders Talk: Winning with Lobbyists, Readers Edition

Deeper Process and Player Understanding; Advanced Contractor and Project Management
Insiders Talk: Winning with Lobbyists, Professional Edition

Agency Rulemaking   NO

Register as Lobbyist

YES

Plan and Implement Agency Rulemaking Campaign
Insiders Talk: Guide to Executive Branch Agency Rulemaking Policy, Procedure, Participation, and Post-Promulgation Appeal

Training In Applied Skills
Live or Video Seminars @ Lobbyschool.com

How to *Successfully* Lobby State Legislatures—Overview

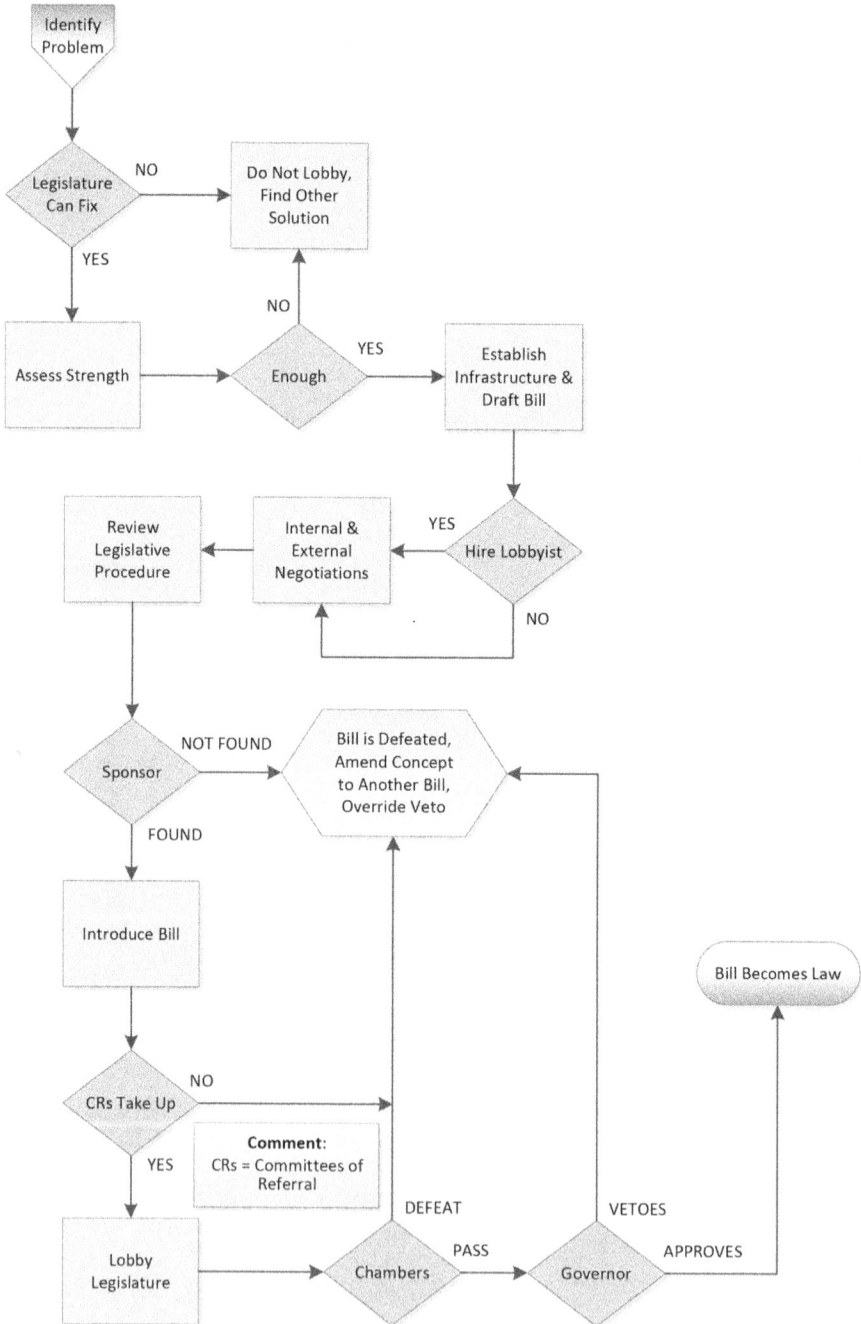

Identify Problem

Legislature Can Fix
- NO → Do Not Lobby, Find Other Solution
- YES ↓

Assess Strength → Enough
- NO → Do Not Lobby, Find Other Solution
- YES → Establish Infrastructure & Draft Bill

Establish Infrastructure & Draft Bill ↓

Hire Lobbyist
- YES → Internal & External Negotiations
- NO ↓

Internal & External Negotiations → Review Legislative Procedure

Review Legislative Procedure ↓

Sponsor
- NOT FOUND → Bill is Defeated, Amend Concept to Another Bill, Override Veto
- FOUND ↓

Introduce Bill ↓

CRs Take Up
- NO → Bill is Defeated, Amend Concept to Another Bill, Override Veto
- YES ↓

Comment:
CRs = Committees of Referral

Lobby Legislature → Chambers
- DEFEAT → Bill is Defeated, Amend Concept to Another Bill, Override Veto
- PASS → Governor

Governor
- VETOES → Bill is Defeated, Amend Concept to Another Bill, Override Veto
- APPROVES → Bill Becomes Law

TABLE OF CONTENTS

CHAPTER 3: DEVELOPING THE LOBBYING CAMPAIGN

CHAPTER 4: HIRING AND WORKING WITH CONTRACT LOBBYISTS

CHAPTER 5: NEGOTIATING WITH SPECIAL INTERESTS

CHAPTER 6: NAVIGATING LEGISLATIVE PROCEDURE

PART II. MEETING THE LEGISLATURE – IMPLEMENTING YOUR LOBBYING CAMPAIGN

CHAPTER 7: MAKING SUCCESSFUL LOBBYING VISITS (STEPS 1 – 6)

Chapter 8: Working with Legislative Committees (Steps 7 – 9)

Chapter 9: Post-CFR and Post-Session Follow-Through (Steps 10 – 25)

FOREWORD

Robert Guyer's *Guide to State Legislative Lobbying*, 4th edition is a timely and important update to this comprehensive lobbying handbook. Gridlock in Congress has led states to consider issues that traditionally were in the federal domain. In today's political environment, federal lobbying isn't enough, making this handbook even more relevant for advocacy professionals across the country.

About 10 years ago as a regional government affairs manager responsible for 15 western states, I attended Bob's two-day seminar. Although I was already a successful and fairly well-seasoned professional, I hoped that the class might offer a few new tips or help me polish existing skills. However, the class, *Guide*, and materials collectively provided a far more extensive learning opportunity than I anticipated.

Building on my previous successes and failures, the training helped me hone strategies for dealing more effectively with my increasing responsibilities. I learned to better identify potential coalition partners beyond natural allies, to more accurately assess my chances of success prior to embarking on a new lobbying effort, and improve my process for hiring and evaluating outside lobbyists. Most importantly, Bob's foundational emphasis on trust through credibility and honesty instilled a greater level of confidence in my own approach to working with lawmakers.

I have been involved with state legislative politics and lobbying for more than 30 years, beginning as an intern during my senior year in college. Today I manage a national state and local lobbying program for a major U.S. wireless carrier. I am confident that whether this is your first time lobbying or you are at the pinnacle of your career, *Guide to State Legislative Lobbying* and Bob's training will increase your effectiveness in advocating for your desired outcome.

Russell J. Sarazen
Senior Director, State Legislative Affairs
T-Mobile US

Insiders Talk
How to *Successfully* Lobby State Legislatures
Guide to State Legislative Lobbying, 4th Edition

This book is a revised, updated, and expanded how-to, hands-on primer describing a basic, simplified model for passing a law. It offers a coherent methodology for developing, implementing, and leading an effective state legislative lobbying campaign.

You are likely reading it because either you or your course instructor realize(s) that the state legislature can do basically anything it wants to you or for you. Government regulates land use, individual contracts, torts, and business and property transactions. It grants privileges such as licenses to operate a business, practice a profession, drive, and marry. It defines crimes and prescribes punishment. Finally, it takes money from many through taxes and gives it to others through government benefits.

As of this writing, the future for state legislative lobbying is exciting! The federal government by default or plan is returning to the states some of the domestic authority taken during the New Deal. Less and less will Congress solve domestic matters; states will be expected to find their own solutions. Associations will find themselves spending less time in Washington on domestic matters and more time in state houses as power once centralized in Washington is decentralized among the states.

This shift in authority will add more work to state legislators who already have too many bills to review, too little time to review them, and too few resources to research the information needed. Legislators will rely more and more on lobbyists to provide the information they need to vote responsibly.

The lobbying principles described in this book apply to all state legislatures. However, because specifics vary from state to state, this book is designed to be used in conjunction with the rules of your state. Obtain a copy and use them.

Lobbying is an art and a science. If this is your first lobbying experience, I urge you to follow the suggested sequence of steps in this book. Once you gain more experience, you will be better able to organize the steps that meet your needs.

A solid grasp of lobbying fundamentals does not guarantee you will "win" in your state capital, but practicing them does improve your likelihood of success and decreases the associated costs. Tommy Neal for the National Conference of State Legislatures writes,

> Of all the games in town it would be difficult to find one more mysterious, unpredictable and least understood than the state legislative game. It is, however, a game not to be taken lightly . . . One thing that makes it mysterious, unpredictable and difficult to understand is that it is not a rational process. You might think otherwise. But in the everyday world of legislative bodies, nothing works quite the way you expect it to.[1]

How to Successfully Lobby State Legislatures, Guide to State Legislative Lobbying, 4th edition will help you navigate this logical but often wholly irrational process; a process indispensable and critical to your wellbeing and that of your principal or purpose.

Robert L. Guyer

ACKNOWLEDGMENTS

I thank Laura K. Guyer, Ph.D. for the hundreds of hours we labored together over the 1999 first edition of this text. She edited many drafts and extracted from me what I really wanted to say. Her expression of my ideas continues to influence successive editions. Michael H. Hoffmann designed the covers, flowcharts, and layout for the first edition. Katherine Lee Amy, my beloved wife, encourager, and proofreader redesigned the flow charts and helped me rethink and redo earlier versions to create this 4th edition.

All of my books are better than what I otherwise could have done due to the contributions of practitioners. I thank all of them for their comments, anecdotes, and suggestions, great and small. Some allowed attribution while others preferred anonymity. All of the unattributed quotes are from former *Lobby School* participants. In particular I thank manuscript reviewers Justin Elliott, Lobbyist – Government Affairs, American Physical Therapy Association (Washington, D.C.) and Michael Sanderson, Executive Director, Maryland Association of Counties.

I especially thank Chris Micheli, Principal, Aprea & Micheli, Inc., (Sacramento) for his thoughtful edits and suggestions. His superior fluency in English, eye for punctuation, clarity of thought, sentence construction, grammar, and technical knowledge greatly improved the utility and readability of this book for practitioners and students of state advocacy. I offer my humble gratitude to them all.

PART I. PREPARING TO MEET THE LEGISLATURE – BUILDING YOUR LOBBYING CAMPAIGN

Chapter 1: Overview of Lobbying

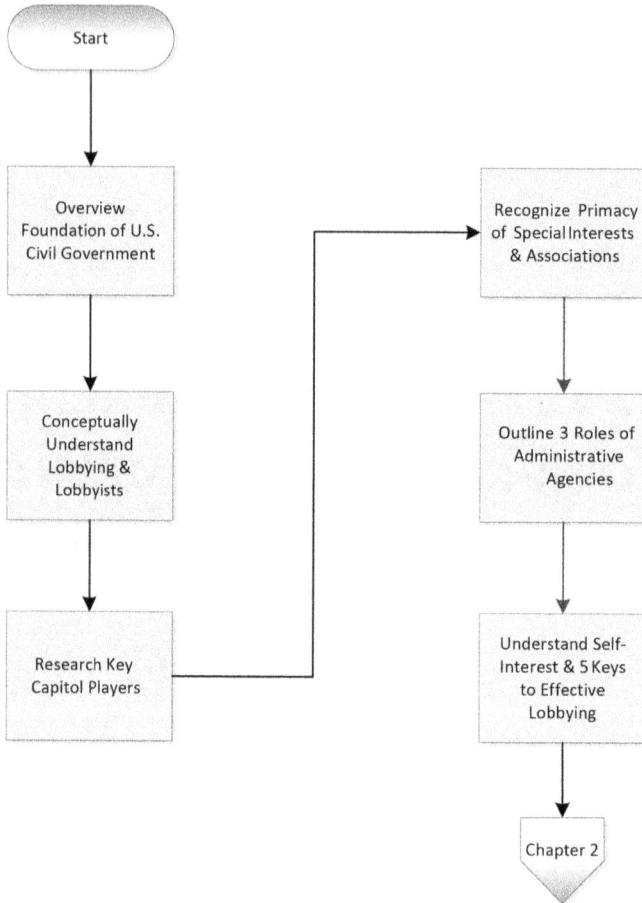

```
                    ┌─────────────┐
                    │    Start    │
                    └─────────────┘
                           │
                           ▼
    ┌──────────────────┐                    ┌──────────────────┐
    │     Overview     │                    │ Recognize Primacy│
    │ Foundation of U.S.│───────────────────▶│ of Special Interests│
    │ Civil Government │                    │   & Associations │
    └──────────────────┘                    └──────────────────┘
           │                                         │
           ▼                                         ▼
    ┌──────────────────┐                    ┌──────────────────┐
    │   Conceptually   │                    │ Outline 3 Roles of│
    │   Understand     │                    │  Administrative  │
    │   Lobbying &     │                    │     Agencies     │
    │   Lobbyists      │                    └──────────────────┘
    └──────────────────┘                             │
           │                                         ▼
           ▼                                ┌──────────────────┐
    ┌──────────────────┐                    │ Understand Self- │
    │   Research Key   │                    │ Interest & 5 Keys│
    │  Capitol Players │────────────────────│   to Effective   │
    │                  │                    │     Lobbying     │
    └──────────────────┘                    └──────────────────┘
                                                     │
                                                     ▼
                                              ┌───────────┐
                                              │ Chapter 2 │
                                              └───────────┘
```

CHAPTER 1

OVERVIEW OF LOBBYING

Understanding why you can successfully affect the legislative process requires some basic understanding of the United States' form of civil government. The beginning of our understanding is appreciating the United States Constitution influences directly and by example the structure and function of state government. And it establishes our rights as U.S. citizens to influence those whom we entrust with political power.

LAYING THE FOUNDATION – CONSTITUTIONAL STRUCTURE OF U.S. FEDERAL AND STATE GOVERNMENTS

The U.S. Constitution establishes the Federal government as a representational democracy called a republic. Following the Federal model, every state government has three branches of government: legislative, executive, and judicial. The legislative branch of state government is comprised of elected representatives from the legislative districts in a state. It "is responsible for translating the public will into public policy for the state, levying taxes, appropriating public funds, and overseeing the administration of state agencies."[2] Translating public will into public policy enables legislatures to make laws on any topic, except as limited by Congress, and state and federal constitutions.

3

The executive branch solely and exclusively implements statutes enacted by the legislature and has limited but critical participation in the legislative process. The legislature enacts statutes but cannot implement them; the executive branch implements statutes but cannot enact them. This distinction will become more central and important as we proceed. The judicial branch, or court system, evaluates the conduct of individuals relative to laws and has limited review of the actions of the legislative and executive branches.

Governments in the United States are strikingly different from other democracies worldwide. Many foreigners feel the U.S., by separating its legislative and executive powers and encouraging all citizens to participate, creates a system that is unpredictable, inefficient, disorderly, aggressive, contentious, and fosters conflict. Yet our Founders rejected England's system of a Parliament that both makes and implements laws. The Founders, following Montesquieu, held that uniting legislative and executive powers in the same body results in tyranny.[3] Separation of powers is a sacrosanct principle of U.S. government, restraining tyranny and promoting liberty – even amidst a seemingly chaotic system.

Arising from an awareness of the human soul, an ingrained distrust of state power, and the belief government must be accountable to the people, the Framers sought to establish and maintain the people's control of government by designing a system of open citizen participation. Thomas Jefferson said, "If once they [the people] become inattentive to the public affairs, you and I, and Congress, and Assemblies, judges and Governors shall all become wolves . . ."[4] Consequently, per the Framers' design, people do participate in government as lawmakers, citizens, interest groups, and others to support a range of positions.

Lawmakers are answerable to the people who give lawmakers their jobs and can take away those same jobs. Lawmakers' desire to protect their jobs leads to their accountability to voters, thereby providing opportunity to individuals and groups to influence government.

Citizen effort to affect government is called by various terms such as *influencing, persuading, petitioning* and, most commonly, *lobbying*.

Because our system is open to citizen participation and responsible to the citizenry, it is designed to be influenced, that is, it is designed to be lobbied. Most simply stated, lobbying is telling your elected representatives about your needs and then motivating them to help you satisfy those needs through the enactment of legislation.

If you have or expect to have some vital interest before the state legislature, you will likely try to influence the outcome of that issue, as it is considered. You will then join the ranks of the tens of thousands participating in democracy as lobbyists, U.S. style.

LOBBYING AND CITIZENS' RIGHTS

Lobbying is a simple concept. It is the active expression of a citizen's right to influence government. This underlying right is so fundamental to the United States' system of government that it is guaranteed by the First Amendment to the Constitution, "Congress shall make no law . . . abridging . . . the right of the people peaceably to assemble, and to petition for redress of grievances." Similar language appears in most, if not all, state constitutions.

U.S. Chief Justice Charles Evans Hughes stated, "The maintenance of the opportunity for free political discussions to the end that government may be responsive to the will of the people and that changes may be obtained by lawful means, an opportunity essential to the security of the Republic, is a fundamental principle of our constitutional system."[5] In his 1964 classic, *Lobbying and the Law*, political scholar Edgar Lane wrote, "Lobbying is not an American invention."[6] Lobbying has long been one of the means by which citizens can bring their needs to government. However, Lane continued, "The American experience is unique in the degree to which diverse interests have proliferated and sought political expression. It is unique in the degree that our institutional arrangements were intended to conduce and have conduced to this end."[7]

Lobbyists and lobbying have changed a great deal over the 150 years since the term lobbyist was first coined. Lane noted, "The term 'lobby-

5

ing' has been in common use for more than one hundred years. Throughout the nineteenth century, it meant face-to-face efforts by paid agents
to influence legislators to vote in their clients' behalf, often by corrupt or
covert means."[8] Lane continued,

> Eighty years ago, lobbying meant personal solicitation of legis-
> lative votes, usually, but not always through the agency of hired
> lobbyists, of whom there were relatively few. These men traded
> on their privileged entree to committees, their specialized
> knowledge of the legislature's procedural lacunae, their skill as
> hosts, and not infrequently their adeptness at honest argument.
> And when all else failed, they were prepared to buy their cli-
> ents the legislation they needed. Overt corruption was common
> enough to justify [the] general comment that 'lobbying methods
> were unscrupulous.'[9]

Some people still think lobbying is unseemly because certain tactics of
the early lobbyists, such as bribery, were criminal. Distaste arises today
when lobbyists are found engaged in controversial activities such as paying for legislators' trips, providing legislators with honoraria for speeches
to special interests, and using questionable methods to make campaign
contributions. However, today's effective lobbyist has moved away from
influence peddling and "shady deals" in "smoked filled back rooms" to
become a teacher, communicator, negotiator, and motivator. Lobbying
has changed.

> The staple work of the representatives of major interests con-
> cerned with legislation began to center around detailed, tech-
> nical craftsmanship in the drafting of bills, the gathering of
> statistics and descriptive material, collection and analysis of leg-
> islation and legislative documents from all over the country, the
> careful bill-by-bill scrutiny of all that was fed into the legislative
> hopper session by session, the assembling of briefs on pending
> proposals and the formal appearance before legislative commit-
> tees, the preparation and dissemination of large quantities of
> printed material presenting a point of view for the education of
> the members of an interest group or for the general public. The

conduct of this sort of work required both more professional and more routine skills than the old-style lobbyist possessed.[10]

Constituency, that is, a district's voters, is the most powerful force in state lobbying. However, constituents vary greatly in relative levels of importance, as discussed in Chapter 3 and in the rest of the book. Today's power-lobbying relies on constituents to provide the facts, figures, and motivation to inspire lawmakers to develop responsive public policy.

LOBBYING IN TODAY'S UNITED STATES

Everyone involved with the development of legislation influences its outcome. Generally, people interested in legislation belong to one of two groups. The smaller consists of members of the legislature, legislative staff, and regulatory agencies; agencies because, for all practical purposes, they are *technical* staff to lawmakers. As we proceed through this book you will see how agencies affect you in the legislature, before the Governor, and with the implementation of your bill into day-to-day reality, or not.

The larger group is populated by those who either advocate for or against proposed legislation. Each of these two large groups has subgroups with their own conflicting and competing goals. And, each lawmaker and lobbyist has his or her own political or personal agenda that influences the position taken on proposed legislation.

"Legislatures respond; they seldom lead."[11] Rather than being originators of bills, "Legislators work almost exclusively as boards of review to judge proposals brought forward by various groups."[12] Most ideas for legislation come from citizen activists, businesses, unions, associations, state agencies, the Governor, and any number of others interested in changing the law, and finally lawmakers themselves.

Today depending on the state, during a regular session bills can number from a few hundred to over 10,000 and deal with hundreds of topics. A legislator at best can be knowledgeable about no more than a few; and, there is never enough time in a legislative session for a lawmaker to become an expert in more than one or two. Thus, he or she faces voting on a number of bills from a myriad of unfamiliar topics.

For this reason, education and strong communication skills are the foundation of effective lobbying. Legislators know they will be more effective when they learn the pros, cons, and especially the politics surrounding bills on which they vote. This is especially true for bills assigned to committees on which they serve.

Lawmakers expect every bill to have supporters and opponents who will present good technical and political reasons to support their positions, pro and con. Therefore, lawmakers listen carefully to both sides of an issue before taking a position. Usually, petitioners lobby to secure support from individual legislators and the Governor for their issues. Remember, *lobbying is teaching* legislators about your issue and providing the political and technical facts needed to convince them to support your view rather than those of your competitors.

DIFFERENCES BETWEEN FEDERAL AND STATE LOBBYING

The U.S. Congress and each state legislature have different legislative environments requiring different lobbying approaches. For several reasons, lobbying in the states is much less resource intensive than in Washington, D.C.

First, there are fewer members in a state legislature than in Congress; thus there are fewer legislators to search out and lobby. On average a state legislature has approximately 140 elected members, of these 40 are Senators and 100 are House members.[13] State-specific numbers of legislators vary considerably and range from Alaska's 20-member Senate, to Nebraska's 49-member unicameral legislature (all called Senators), and New Hampshire's 424 lawmakers, of which 400 are in the House. In contrast, the U.S. Congress has 535 members; 100 Senators and 435 Representatives. These numbers show there are almost four times as many lawmakers in Congress to be lobbied as there are in the average state legislature.

However, you will lobby few, if any, of the 80 to 90 percent of lawmakers who vote pretty much in accord with committee recommendations or as instructed by party leadership. Your focus is on the 10 to 20 percent of lawmakers who can affect your bill, that is, those found on the *committees of referral* who will vote on your bill, and perhaps the caucus and chamber leadership.

Second, state legislators are much more accessible than are members of Congress for two main reasons. First, given the shorter duration of state legislative sessions compared to Congress, state lawmakers are more available to their constituents because they spend more time living at home. Second, state lawmakers have fewer constituents with whom to interact, so you have less competition for his or her limited amount of time. Compare the U.S. Senator from California who has 39,500,000 (2019) constituents and lives in Washington, D.C. for most of the year to the California State Senator who lives at home and has 931,000 (2019) constituents. Increased lawmaker accessibility in the states means you need fewer resources to lobby effectively.

Third, state legislators have few if any personal staff and committee staffs are small. Thus, their accessibility to lobbyists and constituents is increased. In contrast, members of Congress have large numbers of personal staff and committees have additional staff. A U.S. Senator's staff is larger than the entire staff of a smaller state's legislature. The large size and number of staff often seem to interfere with citizen contact with elected Washington representatives. Thus, more time, money, and other resources are required to lobby federal legislators.

Fourth, in most states, legislatures are in session only a few months per year and legislators know they have little time to accomplish much. On the other hand, Congress meets in session for the entire year and this, along with other factors, often leads to a sense the resolution of most issues can wait, and wait, and wait. In Congress next year is soon enough. Resources are saved when an issue is resolved in the state legislature in weeks or months rather than in the years Congress normally requires.

Fifth, at the state level, pressures on lobbyists to make campaign contributions and the expected size of those contributions are much less than at the federal level. This difference is due to the fact costs associated with running a state district campaign are normally far less than for a Congressional seat.

Sixth, experienced lobbyists know some successful federal lobbying techniques may not be appropriate for state lobbying. While I don't agree with his tone, the following does provide insight,

> Lobbying at the federal level is much more sophisticated, requiring more support staff and expertise than at the state level, where lobbyists frequently carry their offices in their hats. The state government lobbyist slaps a legislator on his back and says, 'I'm a good old boy and you're a good old boy. Why don't you vote for me?' In the Congress, lobbying is, more properly, an educational process.[14]

Experienced lobbyists also know lobbying style differs from state to state. Successful state lobbyists acquaint themselves with the environment of each state legislature and utilize the lobbying style preferred in that state.

Finally, what Congress considers important for lawmaking isn't what states consider important, and vice-versa. *CQ* [Congressional Quarterly] *Roll Call* comments,

> One clear element of state priorities is how different they are from those in Congress. For example, while education issues are prevalent in the states, it is not an issue that has seized the national agenda in the last year . . . Similarly, many states are also addressing crime, prisons, and marihuana policy to varying degrees, all issues that have not garnered a great deal of federal attention.[15]

Other differences include, for example, 40 states require *germaneness*, that is, everything in a bill must relate to a single subject. Congress mixes entirely unrelated topics in one bill. Forty-nine states by law must balance their budgets thereby limiting how much the state can spend; while Congress spends and spends money it doesn't have burdening taxpayers today and far into the future.

KINDS OF LOBBYISTS

Lobbyists fall into one of two groups, contract and in-house.

Contract lobbyists sell advocacy services on the open market to any number of clients. This is the most demanding in terms of hours and stress but the most financially profitable form of lobbying. Chapter 4, *Hiring and Working with Contract Lobbyists*, is the primer for working with contract lobbyists.

In-house lobbyists are permanent employees working for a single principal; often paid less than contractors but with less stress, more job security, and, in most cases, better working hours. They are:

- Administrators of lobbying contracts: Contract management, not advocacy is their main job. Seldom are they in the capitol for legislative business.

- Image representatives: They bring members of associations, unions, or public interest groups to the capitol. Often making uncompromising political statements, not lawmaking, is their main purpose.

- Advocates: They generally do the same work as contract lobbyists but, being permanent employees they generally have less pressure on them to produce legislative results. When not lobbying some principals may assign them to non-lobbying duties such as meeting planning, member services, etc. A major-league Mid-Atlantic lobbyist adds,

You will be the constituent services representative for your company or industry. When politicians, staff or regulators need information from your employer or assistance on a matter, you are that voice. Be honest, respond quickly (24/7, no exceptions), and when possible, make the politician look like a hero. The goodwill this buys is priceless, far exceeding that of PAC contributions if done right. Go above and beyond to fix a problem that a politician's constituent calls their office about and give the credit back to the politician. That's political gold and not forgotten.[16]

Categories of lobbyists, contract or in-house: By level of influence, a lobbyist falls into one of three categories: spectator, minor-leaguer, or major-leaguer.[17] The category below is determined primarily by the sum gravitas of their clients, employers, or associations' members.

- Spectators: They provide their principals with information beyond that found in the capital's *Today in the Legislature* news-letter and observe public or coalition meetings.

- Minor-leaguers: Often they are skilled, fully competent lobby-ists who, upon obtaining their first big-name client or employer move to the majors.

- Major-leaguers: Their principal(s), competency, relationships, and at times campaign contributions lead to considerable influence.

While other categories also exist such as registered lobbyists, non-registered advocates providing services just short of that defined as lobbying, constituent-advocates, for our purposes, the above is a good start for our discussion.

KEY PLAYERS IN STATE LEGISLATION

Federal-state similarities of function and, to a degree, form continue with the relative importance of players and key elements of lobbying.

However, the focus of this book is state government. Through the remainder of this text we will discuss and expand on the players, but for now know the key players in the state legislative process, by ranking of relative *political* importance, are:

1. Special interests
2. Legislative staff
3. Agency staff
4. Lawmakers
5. Governor
6. Media
7. Public

As to your bill, note lawmakers, while *primary* in *constitutional* importance because they alone make enactments, are *quaternary* in *political* importance. Ranking of relative political importance indicates where you will spend your time and effort. You will invest most of your effort lobbying special interests and the least with the general public.

LEGISLATIVE CAUCUSES

A caucus is a group of lawmakers uniting around a common interest to produce specific results. The most common interest is political party. One party constitutes the chamber's voting majority and the other party is the voting minority. Infrequently, third-party lawmakers, such as Green, Constitution, or Libertarian parties, will work with, that is, *caucus* with, the major political party with which they feel most connected.[18] Per the National Conference of State Legislatures (NCSL) " . . . one-third of states have no caucuses other than party caucuses."[19]

Party caucuses are staffed, funded, and politically powerful. "Much of what you see in committee and on the chamber floor reflects what the majority caucus earlier decided to do. Most caucus decisions are made in private with only selected invitees; they are often—but now always—closed to the public, media, and of course the opposing party. Being invited to a party caucus meeting is a great opportunity for you and your contract lobbyist to gain momentum for your bill."[20]

However, in two-thirds of the states, non-party caucuses exist, such as a Black Caucus, Women's Caucus, Prayer Caucus, and so on. "Non-party caucuses might favor the legislative initiatives of one party more than those of another, but they usually try to distinguish their ideals and goals from party interests. The increasing diversity of the membership in the state capitol since the early 1970s has spurred the development of non-party caucuses, resulting in greater influence in organizing legislative affairs."[21] According to NCSL,

> The most numerous and longest lasting nonparty caucuses are those based on demographics. They emerged in the mid-1970s as the number of blacks, women and Hispanics elected to legislatures began to increase. Today, 35 states have black caucuses, 23 have women's caucuses and 16 have Hispanic/Latino caucuses. Nineteen states have Native American caucuses tied to a national network . . . The majority of demographic caucuses, according to their websites, are open to all legislators, regardless of party, race/ethnicity or religion. But in fact, Democrats have long dominated the larger racial/ethnic caucuses—in some cases, to the point of excluding the other party.
>
> By and large, however, most caucuses are both bipartisan and bicameral. About half of the nation's legislatures have caucuses focused on regional needs and interests: the Everglades in Florida, for example, or the coastal counties of Maine, Massachusetts, Oregon and Washington, or rural and agricultural areas, such as Alaska's Mat-Su Valley and California's Inland Empire . . . Some caucuses are organized around the interests of certain industries or sectors, from arts, culture, aviation and aerospace to coal, fisheries, manufacturing, steel and vineyards.[22]

For the remainder of this book the word *caucus* refers to the majority and minority political party caucuses. The *Insiders Talk: Winning with*

Lobbyists books discuss caucuses and caucus staffs as lobbying targets in more detail.

SPECIAL INTERESTS AND ASSOCIATIONS

Special interests are individuals, governments, corporations, churches, labor unions, charitable organizations, associations, or groupings of special interests. They are the primary forces affecting your bill. They drive the capitol and the capital. They write most bills, maximize consensus and minimize controversy among players, line up bill sponsors and co-sponsors, provide talking points to lobbyists and legislators, work bills through committees, obtain and keep votes, lobby the Governor's office, and participate in executive agency rulemaking to implement legislation. They capture, focus, and direct lawmakers' supporters, voters, and constituents, including other interest groups, as discussed below. After their home-folk are taken care of, lawmakers are almost exclusively motivated by the special interests that help to put and keep them in office.

One person, even if he or she has a close relationship with a lawmaker, usually makes little difference when lobbying an entire legislature. However, there is a tool that can be used to multiply the potential of your political power. That tool is to join an association which can aggregate political power. At the most basic functional level, all special interests are associations.

Each person has a small amount of political power beginning with his or her right to vote. For this reason, those who don't vote don't count because they have no political power to leverage. Several other factors including relationships with others, place of residency, party affiliation, wealth, and education add to that initial power. One vote usually makes little difference in an election or to a lawmaker, although sometimes one or a few votes can win an election.[23]

An association may be permanent, such as a labor union, or it may be temporary, such as a group united to support or oppose a one-time issue.

The members of an association may be individuals, organizations, or a coalition of many associations. Without respect to the type of association formed, the goal of all associations is to unite many smaller influences into one stronger political force.

Associations and their members engage in most of today's lobbying. Associations form to advance their members' narrow and specific interests. That is, associations exist to promote a seemingly almost innumerable number of *special interests* ranging from animal welfare to zoning.

Legislators want to do the most good for the largest number of their supporters and friendly voters. Therefore, they would rather interact with associations representing many people than with individuals. As you venture into the political arena with your issue, you will find many other associations are lobbying their issues. When they learn about your issue, some will support your cause and some will oppose it, depending on how much your issue affects them.

You must decide if you will join an existing association or form a new one. The formation of a new association can send a strong message to others. A new association, formed to work on a single issue, shows there is focus and member commitment to that issue. Often, established and well-known organizations will form a new *ad hoc* association when there is a need for a group on a single issue. Their commonality is associations exist to advance their members' special interests in a particular topic. For this reason, associations are properly called *special interests*.

The American Society of Association Executives defines an association as, "A group of people banded together for a purpose."[24] By numbers of organizations among the Internal Revenue Code 501(c) category of 29 kinds of non-profit[25] associations, are: 1,052,495, (c)(3) (charitable)[26]; 86,451(c)(4) (civic, social welfare)[27]; 54,425 (c)(5)(labor and agricultural)[28]; and 66,985, (c)(6) (business leagues)[29]. Lobbying is a significant activity for many of these organizations and 501(c)(3) organizations in particular are discussed in Chapter 2.

16

The lobbying principles described in this book have been tested within the context of associations and will be presented from that perspective. To be effective, you must become a member of an association.

In addition to associations, the U.S. has 18,500 businesses with 500 or more employees[30] most of whom will work with government to promote their self-interests. We will functionally speak of the interests of associations and those of corporations, state and local governments, and even individual citizens under the broad heading of special interests.

Special interests are the single greatest influence on achieving your legislative goals and with which most of your lobbying will be done. Their importance will be stressed throughout the remainder of this book.

LOCAL GOVERNMENT

Local governments, that is, municipalities, counties, school and other districts, other local subdivisions of government, and associations of local governments are significant political players. For example, "There are 732 lobbyists registered on behalf of city and county governments in Texas. Overall, they account for 42 percent of the 1,741 lobbyists registered with the Texas Ethics Commission."[31] "In many states, local governments spend more on lobbyists than both business and unions."[32]

Elected *state* officials, who themselves often were once local officials, pay great attention to elected *local* officials, many of whom they already know. Further, they may represent overlapping constituencies, that is, the ones who are paying for state and local governments. These same voters put and keep both sets of elected officials in power.

State and local officials, especially when of the same party, share common interests and values, and influence each other. "When any elected member or key staff member from a local elected entity is concerned enough about an issue to contact a lawmaker or executive branch official, they are likely to pay attention—after all, keeping their constituency happy is how most politicians stay in office."[33]

17

For purposes of this book, we will treat local governments as *special interests* competing for state money, benefits, and advantages over their opponents. Your lobbying planning and coalition building must account for the influence of local governments, pro or con, on your legislative effort.

LOBBYING ADMINISTRATIVE AGENCIES

The President of the United States and state Governors, as the chief executives of their respective executive branches, have bureaucracies to assist them in the administration of the laws they, as chief executives, have been elected to carry out. These bureaucracies, called executive, regulatory, or administrative agencies or departments, implement laws to regulate activities such as education, welfare, tax collection, and environmental protection, among many others.

Federal and state administrative agencies meet their responsibilities to citizens by promulgating rules. Citizens, per the First Amendment and state equivalents, can lobby agencies to affect the rules they make. However, just as federal differs from state legislative lobbying, so too agency lobbying differs from legislative lobbying.

Administrative agency lobbying is much more technical than legislative lobbying because the purpose of an agency rule is to implement the broad goals of a state statute. By law, the legislature mandates *what must be done* and then delegates its authority to an agency to determine *how it is to be done*. Like statutes, agency rules are laws and legally enforceable. For example, the legislature may decree public health is to be protected from a communicable disease found in fish. The state health agency will then determine how to implement this legislative goal. The outcome may include the promulgation of regulations regarding the water bodies in which to ban or limit fishing, establishment of allowable concentrations of species of bacteria, or limits on quantity and quality of discharges into state waters.

When compared to the legislature, agencies operate under many more procedural restraints. Although the legislature is governed by certain self-imposed rules of procedure, agency rulemaking is governed by strict requirements found in the state administrative procedures act and rules implementing the act. A lobbyist must understand the strict procedural limits under which agency rulemaking operates. These include requirements for notice, conduct of public meetings, citizen comment, and many other measures.

There are far fewer persons to lobby in an administrative agency than in a state legislature. Unlike the many legislators who come to the state house reflecting the diversity of the state's constituencies, decision making in an agency is conducted by a small number of homogenous career administrators charged with implementing the legislature's directions and the agency's own agenda. Agency lobbying requires the provision of technical presentations to a small number of highly educated agency experts.

As civil servants, agency staffs are less susceptible to political pressure than are state legislators who can be voted out of elected office by unhappy constituents. Unlike legislators who face periodic elections, the jobs of civil servants are secure. This enables them to give less attention to the political consequences of their decisions as they focus on technical issues surrounding the implementation of legislative policy embodied in state statutes.

Finally, depending on the state, agencies can have profound influence on your bill becoming a law for three reasons. First, the legislature relies on agency advice as to the *technical* considerations as well as the many kinds of impacts of the laws they make. Impacts include economic, environmental, impact on state and local budgets and whatever state law requires be considered, especially in agency implementation of the statutes. Seldom will legislators contradict agency *technical* guidance as to what the legislature should do with your bill. If the agency opposes your bill, overcoming its objections is extremely difficult.

Similarly, the Governor upon receiving an *enrolled* bill will solicit agency guidance as to either allowing a bill to become law or vetoing it. This means, even if you overcome agency objections before the legislature, an extremely unlikely occurrence, the agency will yet prevail when, upon agency request, the Governor *vetoes* your bill.

Thirdly, for all practical purposes you don't have a (functioning) law until the agency says you have a law and you don't know what the law means until the agency tells you what it means. They do this through agency rulemaking and enforcement. Rulemaking agencies write about 10 pages of agency law for every page of statutory law and it's those 10 pages telling you what you really have. Or the agency may decide not to adopt implementing rules and you have nothing. Or the agency may adopt rules and then not enforce the rules which means you have something in theory but not in practice.

What the legislature gave you, an agency can take away and what the legislature wouldn't give you, an agency might. You have to lobby the agency in the legislature, before the Governor, and finally before the agency itself. Lose in any one of the three arenas and you fail.

FIVE KEYS TO EFFECTIVE LOBBYING

Effective lobbying is:

1. Campaign based
2. Established on trust
3. Likeability rooted
4. Education centered
5. Constituent driven

Campaign based. A campaign is a series of planned aggressive activities designed to maximize the chances of achieving a goal. Basic steps are described in this primer and greatly expanded upon in the *Campaign Method for More Effective State Government Affairs* seminars and my other books, and videos.

Established on trust. As explained in Chapter 3, lobbying is *legislative sales*. At the foundation of selling are likeability and trust. Being likeable gets you in their front door, but you have to earn their trust to stay there. Trust rests upon: scrupulous honesty, accuracy, and credibility. Integrity, consistency, truthfulness are virtues on which an effective lobbying campaign rests. One lie, one half-truth, one misstatement of fact *corrected too slowly* will sink a lobbying effort.

Likeability rooted. If they like you, they will *want to trust you*. Likeability is "job number one" in lobbying. If lawmakers (and staff) like you as a person, they may listen to you; and, if they listen to you, they may do what you want. But if they don't like you as a person, they won't heed a word you say and they may vote against you out of spite. Be likeable and respectful at all times.

Education centered. The most important education you provide is how your bill is good for the lawmaker, electoral district, and state overall. Information that doesn't help lawmakers and staff do their jobs such as white papers, press releases, brochures, and association backgrounders end up in the trash. We will discuss this more in Chapter 7, however for now keep in mind *technical facts* are for agencies and *political facts* are for legislatures.

Constituent driven. In order of relative importance, home-folk influencers are: the lawmaker's supporters, his or her voters (not the other party's), those who could become supporters or voters, registered voters who don't vote, and finally the other party's voters. Those who are not registered to vote don't count at all.

SELF-INTEREST IS THE ENGINE OF GOVERNMENT

Politicians, as well as most everyone else in the capitol trying to influence lawmaking, are driven first by their own self-interests. James Madison and his allies, as well as my experience, view *self-interest as the recognized engine of political and social life*.[34] Lawmakers are more likely to support positions that advance their self-interests and oppose those that run contrary to them. This is why we model lobbying as *legislative sales*, that is, meeting lawmakers' needs with what we are offering.

"Gimme, gimme, gimme. I want, I need. It's going to be the end of (fill in the blank) unless you do what I want," generally is a losing approach to lobbying. It's best to work with the principle *customers buy to meet their needs not yours*. Nobody cares what you want until you make them care and you do that first by catering to their self-interests. Once their self-interests are taken care of then you can move on to yours.

For each lawmaker (and special interest) ask, "Why would that lawmaker give me his or her vote?" Until you can answer that question, you are not likely to get the vote. And catering to their self-interest is the starting point for developing the answer.

SUMMARY CHAPTER 1

Lobbying is influencing lawmakers. The U.S. system of a republic founded upon representational democracy is designed to be influenced by any citizen participating in the process of legislation. Legislators need political and technical information about the bills on which they must vote and they want to know their constituents' interests.

Although the fundamentals of lobbying are the same, lobbying style will vary based on federal, state, legislative, or agency environments. Now that you understand you can influence your state elected representatives, you next assess your political potential as a player in the legislative arena, as discussed in our next chapter.

Chapter 2: Assessing Your Chances of Lobbying Success

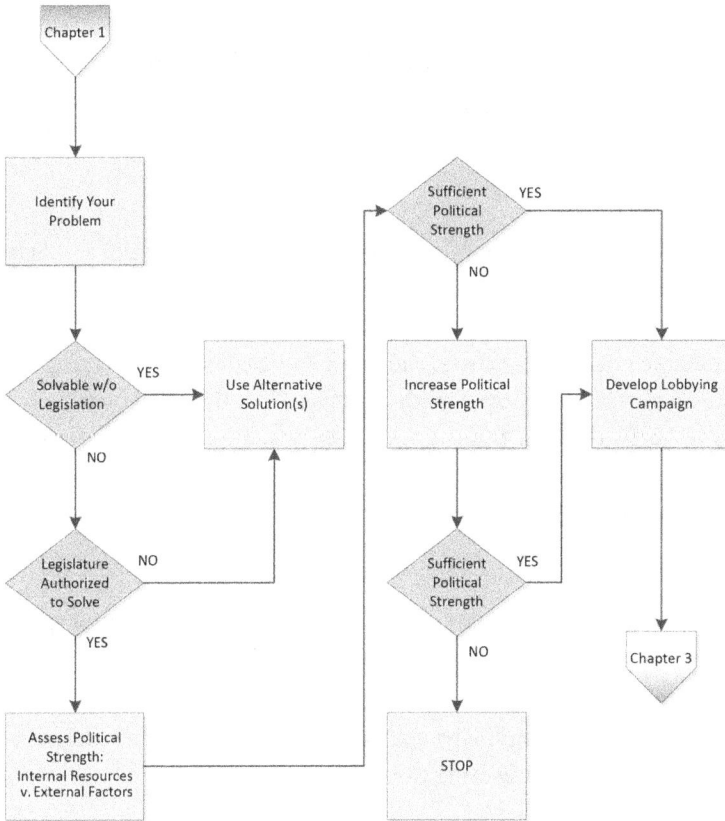

================ CHAPTER 2 ================

ASSESSING YOUR CHANCES OF LOBBYING SUCCESS

Before embarking on your lobbying project, you should assess your chances of success. If you have sufficient resources to overcome normal obstacles to legislative enactments, then you will lobby. If you don't have a reasonable chance of success, then you may be better off staying home. If you nevertheless proceed with insufficient political power, you may find yourself worse off than if you never went to the legislature at all. So how do you know if you have sufficient political strength to proceed? You start by answering four questions.

FOUR QUESTIONS TO ESTIMATE CHANCES OF LOBBYING SUCCESS

The first steps in determining your chances of success and, therefore, whether you should lobby, are answering the following questions:

1. What is my problem?
2. Can my problem be solved without the state legislature?
3. Does the state legislature have the authority to solve my problem?
4. Will the state legislature solve my problem for me?

First, "What is my problem?" You must identify and explain your problem clearly so those who know little about you or your issue can understand it quickly. As you think through your problem, you may find you have more than one. If this is the case, consider each one separately.

Second, "Can my problem be solved without the state legislature?" Some issues, by nature, lie beyond the scope of what the law considers to be appropriate for state intervention. The legislature cannot solve every societal problem nor is it designed to redress every wrong. Before investing time and money to lobby, research possible non-legislative solutions. Could a private or other public institution be better able to help you? For example, you may seek certification by a private professional organization rather than ask the legislature to enact a licensure law. By citizen initiative, you may create a law. You may find a better solution in federal or state court, administrative agency rulemaking, or declaratory order.

Third, "Does the state legislature have the legal authority to solve my problem?" The power of state legislatures is limited by the federal and state constitutions. Further, the Federal government sometimes takes legislative jurisdiction away from states when it decides to "occupy the field" in an area of law. When the Federal government occupies the field, it deprives the states of regulatory authority in a particular matter.

Several resources can help you answer the second and third questions. Contact professional, industry, trade, or labor organizations specializing in your issue. Speak to local legislators; conduct a library or Internet search (next chapter). Contact the administrative agency that would regulate your activity, and contact an attorney or a contract lobbyist. Because contract lobbyists are so involved with the legislature and because they can help you with every aspect of your legislative challenge, Chapter 4 discusses them in detail.

You must complete the homework related to your problem before proceeding to the legislature. By clearly identifying your problem and its possible solutions before lobbying, you can optimize your expenditures of money, time, relationships, and political capital.

When your answers to the first three questions show you have a clearly defined problem which the legislature can solve, then you are ready to consider the fourth question, "Will the state legislature solve my problem for me?" The answer to this question will be determined, in large part, by your political strength.

ASSESSING POLITICAL STRENGTH

Political strength is the difference between the strength of your internal resources and the strength of external factors. You must identify as many internal resources and external factors as possible; then estimate the relative strength or weight of each one. If you go to the legislature without sufficient political strength, you can end up far worse than if you never went there at all, a fate which we touch upon later in this book.

Because a dynamic synergism exists among the internal and external elements, the strength of one can compensate for the weakness of another. Consequently, the presence or absence of a single resource or factor cannot be used to determine absolute political strength or weakness.

INTERNAL RESOURCES – WHAT YOU HAVE TO WORK WITH

An association derives political strength from its members. You can assess the internal strength of your association by considering:

1. Intra-association member consensus
2. Member motivation
3. Relationships
4. Places where members live and work
5. Shared characteristics with legislators
6. Membership size and geographic distribution
7. Reputation
8. Technical, lobbying, and negotiating skills
9. Ability to form alliances and coalitions
10. Money

1. *Intra-association member consensus.* This is the bedrock upon which to build your legislative effort because consensus translates into cohesiveness leading to member motivation. Consensus building begins when the leaders of each sub-group within the association reach agreement on the nature of the problem and its legislative solution. Then, as a unified body, they explain the problem, offer a solution to the general membership, and ask for member support. Once member support has formed, the association formally adopts goals and a proposed legislative solution and communicates them to the entire membership.

At the conceptualization stage, member consensus usually runs high. As time passes during the process of developing a series of concrete actions to be taken, consensus may weaken. You must work to maintain it, and two of the most effective tools are communication and member involvement.

The association must maintain ongoing and candid communication with its members. Early and ongoing member awareness of the association's activities will help curtail misunderstanding and avoidable disagreements. Effective communication, for example, will help to prevent an uninformed association member from contacting his or her legislator to object to the bill the association is lobbying. An apparent intra-association conflict burdens the bill with unnecessary controversy and reduces the likelihood of accomplishing your goals. Lawmakers don't want to get involved in family feuds, but your opponents will seize upon them.

Member participation in the lobbying effort leads to member "ownership" which builds cohesiveness, maintains consensus, and willingness to contribute resources including labor, political capital, and money. Involve as many members in lobbying activities as possible. Ask less participatory members to become more involved by writing a letter, visiting a legislator with whom they have a constituent relationship, or accompanying one of your association lobbyists on a lobbying visit.

The consensus you build must be real, that is, more than mere acquiescence to the association's legislative goals. To be useful and productive, consensus must lead to member motivation.

2. *Member motivation*. Members must be motivated to work to accomplish your association's goals. In permanent associations, motivation to work on a single issue is often more difficult to achieve and maintain because members have so many other issues in which to become involved. On the other hand, in temporary or *ad hoc* associations formed in response to an immediate and specific concern, members are usually highly motivated and focused to work on their common single issue.

Motivation is difficult to measure. However, you can estimate the degree of motivation by testing the willingness of members to contribute their resources to support the lobbying effort.

Develop a checklist clearly identifying types and amounts of resources members must contribute to implement a successful lobbying campaign. Determine how many and which members should participate in the project. Estimate the time requirements and amount of money members will need to contribute. Will members encourage other individuals, associations, and legislators whom they know to take action on behalf of the association's goals? Once you have completed the checklist, ask your members to commit the necessary resources. Then, determine whether your needs will be met.

Achieving consensus is only the first step in initiating your lobbying effort. Consensus must manifest itself clearly as member motivation. If you find your members actively support and will contribute resources to the association's effort, you can proceed to assess other internal resources. Throughout the lobbying campaign, you will need to nurture consensus and motivation and answer complaints and doubts. Once your association reaches consensus and you are satisfied your members are sufficiently invested, you can then evaluate the following remaining resources.

3. *Relationships*. Those who influence legislators have established positive personal relationships with them. Because they are members of a community, legislators develop relationships with family, friends, acquaintances, neighbors, political allies including fellow legislators and lobbyists, co-workers, clients, employees, members of their places of worship and social clubs, and colleagues in professional societies and

labor unions. Each relationship provides an opportunity to influence a legislator. As you estimate the political strength of your association, carefully determine the number, type, and depth of relationships each association member has with different legislators.

If your members don't have relationships with their districts' lawmakers, then they have to build them. Encourage each member to ask itself this question, "Is my lawmaker my friend, and if not, then why not, and what am I going to do to build the relationship?" Building relationships is easy and can be fun. Chapter 7, section *Why Will Lawmakers Listen to Me?* lists seven reasons why their districts' lawmakers are inclined to talk to them. Get each member to set up a 10-minute face-to-face appointment with the lawmaker or staff to introduce themselves and to say why they are interested in the lawmaker, district, and state government. In time they will visit with a completed Appendix 2, *Suggested Lobbying Visit Leave Behind.*

4. *Places where members live and work.* A lawmaker's first concern is for the people who live and work in his or her electoral district. In order of importance these are:

1. Supporters
2. Lawmaker's voters
3. Voters who could become supporters
4. In-district employers
5. People who just happen to reside in the district
6. In-district non-voters
7. Opponent's supporters and voters

Legislators, who hold their offices at the pleasure of their districts' voters, respond attentively to the concerns of those who put and keep them in office. Thus, they are more inclined to support your message when championed by 1 through 4 above; and 1 through 3 because they vote. In-district employers, 4, are important because they directly impact the overall wellbeing of the district, are potential sources of campaign donations, and because their employees will vote to keep their jobs. Least influential are 5 and 6. Group 7, aka "the enemy," may harm your lobbying effort.

5. *Shared characteristics with legislators.* An association member who shares characteristics with a lawmaker can be a more effective lobbyist for that legislator. Shared political party, political or social views, occupation, race, ethnicity, gender and many other characteristics can favorably predispose a legislator toward your association member and, therefore, your issue. Shared characteristics are at the foundation of successful *affinity marketing.* Constituency is the most basic shared characteristic.

6. *Membership size and geographic distribution.* In general, the greater the number of members in your association, then the greater will be its influence. In part this is because legislators seek to do the most good for the state overall which approximates to benefitting the greatest number of people; thus, they often place greater significance on issues belonging to associations with large memberships. Realizing this, you can increase your political strength by making your association as large as possible such as joining with other associations in a coalition.

Further, political strength expands when your members reside in a number of different electoral districts. However, some districts will be very important for one issue, but unimportant for another. Only 10 to 20 percent of lawmakers matter for any bill. This is because districts that matter are represented by lawmakers sitting on committee(s) considering your bill.

7. *Reputation.* Reputation directly affects how much attention you will receive in the capital and degree of respect and trust you can leverage. Assess your group's reputation by asking these questions:

- Do legislators respect my association or its members?
- What opinions do they have about us?
- Is my association or its members seen as influential or are they unpopular?
- If unpopular, how can we remediate our reputation?
- Do we want to remediate our reputation?

The reputation of your members directly affects the power of your association and its political influence. Respected community and organization leaders publicly supporting your association add their public images and goodwill to your organization and issue thereby making both more attractive to others. On the other hand, if your association, lobbyist, or members are considered hostile to the particular lawmakers you want to influence, then you may ask a more acceptable ally to take the lead on making particular contacts.

If your group is unpopular with lawmakers do you want to fix their perception? Some organizations refuse to talk civilly, much less find common ground, with lawmakers whose principles or party they find offensive. Rather than achieving pragmatic "half-of-the-pie" legislative goals, they believe their members prefer to see them opposing a foul philosophy as an end in and of itself.

However, unless an incurable animosity exists between you and a particular lawmaker, most will work with opponents sharing common interests, even if momentary. Dislike is no reason to stop a mutually beneficial deal and lawmakers are dealmakers. Phillip Stanhope, First Earl of Chesterfield, observed, "Politicians neither love nor hate. Interest, not sentiment, directs them." If your organization can help the lawmaker achieve what he or she wants, you may effectively work together on that topic at least. This is the foundation of coalitions which are mentioned throughout this book.

8. *Technical, lobbying, and negotiating skills.* Legislators place greater confidence in the statements made by persons with specialized training or experience. When association members have highly specialized, professional, or technical credentials, especially in the subject matter of the proposed legislation, you will have added political strength. For example, a farmer with a master's degree in entomology will be more persuasive than a "weekend gardener" when speaking about the impacts of pesticides on agriculture. Because executive agencies' professional staffs are for all practical purposes technical staff to the legislature, your expert speaking to and being respected by the agency expert can influence the agency to recommend favorably your position to the legislature.

31

You will have increased political strength if some of your members have previously participated in lobbying or legislative negotiations. You should explore how the skills and relationships of your members can be used to advance your issue. Use the negotiating experience of your members to help the association make good decisions. Encourage those with lobbying experience to teach other members to become more effective lobbyists. The *Lobby School* also provides this training. Chapter 5 discusses negotiation skills development.

9. *Ability to form alliances and coalitions.* Your members are likely to hold memberships in other associations. Ascertain their ability and willingness to leverage these relationships to help you build alliances with other associations. However, don't be surprised if some members resist "cheapening" for political advocacy their professional relationships, that is, "professional" in the purest traditional sense of the word.[35]

A coalition dedicated to a single issue can be most effective. However, while coalitions multiply influence, they exist for advantage, not love, loyalty or debt. They are filled with intrigue and side-bar deals. Everyone who understands how coalitions work is regularly doing their own cost-benefit calculations about remaining in the coalition or throwing another partner "under the bus" to achieve their own ends. A major-league Mid-Atlantic lobbyist, however, qualifies this observation, "Working with and building coalitions in the effort of passing, or killing, a bill was a very different experience during my ten years as an in-house lobbyist versus my subsequent years as a contract lobbyist. Overall my experience in-house for a large energy company delivered favorable results with fair weather friend coalition building. In the world of contract lobbying, I did not find that to be the case.[36]

10. *Money.* Money is power; not the only kind of power, or even the most influential form of power. However, lobbying costs money, contract lobbyists cost money, operating even an *ad hoc* association costs money, compliance with state lobbying ethics requirements costs money, and so much more. While "sweat equity" can accomplish much, money can mitigate somewhat deficiencies in the above. And donations are a direct indicator of each member's true commitment to the lobbying campaign.

External Factors – What You Have to Get Past

Once you have evaluated internal resources, you evaluate external factors that support and oppose your bill, within and external to the legislature. These factors are largely beyond your control and include:

1. How broadly compelling is your issue?
2. How little change you can accept?
3. Who are potential winners and losers?
4. Does the partisan composition of the legislature help or hurt?
5. Will the session's legislative theme advance or impede my bill?
6. What does the gross rate of bill passage portend?

1. *How broadly compelling is your issue?* Begin your external assessment by estimating the amount of support organically existing for your issue and the amount of support to be cultivated. Lawmakers often hesitate to support controversial bills or bills benefitting a few at the expense of many. Therefore, make your bill as non-controversial and widely beneficial to others, as possible. If you can honestly associate your issue with commonly supported causes or beliefs such as children, health, environment, or better jobs, then the goodwill associated with these topics may broaden your support.

2. *How little change can you accept?* The less you ask for, the more likely you will get it, but *do not ask for less than you need*. This isn't like buying a car or house, employing a negotiating technique intending to ask for more and settle for less. During the legislative session, and especially the closer to *sine die*, (i.e., the last day of the session) there is too little time and too much to do to play games. Ask for what you want. Once the legislature has given your issue attention, it may not want to address it again for years.

3. *Who are potential winners and losers?* Every law has winners and losers; and most lobbying is a zero-sum game. One side wins at the expense of the other because state resources are limited and the pie isn't going to get any bigger.

When evaluating external factors, determine who might support or oppose your bill. Besides your association's membership, who else will benefit if your bill becomes law? Who will lose? Assess the significance of the impact of the win or the loss on other persons, as this will predict the magnitude of their support or opposition to your proposed legislation. Consider the political risks for each of those who support you. Will supporting your bill, for example, result in a lawmaker losing the support of other legislators or interest groups for bills he or she considers important? Will opposing you diminish another interest group's ability to work on more important issues before the legislature?

4. *Does the partisan composition of the legislature help or hurt?* The degree of partisanship within each chamber and in the legislature can greatly affect the likelihood of your success. In solidly one-party controlled legislatures, the likely outcome of many bills can be immediately estimated. Liberals who lobby a conservative legislature or conservatives who lobby a liberal legislature should know they face opposition before they mention their issue. On the other hand, partisans who lobby fellow partisans do better.

If your association usually supports one political viewpoint, you must consider the popularity of that view within the current legislature. Unless your organization is so partisan you refuse to even talk to the opposing party, there is no reason you can't have a civil understanding such that given the right conditions, you can work together on a different bill.

On the other hand, there are issues transcending partisanship and concerns on which all parties largely agree. For example, stopping human trafficking and sex slavery are largely non-partisan and bills put forward by the *Polaris Project* (https://polarisproject.org/) sail through legislatures. Although not quite as universal in bipartisan support, *The Campaign for the Fair Sentencing of Youth* (https://www.fairsentencingofyouth.org/) seeks to end juvenile life without parole for youthful offenders. Other points of agreement, such as reducing poverty, differ not as to philosophy but on mechanism.

5. *Will the session's legislative theme advance or impede my bill?* The legislature and the Governor set goals well before each legislative session

establishing a session's theme. In one session the theme may consume the legislature, while in another, the theme will be more subdued. The theme is important because it affects the types of proposed legislation the legislature will favor in a given session. You must discover the session's theme before drafting or lobbying your proposed bill. Legislators and others acquainted with the legislature, especially those in the majority party, can accurately estimate the forthcoming year's theme and its likely effect upon your legislative proposal.

Once you know the theme, ask yourself, "How well does my issue fit within it?" If your issue advances the theme, then the likelihood of enactment is greater than if it does not. If you cannot fit your issue into the session's theme, then:

- Redraft your bill to advance the legislative theme.
- Break your bill into a series of smaller bills. Small bills may sometimes be enacted even when the session focuses on a different theme.
- Wait for a later, more favorable session.
- Proceed regardless of theme if your bill is necessary this year.

6. *What does the gross rate of bill passage portend?* Each jurisdiction has its own gross rate for bill enactment. Some states enact most bills while others enact few. Knowing your state's gross bill enactment ratio provides a general estimate of probability of enactment. Further, by comparing the issues in your bill to others the legislature has similarly considered, you will gain a more refined estimate about your likelihood of success. For most states, data to calculate enactment rates are available on the legislatures' websites.

This information is critical for a multistate lobbying campaign. Introducing your bill in a state with a high enactment rate improves the likelihood your bill will become law and thereby gain momentum to become law in other states.

In addition to the gross rates of bill passage, you should be aware that bill enactment is affected by sponsorship. For example, a minority sponsor in a partisan legislature is less likely to be successful than is a member of the majority party. As you consider potential sponsors and lobbyists, examine their track records of bill passage.

TAX-EXEMPT ORGANIZATIONS

Tax laws may limit the amount of money that may be spent on a lobbying effort. Federal Section 501 (c)(1–29), Internal Revenue Code (IRC) organizations and state tax law equivalents, as well as organizations receiving government funding, must ensure their expenditures comport with their application for tax exempt status and do not exceed federal and state limits on spending for legislative activity.[37] This is most acutely applicable to 501(c)(3), IRC nonprofits.

501(c)(3), IRC NONPROFITS MAY LOBBY[38]

"Not only are nonprofits legally entitled to lobby, they are expected to do so. Congress has been very clear nonprofits have a role in society that includes being a voice on issues that matter to people, communities, and the nation."[39]

A nonprofit may freely choose as a matter of its own policy not to lobby. However, its choice should be informed with the full understanding federal law permits 501(c)(3) charities to advocate before the state legislature on behalf of its clients, members, and causes as long as lobbying is not a *substantial* part of its activities.

"A public charity is not permitted to engage in *substantial legislative activities* (commonly known as lobbying). An organization will be regarded as attempting to influence legislation if it contacts, or urges the public to contact, members or employees of a legislative body for purposes of proposing, supporting or opposing legislation, or advocates the adoption or rejection of legislation . . . Substantiality is measured by either the substantial part test or the expenditure test."[40] (emphasis added)

A 501(c)(3) organization that notifies the United States Internal Revenue Service of its intention to lobby can, in most cases, spend more money on lobbying activities than a 501(c)(3) that does not notify the IRS. See Appendix 1.[41]

Private foundations may give money to charities that lobby. However, the gifts cannot be earmarked for lobbying and must be either in the form of general-purpose grants, or meet the requirements of the Foundation Excise Tax Regulations.

501(c)(3) charities desiring to lobby beyond IRS limits may form non tax-exempt organizations under IRS provisions for 501(c)(4), (c)(5), or (c)(6) organizations. Lobbying is a fundamental purpose of these organizations.

WEIGHING INTERNAL RESOURCES AGAINST EXTERNAL FACTORS

Once the internal resources and external factors have been identified and evaluated, you can estimate your political strength by estimating the difference between their respective sums. That is,

Σ (+/- Power internal resources)
$\underline{-\Sigma \text{ (+/- Power external factors)}}$
If Σ +, continue lobbying
If Σ -, wait until time is more favorable

Like a chess game, political strength is the relation between opponents' relative power and positions. A weaker opponent with better position can win the game. And a powerful opponent in poor position can lose the game.

How do your internal resources compare to the external factors? Do you have enough political strength to begin your legislative effort? If not, can you increase it? As you estimate political strength, realize this is a subjective evaluation requiring best judgment.

Assessing your internal resources and external factors places you at a crossroads in the lobbying path as you must now decide whether to continue with your project or abandon it for this year. You may find, although your political strength is insufficient, you have little choice but to move forward because of an urgent need for legislation. Ideally, however, you will move forward only if your political strength seems sufficient.

Increasing Your Political Strength

If your initial assessment suggests insufficient political strength, you can grow stronger. Although you can do nothing about this year's partisan composition of the legislature, theme for the session, or your tax status, you can affect some of the internal resources and external factors.

Highly motivated association members willing to commit to your legislative success can compensate for deficits in other internal factors. You can also increase legislators' awareness of your association and its expertise. By joining with other individuals, companies, or associations who have resources you lack, you can add to your political strength.

Specialized consultants are available to help you in most areas. Especially valuable are contract lobbyists who are experts in advocating legislation and who have a network of political contacts. We discuss them in some detail in Chapter 4. You may be able to reduce opposition and gain support by redefining your issue to make it more compelling or by revising your legislative goals to fit better with the session's theme.

Dangers of Lobbying with Insufficient Political Strength

Going to the legislature with insufficient political strength may leave you worse off than if you never went to the legislature at all. The loss of resources including money, reputation, member motivation, political capital, and so on may be the least of your problems. More powerful opponents may convince a legislator friendly to them to sponsor an amendment to your bill in which the lawmaker says, "I propose we strike everything below the *enactment clause* and put in [your organization's worst nightmare]." Insufficient political strength already makes moving your bill difficult. But far worse, inability to fend off harmful amendments to your bill may result in your worst nightmare becoming law.

Summary Chapter 2

Your assessment of political strength begins with consideration of internal resources and external factors. The dynamic synergism among these variables can enable you to move forward even when some factors are not favorable to you or your issue.

Political strength is the difference between the power of your internal resources and external factors. It is a subjective evaluation. When you have sufficient political strength, or when you are able to increase it sufficiently, you can proceed to develop the lobbying campaign. In the next chapter, you will design the association's infrastructure, develop the lobbying plan, and draft your preliminary bill.

Chapter 3: Developing the Lobbying Campaign

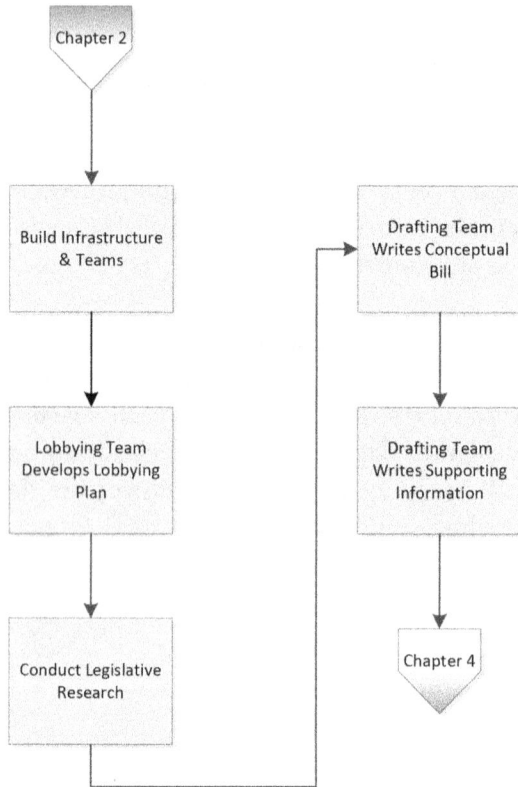

```
        ┌──────────┐
        │ Chapter 2 │
        └────┬─────┘
             │
             ▼
┌──────────────────┐                    ┌──────────────────┐
│ Build Infrastructure │                │   Drafting Team    │
│     & Teams         │─────────────▶   │ Writes Conceptual  │
│                     │                 │       Bill         │
└──────────┬──────────┘                 └─────────┬──────────┘
           │                                      │
           ▼                                      ▼
┌──────────────────┐                    ┌──────────────────┐
│  Lobbying Team    │                   │   Drafting Team    │
│ Develops Lobbying │                   │ Writes Supporting  │
│      Plan         │                   │   Information      │
└──────────┬────────┘                   └─────────┬──────────┘
           │                                      │
           ▼                                      ▼
┌──────────────────┐                        ┌──────────┐
│ Conduct Legislative │                      │ Chapter 4 │
│     Research        │                      └──────────┘
└─────────┬───────────┘
          │
          └──────────────────────────────────┘
```

CHAPTER 3

DEVELOPING THE LOBBYING CAMPAIGN

Although lobbying is a simple concept, its practice involves a systematic progression of activities and decisions. Once you conclude you have sufficient political strength to go forward, your next step is to develop your lobbying infrastructure. The infrastructure is built upon two broad categories of distinct yet interdependent teams: management and functional. Together they plan, organize, and implement your campaign.

In an ideal *member-driven* organization, association or coalition, individual members appoint team participants to serve the association's legislative goals. Their willingness to contribute money and personnel to work on behalf of the association is a direct indicator of commitment. While levels of commitment vary, the sum donation of all contributions is a solid predictor of lobbying fitness.

Having worked for and with smaller organizations, professional and volunteer, I realize how difficult it is to gain sufficient commitment of both personnel and money. Some will have the money but not the personnel requiring them to hire contractors, which I discuss in Chapter 4. However, as good as your contractor is, he or she alone cannot substitute for member involvement, especially in major legislative efforts.

Other associations have less money, but their members are enthusiastic and ready to apply the methodology you are learning herein. To illustrate,

As the . . . Alabama Legislative Session opened, the Chairman of the Senate Education Finance & Taxation Committee addressed all of Alabama's school superintendents. During the Q & A, a superintendent asked what else our association could do to better impact the legislative process. Senator Hank Sanders replied, "You are doing everything right. Your staff works hard and represents you very well and your [staff] lobbyists are well known. Superintendents are talking and meeting with their legislators and legislators want to know what superintendents think. I believe you will see your priorities in the budget that comes out this year because you have a lot of influence. You used to be PITIFUL, but now you are doing everything right."

Senator Sanders' words affirmed the transformation we have made as an organization. Just three short years ago I was hired as the first full-time executive director and began over the next year and a half to add a few staff members and we worked to improve all aspects of our association. I remember in my first weeks the State Superintendent advised me, 'Now Susan, don't think you can do too much—these superintendents never agree on anything. It's like herding cats!' With that warning I searched to learn more about the legislative process. After all, I had been hired to improve our efforts and gain influence in Montgomery. I read 'How to Effectively Lobby Your State Legislature' [Guide to State Legislative Lobbying] by Bob Guyer. I went online and registered for Bob's training. Then I set out to organize our members, establish effective communication, bought every member a copy of his book on how to successfully lobby and hired Bob Guyer to train our superintendents in the Campaign Method of Lobbying.

The Campaign Method of Lobbying took us from PITIFUL towards POWERFUL in just 3 years! I believe Bob Guyer's Campaign Method can work for any organization serious about impacting the legislative process. It made a real difference for me in developing a successful game plan for our association.

Dr. Susan Lockwood, Executive Director (former)
School Superintendents of Alabama

Even small organizations doing the things you are learning can have an impact. I *pro bono* assisted an enthusiastic but almost penniless organization wanting to enable the Medicaid-disabled to stay in their homes rather than being sent to nursing homes. We played a small but important role in enacting Tennessee's *Long-Term Care Community Choices Act*.

Regardless of the kind of organization for which you work, the principles below will help you become more successful than you would otherwise be. I will lay out the ideal, and you will tailor it to your resources.

BUILDING YOUR INFRASTRUCTURE

Teams, starting with the management and functional, form the infrastructure of your lobbying campaign. Then the size of your association and level of member commitment determine the number of individuals to serve on each team. If your association is small, you may need to combine team functions so the necessary work can be accomplished. In that case consider hiring consultants, law firms, and contract lobbyists, or joining with other associations to supplement your resources. By hiring professional assistance or joining a coalition, you can compensate for your lack of personnel.

However, as valuable as they are, all contractors are inherently conflicted, starting with the pressures of other clients, demands from lawmakers, and running profitable businesses. Contractors are supplements; they are not, nor can they be, substitutes for members.

The *Management Team* should be comprised of persons representing each interest group within the association and each having the authority to commit their employers' political, financial, and personnel resources. It initially meets to form and fund the organization. This team organizes the project, commits resources, develops project goals, and appoints members to the functional teams. The Management Team translates association legislative goals into specific outcomes, allocates resources, and develops a rationale and strategy for the project.

Therefore, it should be comprised of politically savvy top managers who understand human nature and know how to work with people, especially those with opposing views. Of course, this team receives counsel from the functional teams and contract lobbyist as it fulfills its mission. Especially in associations whose members are large organizations, these top managers in time will delegate their day-to-day association operating responsibilities to immediate subordinates.

Management Team oversight ensures effective communication among the functional teams, staff, contractors, and with the management team itself. Even the best designed campaign will fail if individuals or teams lose sight of the overall goal or become focused only on their narrow interests or responsibilities.

While many functional teams are possible, we will focus on two critical ones: those who do the lobbying and those who do the writing. The *Lobbying Team* is composed of association members and, if a large enough organization, association staff. Wealthier associations may have staff, legal counsel, and in-house and contract lobbyists.

The Management Team assigns broad legislative goals to the Lobbying Team and provides broad policy direction. The Lobbying Team responds by planning and implementing the lobbying portion of the campaign. They influence the players, that is, special interests, legislative staff, agency staff, lawmakers and the Governor. They meet with supporters and opponents, attend and testify in committee hearings, and otherwise do the face-to-face work in moving your bill.

The *Bill Manager* chairs the Lobbying Team.[42] Appointed by the Management Team, the Bill Manager is responsible for overseeing the day-to-day activities of the lobbying effort. He or she coordinates grassroots lobbying activities of association members and is the designated contact for the association's contract lobbyist(s). The Bill Manager updates the Management Team about the bill's progress so changes can be made in policy or resource allocation. He or she is also responsible for ensuring the association, including its member lobbyists, complies with the legislature's ethical requirements.

The *Drafting Team* writes the bill and supporting information to be given to the legislature. The team should be composed of persons who understand the topic, write clearly and appreciate legal requirements. The initial supporting information and committee testimony will be drafted prior to bill introduction and revised, as needed.

The *Bill Historian* is insurance you hope you never use, but, if you do, he or she can save your campaign. The Historian is always at a moment's notice ready to explain to interest groups, lawmakers, and staff all actual and proposed changes in bill language following its publication. He or she is a detail-oriented person who documents each change and reason why. As your bill advances along the legislative path, there will be proposed and actual changes to its language and concepts. By being able to explain all changes, upon inquiry or challenge, if asked about differences among successive drafts, he or she can save you from appearing dishonest or incompetent.

To illustrate, we were meeting with Congressional staff to discuss our bill. An opponent committee member sent his senior staffer to stop our progress. At a critical moment the staffer calmly asked us, "Industry, why does the draft before us today look so different from your previous draft?" None of us remembered. Upon seeing we had no answer as to why it had changed, he aggressively charged, "Isn't this typical industry deceit, once again trying to slip something past the U.S. Congress?" We appeared to be either nefarious as charged, or we were incompetent; and lawmakers want to partner with neither. Had a bill historian answered, "It was changed on August 21 at the Speaker's request," we would have avoided considerable injury to our credibility and our bill. The Bill Historian is insurance.

Consider adding other functional teams to meet the needs of your campaign. These include grassroots organizing, negotiations, public relations, media, budget, and other activities specific to your project.

THE LOBBYING PLAN

The lobbying plan describes how you will gain support and minimize opposition. It helps to maximize use of resources to increase the likelihood of success. When you assessed political strength, you estimated the power of internal resources versus external factors. As you develop the lobbying plan, consider these thirteen elements:

1. Constituents
2. People and associations
3. Executive agencies
4. Costs and benefits
5. Timing
6. Place
7. Campaign contributions
8. Relationship building
9. Communication with the media
10. Avoiding unnecessary conflicts with your members and special interests
11. Maintaining confidentiality
12. Growing and keeping consensus
13. Social media

1. *Constituents.* The term *constituents* generally refers to persons living in a lawmaker's electoral district. However, these residents vary greatly in political significance ranging from highly influential to utterly irrelevant or even toxic. Lawmakers strive to satisfy their *friends*. In order of importance, constituents are a lawmaker's:

- *Supporters*, that is, persons whom the lawmaker trusts, vote for the lawmaker, and donate time or money. Campaign finance reports reveal most supporters.

- *Known voters*, generally of the same party, but anyone who can say he or she voted for the lawmaker.
- *Could-be voters*, generally opponents, who at times share the lawmaker's views.
- *Non-voters*, they don't vote, so they don't count to really anyone.
- *Opponent's supporters and voters*, worse than not counting, *they are the enemy.*

In addition to influencing lawmakers directly, supporters and voters can be mobilized to carry out letter writing and emailing campaigns, make office visits, develop telephone and social media trees, and use other methods to broaden home-folk support. Properly organized constituents amplify your political strength.

On the other hand, constituent involvement may be wholly unnecessary. This is because most bills with little fanfare quietly move through the legislature, staying within the confines of the capitol. As with the media mentioned below, few capitol players want either constituents or media around as they only add work, complications, and volatility to making laws.

That being said, if your opponents mobilize the home-folk then you also will have to mobilize them. But expect, for other than a hot-button issue, your opponents won't want to spend their resources involving constituents, if avoidable. For this reason, most bills have little or no meaningful constituent involvement.

2. *People and associations.* You must identify persons and groups who can impact for good or ill your effort. Start with the special interests which will be your bill's first line of supporters and opponents. They are corporations, associations, unions, activist groups, and all levels of state and local government. You must predict which groups may oppose your bill for substantive or political reasons. Can you satisfy, undo, or work around their opposition? Locate your potential supporters and find ways to involve them actively in supporting your bill. Find ways to strengthen their support and look for nontraditional allies for your issue. Think broadly and creatively when considering alliances with others.

Next, consider legislative staff, especially committee and personal. Lawmakers normally vote as suggested by their staffs because they trust their staffs and staffs do most of the work processing legislation.

Identify executive agencies that must be lobbied to gain their support for your bill or reduce objections to it. Special interests, legislators, and the Governor give considerable attention to experts within these agencies, as described in the next subsection below.

Consider the Governor's likely response to your bill. Determine whether your bill fits with his or her legislative goals for the session. The Governor may support or oppose your bill depending upon how it fits with his or her agenda.

Fellow state and local elected officials and interest groups in a lawmaker's district can be quite influential with lawmakers. Look at the committees to which your bill will be referred and cultivate relationships, mutual respect, and a good feeling with officials and interest groups who support the committee member.

Finally, consider lawmakers on the committees which will hear your bill. Expect once special interests, legislative and agency staffs, Governor, and constituents support your bill, so too will lawmakers. This approach has important corollaries:

- As first mentioned in Chapter 1, 80 to 90 percent of lawmakers are irrelevant to the success or failure of your bill because they will never vote on your bill, except on the chamber floor, either as instructed by the caucus or otherwise in accord with the reports of committees of jurisdiction. Thus, the few who really matter are found on the committees that will consider your bill, and perhaps the caucus and leadership.

- Seventy percent of the work of getting your bill into law takes place *before* the bill is introduced, as described in Chapters 1 through 6. Activities which largely occur before bill introduction include: assessing and increasing political strength, building infrastructure, drafting your bill and supporting materials, hiring and working with contract lobbyists, negotiating with special interests, and planning your procedural path.

Upon bill introduction, you direct the momentum developed earlier to accomplish the remaining thirty percent, including adapting the above to changing politics, working with lawmakers, legislative and agency staff, and sometimes the Governor and lawmakers' constituents.

- Legislators, while *constitutionally* of prime importance because only they can vote on your bill, are *politically* quaternary in importance in the legislative process.

3. *Executive agencies.* Agencies, the third greatest influence on your bill, are powerful in the legislature for a variety of reasons, including:

- Legislators listen to them.
- Special interests fear them.
- Governors protect them.
- Agencies "veto" enrolled bills and statutes.
- Agencies introduce legislation.
- Agencies employ in-house lobbyists.
- Agencies lobby for their own interests.

Legislators listen to them. As the legislature's *de facto* technical staff, legislators give great weight to agency advice and recommendations regarding *substantive* legislation. Few legislators have the technical expertise to evaluate, much less challenge, agency experts who often hold advanced degrees in the field under discussion in the bill. On the other hand, many legislators distrust agency requests in *appropriations* legislation.

Special interests fear them. Agencies impact special interests because agency approval improves chances of bill passage while agency opposition generally dooms a bill. Next, to implement legislation, an agency adopts highly detailed rules. Agency rules can take away everything the legislature gave a special interest or give it more than the legislature would.

Further, special interests when considering opposing the agency, as a matter of self-defense, generally weigh the threat and burden of agency retaliation. Therefore, special interests seriously consider what an agency wants in a bill as they strive to stay off the agency's "bad side."

Governors protect them. Governors employ agencies to assist them in executing the legislature's directions while accomplishing the Governors' goals. Legislative interference with agencies can lead to a constitutional separation of powers battle, as mentioned in Chapter 1, section *Laying the Foundation - Constitutional Structure of U.S. Federal and State Governments*. Veto messages regularly read, in essence, "Since you lawmakers meddled with (or ignored) my agency – 'BILL VETOED.'"

Agencies "veto" enrolled bills and statutes. In the unlikely event an agency didn't kill a bill in the legislature, it still can "veto" the enrolled bill and statute in a couple of ways.

First, when Governors receive enrolled bills, they ask agencies for advice on what to do with them. The agency can urge the Governor to veto an enrolled bill based on technical facts, cost to the state of implementing the law, difficulty of implementing the law, effect the law would have on state and local governments and other agencies, impact the law would have on the public, any hint of violation of separation of powers, or a combination of these things. Expect the Governor to do as recommended.

Second, if the Governor doesn't veto the enrolled bill, it becomes a statute. However, an agency for all practical purposes can "veto" a statute by not implementing it, either through failure to enter into rulemaking or by not enforcing the rules it does adopt. The net result is until rulemaking is completed, there isn't a law; and nobody knows what the law means until the agency says what it means, as explained in its adopted rules. Furthermore, if the agency won't enforce its rules for reasons of policy, interest, or resources, for all practical purposes the law is without effect.

Agencies employ in-house lobbyists. Agencies introduce legislation using several vehicles which differ in substance and frequency from state to state. Depending on the state, they may introduce bills automatically without a sponsor or the Governor's approval, use legislative bill slots reserved for agency and Governor's bills, or employ surrogate constituent groups to introduce legislation for them. Generally, state agencies may not hire contract lobbyists.[43]

Agencies lobby for their own interests. Agencies lobby for what they want, propose and oppose legislation, work with and threaten special interests, build coalitions, negotiate bill language, and are extremely influential legislative players. Accordingly, agencies have their own lobbyists who, being political, have much broader policy perspectives than the fact-and-law career civil service technical staffs. They can influence the agency's policy makers to support or oppose a bill.

Agency interests are narrower than those of stakeholders and lawmakers and they are largely insulated from political pressure and accountability. Except as mandated by statute, they often have little concern for the economic impacts of their actions upon private parties (as contrasted with affecting the state budget).

To illustrate, the Department included language in an omnibus solid waste bill that could force my principal to cease operations and result in the loss of 1,300 well-paying manufacturing jobs. I enjoyed a friendly relationship with the Department manager responsible for the threatening provision. However, when I told him the Department's proposal could result in factory closure, he said to me, "Bob, the Department doesn't get paid to keep you in business. If you have a bad product, then I guess you'll just have to go out of business."

Immediately, I ran over to the Speaker's office to alert them to the dangers of the Department's proposal. Fortunately, I also had a good relationship with a deputy majority leader who was our member in the house. When I recited to her what he had just said, she unexpectedly stood up from her chair, slammed her desk with her hand, and exclaimed, "The Department doesn't care about jobs. Over here at the legislature we care about jobs." In the end, the bill was fixed to keep my principal in business and 1,300 jobs in her district.

However, influencing an agency on legislative matters may be considered to be lobbying the agency. Lobbying the agency may require registration as an agency lobbyist; even getting a second lobbying license and complying with a second set of ethics rules. Florida offers an instructive example,

> Although properly registered in the Legislature, the lobbyist may not be correspondingly registered in the executive branch for the same principal. This is a gray area; but since the lobbyist is now attempting to influence the outcome of a legislative measure within the state agency, it is highly recommended that the lobbyist become immediately registered within the executive branch notwithstanding the issue being a legislative public policy matter.[44]

Finally, Thomas Jefferson said, "The execution of the laws is more important than the making of them . . ." Although he was speaking of the courts, his comment is quite applicable to executive agencies, too.

4. *Costs and benefits.* Assess the financial, political, social, and personal costs to your association, supporters and opponents, legislators, and others. List the benefits of your legislation and compare them to the probable costs to your association and others. Try to identify the amount of lobbying needed to maintain support and estimate the cost and benefit associated with each new alliance. You will want to draft your bill to minimize costs and maximize benefits for all affected parties should your bill become law. Although "win-win" is an attractive concept, in practice most laws benefit one group more than others.

5. *Timing.* Often, the success of a legislative effort is dependent upon timing. An ill-timed legislative effort may fail despite a meritorious concept. To find the best timing for your effort, answer these questions:

- How difficult will it be to move your bill? The more difficult, the earlier you should start.
- Would a bill advance more readily in another year?
- Can this legislation wait until next year or must you lobby it this session?

- Will friendly lawmakers still be in office or otherwise able to support you next year?
- Is there time to meet critical dates, procedural milestones, and political timelines?
- Are there other time-related conditions to consider, such as impending elections and changes in the majority party?

6. *Place.* Before taking your issue to the state house, consider where the best or easiest jurisdiction might be to obtain precedent-setting legislation. It might be in a sister state or in a major political subdivision of the state, such as an important city or county. Investigate similar legislation passed in states having precedential value to your legislature. Finally, decide which lawmakers to lobby at home and which in their capital offices.

7. *Campaign contributions.* Will campaign contributions be part of your lobbying plan? If so, on a member-by-member basis, determine how your support of a legislator's re-election campaign will garner goodwill or engender an opponent's hostility. If you need the support of legislators with whom your association has *no preexisting connections,* then a large enough campaign contribution may improve their *awareness* of your existence. However, no matter how much money you give a lawmaker it will have little influence on how he or she normally votes, much less changing votes. They will take your money but you won't get a vote.

Legislators vote to please those who put and keep them in office. Accordingly, they listen attentively to their supporters, voters, those who could in time support them, and supportive special interests. They listen to proven friends.

However, because making campaign contributions can be risky, many organizations simply don't do it. "And only about a third of the thousands of interest groups in Washington even have a political action committee with which to give campaign contributions. The other two-thirds give zero dollars to candidates."[45] Further, 501(c)(3) nonprofits are forbidden from making partisan donations of either money or support.

None of the organizations for which I worked made *regular* campaign contributions and donations were of modest amounts. Giving to the losing candidate may make you an enemy of the winner. If the candidate is sure to be elected, then donations won't hurt you as long as the lawmaker stays in office. Knowing donations can be risky, and you aren't going to get a vote for your money, you must carefully consider whether you should do it.

8. *Relationship building.* Positive relationships are the foundation of your capitol lobbying. Relationships that matter are with lawmakers' constituents, interest groups, legislative and agency staffs, lawmakers themselves, and the Governor. Some relationships are more important than others and you will invest more in one relationship than another. All have degrees of importance. But your most important relationships are with lawmakers on the committees likely to vote on your bill, that is, the ten to twenty percent who matter.

Building relationships with elected officials is rewarding, relatively easy, and critical to your success. When a legislator benefits, he or she will work to advance and defend your interests. In the legislature, a lawmaker may sponsor, co-sponsor, or even lobby for your bill. As a member of the legislature, he or she has much greater access to "inside" information and can inform you about the legislature's internal activities surrounding your bill.

Lobbying is *legislative sales.* Your job is to know as much as you can about your customer *before you make your first contact.* Knowing your customer is the foundation of relationship building. And information about your customers is abundantly available. Expect lawmakers to have personal and legislature-assigned websites, social media pages, and instant messaging accounts. Try to subscribe to their social media feeds or pages. Virtually all special interests have websites. The more you know about your customer, the more effectively you will be able to develop an effective sales package for your lobbying visits. Internet research is discussed more below.

9. *Communications with the media.* Consider the pro and con impacts the media could have on your bill. If your group is of kindred spirit to

reporters, they can be helpful to you. Attention from media who are generally unfavorable to you can be quite harmful. On the one hand, your issue may suffer from media attention if it brings unwanted interest to friendly lawmakers or from opposition groups. On the other hand, favorable attention may help you overcome opposition.

Whether you do or do not want media attention, you must be prepared for it. Develop press releases explaining the identity of your association, its members, and its lobbying goals. Select articulate, credentialed, or well-known members of your association to represent you to the media.

10. *Avoiding unnecessary conflicts with your members and special interests.* Your association must ensure its legislative goals and activities do not *unnecessarily* conflict with the interests of your members or allied organizations. Member organizations often have legislative agendas being lobbied by contractors or in-house staff unrelated to your issue. You must coordinate lobbying efforts to avoid sending conflicting messages to the legislature.

The association should also communicate and coordinate activities with special interests whose issues will follow a similar path through the legislature. These other groups will not compete with you on specific issues, but they will compete for the legislature's very limited amount of time, attention, and state funds.

11. *Maintaining confidentiality.* Once you have evaluated your issue and developed the lobbying plan, it should be explained *orally* to all members of the functional teams. Maintain confidentiality about your plan and do not distribute any written details. Too often, by intentional leak or accident, written documents are found in the hands of the wrong people, leading to catastrophic results. Further, you should not discuss your lobbying campaign in public when you don't know who is listening. The Second World War gave us the caution, "Loose lips sink ships."[46] This advice remains useful today as illustrated by presidential counselors giving a *New York Times* reporter, coincidentally sitting at an adjacent table, an accidental scoop by discussing Oval Office strategy while dining outside on a restaurant patio![47]

12. *Growing and keeping consensus.* Consensus propels and controversy kills. Among the most difficult and critical aspects of your legislative campaign is gaining and keeping consensus among those who can impact your bill. These include:

- Intra-organizational (your own organization)
- Intra-segment (parties with similar interests who should be united)
- Intra-coalition (disparate groups momentarily together advancing a one-time common interest)
- Inter-capital players (agreement among special interests, legislative staff, agency staff, Governor)
- Intra-legislature (keeping supportive lawmakers together as they are attacked by your opponents)

To maintain consensus, at times you may feel like you are baby-sitting. Other times you are holding distressed hands. You may be like the vaudeville entertainer trying to keep a series of plates spinning, but you have to do it.

However, loss of consensus or the outbreak of controversy can sink a bill. To illustrate, about to gain a favorable Senate vote, a Senator put a *hold* on our bill. (A *hold* is a U.S. Senate privilege allowing a senator to interrupt anonymously the progress of a bill.) His staff showed us a constituent letter from *one of our own members* objecting to our bill. By the time we cleared up our member's objection, the bill was lost for that Congress. One disaffected member destroyed two years of work for 115 other organizations. Two principles were at play: 1) *consensus propels and controversy kills*, and 2) *lawmakers hate to get involved in family squabbles.*

13. *Social Media.* Social media broadcast that which associations want to say to their members, what lawmakers offer to anyone who will listen, and what interest groups and individuals hope will influence lawmakers. But how important is all this broadcasting? And for us as lobbyists, do social media actually lead to lawmakers' votes, or at least nudge them in the right direction? Some advocates hold that social

media are central to lobbying, others that it is a useful tool, and a few that it is dangerous. Given its potential, I discuss it in some detail in the next section.

SOCIAL MEDIA[48]

A 2019 Lobby School survey of 31 lobbyists found social media are used for the following:

- Mass communication:
  - Association to its members, allied groups, and public
  - Association and individuals to lawmakers
  - Lawmakers to public
- Building rapport and intelligence gathering
- Lawmaker pressure, reward and punishment

Mass Communication:

Association to its members, allied groups, and public. Regular communication with members promotes member consensus which is the bedrock of an effective lobbying campaign, as emphasized in Chapter 2. Consensus precedes member motivation, investment, and action. Social media connect associations with and motivate like-minded groups.

Association and individuals to lawmaker. Cate found 53 percent of Florida lawmakers' staffs say constituents' comments on social media sites are important or very important in influencing lawmakers on matters on which lawmakers don't have a firm opinion.[49] In contrast, 100 percent said in-person constituent visits were important or very important in influencing them.

Social media facilitate inexpensive quick communications with lawmakers. Social media avoid non-constituent screening filters and likely are exempt from public records laws. It is attractive because it offers:

Quicker access to some lawmakers. Lawmakers often manage their own social media accounts and check them more frequently than email.

Access to legislative staff. Virtually all offices manage their own social media. Advocates should balance the convenience of being able to reach an office with the potential downside of annoying the staffs who have to process messages.

Inexpensive contacts. Social media are inexpensive as to costs in terms of money, time, labor and convenience relative to the costs of paid media and human lobbying.

Insulation from public records laws. Social media may be more attractive than emails and hard copy correspondence because, in most if not all states, social media communications are not subject to public records laws. However, at the state level this is an evolving question but for now, social media often avoid public disclosure further making it an attractive communications tool.[50]

Circumventing non-constituent filters. Legislatively provided email services filter out communications from non-constituents. 2020 presidential candidate Joaquin Castro (D-TX) states, "With government email systems that filter out messages from non-constituents and staffers who vet phone calls to the office, social media networks are the best places for direct, one-to-one connections with your elected officials."[51]

Lawmakers to public. Lawmakers intending to stay in office are always campaigning for office, either to keep the ones they have or to move to a higher one. Social media allow lawmakers to market themselves, measure support in their districts and statewide, and identify potential campaign contributors. And, as mentioned in Chapter 7, *lawmaking is campaigning.*

Building rapport and gathering intelligence. Lobbying is a people business and social media have a place building relationships, at least to the depth of being "Facebook friends," and gathering intelligence on lawmakers and opponents. Much information can be found about law-makers on the Internet. Social media can be useful for gathering intelligence on your opposition. Its sponteneity often blunders out secrets.

Lawmaker pressure, reward, and punishment. Advocates use social media to pressure, reward, and punish lawmakers. Pressure can be applied to one person or to a group of targeted lawmakers. Social media can be used to reward lawmakers with public praise, or to chastise them.

How Effective Are Social Media in Getting Lawmakers' Votes? The real question for lobbyists is not whether social media is a valuable tool for communication, gathering intelligence, and exerting pressure, as described above. It is. A few respondents said they have seen it get votes. Most respondents, however, simply see social media as just one more device in the lobbyist's tool box. It's useful, but let's not exaggerate its importance. Even among those who thought social media most useful, with one or two exceptions, respondents had no evidence social media actually got votes.

Cautions and Criticisms over Social Media. Several cautioned about being unable to control one's message and being overly trusting in social media. To this I add, social media falls within a crowd of other much more powerful influences. As to controlling message, the feeling was expressed once communication is put on the web it is open to distortion and media scrutiny.

Social media may nudge a lawmaker, especially in matters in which he or she isn't strongly invested. However, as I discuss extensively in *Insiders Talk: Winning with Lobbyists, Professional edition,* a lawmaker will vote first to ensure personal political longevity by pleasing his or her supporters, voters, and could-be supporters. Those who don't vote and the opponents' voters, *if they have any influence,* have much less of it.

Having a secure seat, the lawmaker will next vote to build a successful legislative career. That means going along with the party caucus and same-party chamber leadership. A lawmaker who votes contrary to either can find him or herself with reduced influence or even stripped of committee assignments thereby denied opportunities to build a record of legislative success. All the social media "friends" or instant messages aren't going to motivate a lawmaker to vote contrary to leadership.

Having a secure seat and good committee assignments, the lawmaker will vote to maintain or gain supporters, both political and financial. Electronic messages aren't going to motivate a lawmaker to risk endorsements from significant interest groups or financial backers.

Social media is just the messenger; it is not the message. Several respondents commented on the use of social media to drive great numbers of communications to targeted lawmakers. However, there is a sinister side to social media. Some of its power comes from intimidation, harassment, humiliation, disinformation and defamation. It is the rule of the mob. Nathan Sykes of TechTalk writes,

> One common form is a wave of angry people—not necessarily even a majority—who mob together and form a community of outrage. The resulting noise can be filled with allegations, both true and false, that do considerable damage to a person's career or health . . . Another pointed use for social media is to further the rapid spread of disinformation. This can be on purpose, with the intent to develop a particularly nasty rumor, or it can be born out of sheer ignorance. People sometimes believe what they're sharing is true and important when, in fact, it is not. This was done in increasing numbers during the last major U.S. election by various sources.[52]

All users of social media, especially lawmakers and staff, must bear in mind social media consists of real people mixed with Astro-turf, spoofing, bots, fake profiles, trolls, and click-farms. "However, I also think it [social media] can be ignored by legislators at times because it can just be a lot of noise and even to a degree misrepresents the general public's true perception of an issue because those who voice their opinions on social media are often times a loud minority."[53] "[T]he most prolific 10% of Twitterers create 80% of the total tweets. In other words, don't be fooled into thinking that the most popular opinions on Twitter represent the most popular opinions offline."[54] And like much found on the Internet, social media should be taken with the proverbial grain of salt.[55]

Ben Nimmo, *Information Defense Fellow, Atlantic Council's Digital Forensic Research Lab,* asks,

> How many social media accounts belong to the person they claim to be? There are millions which don't. There are troll accounts which pretend to be someone else. There are bot accounts which use somebody else's profile picture and name, but are automated to post hundreds of times a day. There are accounts which used to be run by a genuine user, but were hijacked and taken over by someone else. There are accounts which claim to be one person, but are operated by a team. There are cyborg accounts which sometimes post authored content, and sometimes post on autopilot, with no human intervention.[56]

In the same article, David Caplan, *Co-Founder of TwitterAudit,* says,

> At *Twitter/Audit* we've analyzed tens of millions of Twitter users over the past six years. We've tuned our algorithm to recognize bot patterns [to] distinguish fake accounts from real accounts. (sic) Based on our data we would estimate that 40–60% of Twitter accounts represent real people. It's much easier to sign up a fake/bot account on Twitter than it is on other social media platforms, and in many cases it's hard to tell if an account is fake or just inactive. On the other hand, it's a bit easier to define a "real person" on Twitter than it is on, say, Instagram.[57]

Facebook recently has been disabling hundreds of millions of fake accounts each month.[58] Even an instructor in a political practices class I attended told us, since most lawmakers are older males, an effective way for us to get a lawmaker to Facebook "friend" us was to create a phony account with a picture of an attractive woman. President Reagan's fre-

61

quent use of the Russian proverb, *doveryai, no proverya* (trust but verify) should guide all users of social media.

A Case Study in Social Media Backfire. Some social media power rests on intimidation, embarrassment, and mob incitement. A multistate lobbyist provides this case study of a lobbyist who tried to inflame a mob to bully a lawmaker, and indirectly an entire legislature. He writes,

> But what sticks out in my mind more are incidents where a person/group had tried to shakedown a lawmaker with social media. This most often backfires badly.

> This occurred two years ago as (Maryland) was considering revamping their alcohol laws. Maryland has a system that allows only one store per person or corporation—statewide. Meaning that Total Wine can only have one store in the entire state (which is quite sad because their headquarters is in Potomac, MD, with over 500 employees). Safeway, and any other grocer, is only allowed one store to sell alcohol in the entire state.

> This system protects incumbent "mom and pop" liquor stores. And their trade association has incredibly formidable contract lobbyists, the best in the town. Nobody can do anything as it relates to alcohol without their blessing.

> But times, they are a changin,' and the public is definitely supportive of more options/competition, so that's why the alcohol lobbyists stop these democratization of alcohol bills from ever seeing the light of day (a vote in committee).

> Every year there was a big push, grassroots, the whole nine yards, to expand access to alcohol. Two years ago, a bill had been worked that would have allowed existing license holders to open a second store, and it would've removed the cap on a store size (was and still is limited to 10,000 square feet or less, it's an anti-Total Wine law). It was worked hard and eventually passed the alcohol subcommittee, a very hard feat. It passed

with the vote count needed, nothing more. But, of course, you know, a subcommittee vote means nothing legally, but it set the bill up for vote by the full committee.

If you were on the inside, you knew that the bill was going to have enough . . . but just enough . . . votes to pass the full committee. Many "no" votes were never going to change, they had entrenched interests that this bill was against. But that doesn't matter, they said no, but if you have enough votes to pass it, let them be and shore up your yes votes.

Well never to leave well enough alone, a lobbyist (was from a big liquor store chain, and she wasn't "from" Maryland, she was a multistate lobbyist, you know the kind that parachute in as or when needed, but never truly have the strong relationships), she decides to run a campaign finance report of a "no" vote that showed his contributions from the entrenched "mom and pop" liquor store umbrella association, and then post that onto Facebook the day the full committee was set to vote. What a foolish decision (especially for a so-called seasoned lobbyist), and of course it's no secret that people receive contributions from industries that the legislator is supportive of.

This of course greatly infuriated the legislator, but as you know, it brought unfavorable public scrutiny down upon the legislative process.

Politicians may have deeply differing viewpoints, but they tend to stick together as one to protect their ilk. And posting something like that caused legislators on both sides of the issue to pull back, withhold the bill, and it's never seen the light of day again.

All because somebody couldn't leave well enough alone.

It's like finding a bag of money and then seeing a quarter lying across the way between the railroad tracks and reaching over to get it only to be run over by the train. [59]

Future of Social Media. No one polled saw social media declining, and many expected its use to expand. I expect that many of those who responded that they don't use social media for lobbying will incorporate it into their practices.

While many factors will affect the future of social media, I expect an aging lawmaker population and to-be-determined willingness for hands-on direct engagement to affect it most. Respondents commented the lawmaker group that uses social media most is under 40 years old. The National Conference of State Legislatures reported that as of 2015 the average age of state lawmakers is 56 years old with approximately two-thirds of state lawmakers being over 50.[60]

Social media is a tool which, in limited instances, may nudge a lawmaker to take action. However, as emphasized earlier, advocates shouldn't make too much of it.

- *On the one hand,* it cannot trump the human connection coming from a lawmaker looking into the eyes of a real person, especially one he or she knows personally, and realizing his or her vote will have a real impact, for good or for ill, on that person's life. On the other hand, social media are a quick way to broadcast information, from lawmakers to voters and from interest groups to lawmakers.
- *On the one hand,* speaking face-to-face to a lawmaker may have an impact living beyond the moment. On the other hand, social media posts may become irrelevant by the end of the day, if not within hours.
- *On the one hand,* the real person a lawmaker talks to is just that, a real person. On the other hand, social media consists of real people mixed with Astro-turf, spoofing, bots, fake profiles, and click-farms.
- *On the one hand,* face-to-face lawmaker-advocate interaction fosters civility, dialogue, and respect. On the other hand, the anonymity of social media brings out trolls, sometimes paid, disrespect, and even threats.
- *On the one hand,* a lobbyist accompanied by a few constituents

is generally impactful. On the other hand, an organized social media effort may flood an office in a few hours with thousands of posts to create an impression. Sophisticated staff will be able to discern what's real and what's to be ignored.

Social media are valuable tools. But so are your cellphone, pen, and business card.

CONDUCTING LEGISLATIVE RESEARCH

You must discover and utilize available information about the legislative process, individuals and interest groups, government agencies, committees, and legislators who will affect the outcome of your bill. As Francis Bacon said in 1597, and subsequently repeated for centuries, "Knowledge is power." Initially, conducting research may seem to be an intimidating task. However, today's technology has simplified the process and expanded the amount of information available.

Lawmakers may maintain capitol and district offices staffed by employees who can answer your questions on a variety of issues. A legislative aide who manages the day-to-day activities in the office can schedule an appointment with the legislator, or even better with his or her staff, for you to discuss your topic of interest. Legislative aides with access to state resources and personnel can provide you with valuable insight about the political environment in your state capital.

The local library may provide information about state representatives, state and local agencies, and interest groups. References describing the basics of the political process, such as how a bill becomes law, are available, as are books to help you draft your bill.

Many state government activities are conducted with or through local government. Consequently, local government and agency officials are often well informed about state issues and can provide you with information about current topics as well as possible future legislation.

Your state likely publishes statewide guides, often hardcopy or digital. These guides show the geographical areas of each elected official's electoral district in addition to the electronic email and mailing addresses, fax and telephone numbers, lists of state agencies and representatives, and districting information. The Office of the Senate Secretary or House Clerk may publish manuals with current information, biographical data, and other relevant facts about legislators, committee assignments, and political activities.

Legislative services agencies are a valuable resource for groups interested in drafting their own legislation and supporting information for presentation to their sponsor. One legislative services agency, known in some states variously as *Legislative Services Bureau, Office of Legislative Legal Services, Legislative Counsel, Bill Drafting Services,* or similar names ensures bills are correct as to form and law. Although these offices work primarily with lawmakers and not directly with citizens, expect the legislature's website to provide the bill drafting manual and models on which to pattern your bill and supporting information.

Major political parties' local and state offices may provide information about current and prospective candidates, party positions on issues, candidate campaigns, and local opportunities for involvement with the party. These offices are listed online with other political groups and state agencies.

If you can get the lawmaker's election campaign manager to speak to you about the legislator, you can gain a trove of insight into your customer. However, managers may in the interest of privacy rebuff your efforts. Similarly, the lawmakers' families and friends have valuable information they may or may not be willing to share with you.

Finally, contract lobbyists understand the process and players, and, as stated throughout this book, can be tremendous help to you, and, at times, they are even indispensable. They are the topic of our next chapter.

Internet Research

The Internet is an invaluable source of information for most topics related to lobbying your bill. State legislatures maintain home pages providing information about individual legislators, list state government directories, describe bill drafting procedures, and provide chamber rules. Home pages offer links to sites related to the state's government; topics range from agencies to personnel matters. During the legislative session, status of bills, journals, meeting notices, and legislative calendars may be listed.

Sample bills in the proper format can be obtained from web sites in each state. Although sample bills may be downloaded to use as models, you should obtain an official paper copy since electronic versions may not show chamber coding, bill summary, tables, or other necessary information.

There are hundreds of great websites for Internet research and I will touch upon just a few. One of the better web sites for finding pertinent state information is the *FindLaw* web site. Through this site you can access information from each state's directory and the executive, legislative, and judicial branches of government. Listings show email addresses, committee names, memberships, and positions of leadership within the legislative branch.

Cornell University offers a web site that provides political information. You can retrieve federal and state constitutions, state statutes by a variety of topics, pending bills, and directory information by state. There are links to sites related to local and national politics of each state, as well as to other political topics.

Project Vote-Smart, sponsored by persons along the political continuum, tracks and researches state and federal political activities. From the web site, you can find information about local legislators, biographical and contact data, bill tracking information, and a variety of links to state and federal sites. It also provides information about legislators such as their financial donors, current issues, candidate positions, voting records, and candidate evaluations by interest groups. In addition, *Ballotpedia, National Conference of State Legislatures, National Governors Association,* and *MultiState* all provide valuable information.

States publish information to help you find groups previously interested in legislative topics similar to yours. You may find lobbyists, organizations and issues for which they lobby, and perhaps financial disclosure information. The information is public record and may be obtained from the lobbyist registration office Internet data base.

Given the abundance of information available, you can know the environment in which you will be working, history of legislative actions on your issues, and lawmakers' voting records. You can find names of lobbyists and organizations interested in your or similar issues. You can find who gives money to whom and ratings of lawmakers by interest groups. In other words, much of the information you need to know is plentifully available.

DRAFTING YOUR CONCEPTUAL BILL

A *bill* is an idea in written form publicly presented to the legislature for enactment. Until it takes concrete form as a bill, it remains just an idea. "No law shall be enacted except by bill" is a common phrase in state constitutions and is the practice in all states.

All bills follow a prescribed procedure when introduced into the legislature. Legislative procedure ensures the *formal processes* of making laws are orderly, fair, and open to the public.

Until introduced into the legislature, your bill belongs to you. You can add or subtract ideas, revise its language, change its purpose or goals, or otherwise alter it for your best interests. However, once *your bill* is introduced into the legislature, it becomes *their bill* and you are just one more special interest trying to influence its direction. You assessed your political strength before going to the legislature to estimate your ability to affect, if not control, the bill once it is no longer yours.

A well-drafted bill is:

- Advancing the session's legislative theme (first mentioned in Chapter 2).
- Narrow in scope so only one committee could naturally have subject matter jurisdiction.
- Short and easy to process. (You may need multiple small bills for bigger topics.)
- Non-controversial and therefore eligible for unanimous consent.
- Not asking for money in order to avoid money committees. See if you can put the substance in one bill and request the money in the budget or a supplemental appropriations bill.
- Not affecting state or local governments to avoid the Government Operations Committee.
- Benefitting as many lawmakers and special interests as possible.
- Anticipating months or years of agency rulemaking to implement your law.

Because your bill's language evolves several times before it is introduced, you should not be concerned initially with details of prescribed form. Your main sponsor and the legislature's Legislative Counsel will ensure its form is correct before it is introduced. Your initial efforts should be to write a well-analyzed, legally correct, and effective document in the general form of a bill. Duncan L. Kennedy, former Revisor of Statutes for Minnesota, wrote, "Bill drafting must have the accuracy of engineering, for it is law engineering; it must have the detail and consistency of architecture, for it is law architecture."[61]

The Drafting Team writes the association's bill and supporting information using data provided by the Lobbying Team. These data include an assessment of the inadequacy of existing law, the association's legislative goals, and reasons for enacting a new law. The political context in which the bill will be written must be provided and the Lobbying Team must show how the association's goals fit within those of the legislature's themes for the forthcoming session. Finally, the Lobbying Team must identify the bill's likely supporters and opponents, examine the opponents' arguments, and provide rebuttals to each objection. Once this information has been provided, the Drafting Team can begin its work.

Your draft bill will have three main components: title, enacting clause, and body. The title and enacting clause are relatively simple and may be written quickly. The title should clearly show the purpose or subject matter of the bill and begin with language such as, "An Act to/concerning/relating to ____" or "A bill to be entitled ____."

The enacting clause conveys the intent of the legislature to make the bill state law. It declares, "Be it enacted by the General Assembly" or "Be it enacted by the people of the State of____." The exact language of the enacting clause is prescribed by the state's constitution.

The body clearly identifies sections to be enacted, repealed, or amended and requires the greatest amount of time to write. If new sections are created, they must be clearly identified as, "New Section" or "Section____ of the code is created to read" followed by the new language. The repealed sections must be identified as, for example, "Section____ of the code is hereby repealed."

If writing an amendatory or repealing bill, the affected sections of existing law must be denoted and shown in full within the body of the bill. Amended sections must be identified as, "Section____ is amended to read as follows . . ." or similar wording.

Amended sections must clearly show changes in language. Although the coding varies among states, additions are usually indicated by underlining, by **bold letters**, or by using all UPPERCASE LETTERS. Deletions are indicated by strikeout, [bracketing], *italics,* or other convention.

Before putting pen to paper, the Drafting Team should obtain copies of several previous bills from each chamber of the legislature to use as models for your proposed legislation. If your state posts bills on the Internet, you should still go to the Clerk of the House or Secretary of the Senate to secure paper copies. Unfortunately, the digital format does not always show the complete information and correct appearance of the state's bills.

Throughout the process of engineering the law, the Drafting Team should use these questions below, derived largely from Revisor Kennedy, to improve their decision-making and bill drafting:

1. Do existing laws already accomplish some of what you desire?
2. Is it better to amend an existing law or create an entirely new act?
3. Should the bill be drafted as a stand-alone or free-standing bill; or should it be an amendment to another bill?
4. Can you draft the bill to relate to the themes of the forthcoming legislative session?
5. Can you draft the bill to decrease the likelihood of referral to unfriendly committees or too many committees?
6. Once enacted, will this law create conflicts with existing law or produce unintended results? (Always brainstorm because unforeseen consequences bring unexpected opposition!)
7. Have the constitutional and statutory limitations and court precedents on legislation been observed?
8. Are the provisions of the bill integrated with existing law?
9. Is the use of words consistent with the language in existing statutes?
10. Are the titles of public officers, agencies, and institutions stated correctly?
11. Does the bill embrace only one subject in states having a single subject rule?
12. Is the title an appropriate expression of the subject of the legislation?
13. Is each distinct part of the bill a separate section?
14. Is the enacting clause in proper form?
15. Are amended sections of existing laws set forth in full?
16. Are all conflicting laws repealed by chapter and verse?
17. Are references to the statutes accurate?
18. Does the bill need an effective date that differs from the date specified by the state constitution?

19. Should provisions within the bill become effective at different times?
20. Is a state appropriation needed to implement the bill?
21. Should the appropriation be placed in this bill or in a specific or general appropriations bill?
22. How will funding be continued over time?
23. Is the style of the bill clear and the language understandable?
24. Can the bill be shortened, simplified, or made clearer?
25. Will the law be enforceable? How and by whom?
26. Does the bill clearly direct agencies to adopt favorable rules to implement your law or does it give them discretion to adopt rules that would reverse your legislative success?

Finally, draft the bill looking not to just the end of the legislative session but to years of future agency rulemaking. This is because, while legislatures are constitutionally authorized to enact laws and appropriate money, they are constitutionally barred from implementing anything. Implementation belongs solely to executive agencies. The net result is for every page of *statutory law*, agencies promulgate ten pages of *administrative law* implementing the statute and they may take years to do it; and both are equally law. Chapter 9, section *Executive Agency Rulemaking*, discusses this more.

Draft Your Conceptual Bill Yourself

The hard part of bill drafting is not putting pen to paper. Any competent consultant can do that for you. The hard part is achieving consensus among parties having a legitimate interest in your issue, starting with your association members. As parties work together to draft the bill, balancing each party's competing interests, a lowest common denominator consensus emerges. Nobody gets everything they want but everybody gets something they can live with, and all agree that's better than what they have now.

Laboring over each word and arguing possible interpretations of the language bring organizational unity as ideas are translated into specific, meaningful terms. Bill drafting is so central to establishing the cohesiveness of the association it should not be left in the hands of consultants. Once you achieve intra-interest group consensus then your consultant can draft the bill.

DRAFT SUPPORTING INFORMATION

While both numbers are very small, more people in the legislature will read your supporting information than will read your bill. Your bill may be among thousands introduced into the legislature during the session; unless it is of vital importance to lawmakers, few will read it. Among those who do read it, even fewer will remember what it says. There are just too many bills and too little time. I discuss this in greater detail in Chapter 6.

To help lawmakers recall the important points in your bill, you should provide supporting information explaining why your bill should be enacted, identify its main points, and provide the rationale for each one. This information should be short, specific, and exceed no more than two pages. You must show each lawmaker how they, their districts, and the state overall benefit from your legislation. Give copies to your bill's main sponsor(s) and co-sponsor(s). The main sponsor may, in turn, attach a copy of the supporting information to his or her *bill drafting request* (BDR) submitted to Bill Drafting Services, Office of Legislative Counsel, or similarly named office in charge of composing bills. This information may help the drafters incorporate your ideas into the bill to be introduced.

Prepare model letters and press releases tailored to the needs of each sponsor to give to respective constituents and local press explaining the member's reasons for supporting your bill. Well-developed, easily understood, and concise supporting information can significantly increase your bill's likelihood of success in the legislature.

Shortly before the legislative session begins, the Drafting Team will prepare written and oral testimony for you to present at the committee hearing(s) on your bill. The oral testimony will be an abridged version of the written, and both must be presented in the formats established by the committee. Ask the staff of the committee of subject matter jurisdiction for a copy of a well-formatted written presentation and inquire about the format and customs for oral testimony. We discuss committees and committee testimony in Chapter 8.

You want to make it as easy as possible for the legislature to do what you want. Legislators, and especially legislative staff, welcome from trustworthy sources competent, high-quality work that *helps them do their jobs.* Appendix 2, *Suggested Lobbying Visit Leave-Behind* may be all a lawmaker or staffer needs to decide on how to vote. Because lawmakers first vote politics, that's pretty much all many want to know. Your materials should give them political cover by proving to supporters and detractors that their decisions to support you are just good political and economic common sense.

Helpful materials include your drafts of committee reports, bill summaries and analyses, fiscal notes, letters to constituents, talking points, and the like. They may use none of what you offer, or they may use much of it. Nevertheless, offer, offer, offer, until they make clear they don't want to hear from you.

However, the legislature does not find the following kinds of materials helpful: association press releases, white papers, position statements, newsletters, and similar materials not directly applicable to the particular bill which committee staff is processing. Congressional and state legislative staffs have told me they throw these kinds of materials into the trash as soon as the advocate presenting them leaves their offices.

SUMMARY CHAPTER 3

Developing a successful a lobbying campaign requires sufficient commitment of personnel and resources, careful organization, research, and planning. Distributing the work among teams gives buy-in and ownership of activities and optimizes member contributions. Planning enables the project to move forward and provides opportunities for all to give input to the lobbying project. Research ensures the bill will be comprehensive, without conflict, and legally correct.

With a lobbying plan, draft bill, and supporting information in hand, the Management Team is ready to consider the hiring of a contract lobbyist. If you do not hire a contract lobbyist, then your Lobbying Team can begin to lobby special interests, prospective sponsors, legislators, and the Governor. However, you will be working extensively with contractors, whether or not you hire one yourself. The more you understand them, the better you will survive them. We discuss contract lobbyists in the next chapter.

Chapter 4: Hiring and Working with Contract Lobbyists

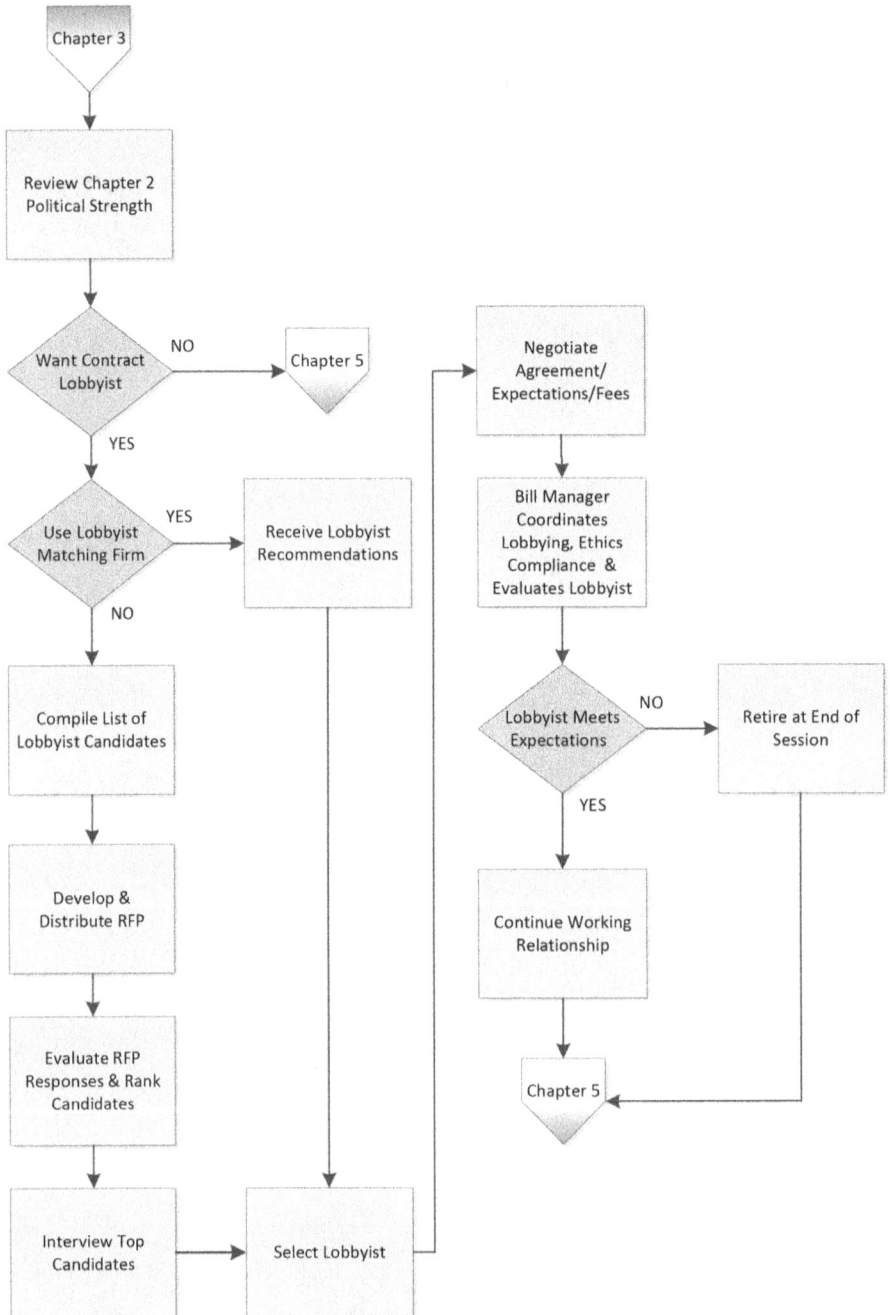

```
            Chapter 3
                │
                ▼
    ┌───────────────────────┐
    │  Review Chapter 2     │
    │  Political Strength   │
    └───────────────────────┘
                │
                ▼
          ╱───────────╲         NO
         ╱ Want Contract╲──────────────▶ Chapter 5 ──────────┐
         ╲  Lobbyist    ╱                                      │
          ╲───────────╱                                        ▼
                │ YES                          ┌───────────────────────┐
                ▼                              │  Negotiate            │
          ╱───────────╲      YES              │  Agreement/           │
         ╱ Use Lobbyist ╲────────▶ ┌──────────┐ │  Expectations/Fees    │
         ╲ Matching Firm╱          │ Receive  │ └───────────────────────┘
          ╲───────────╱           │ Lobbyist │            │
                │ NO              │ Recommen-│            ▼
                ▼                 │ dations  │ ┌───────────────────────┐
    ┌───────────────────────┐    └──────────┘ │  Bill Manager         │
    │  Compile List of     │          │       │  Coordinates          │
    │  Lobbyist Candidates │          │       │  Lobbying, Ethics     │
    └───────────────────────┘          │       │  Compliance &         │
                │                      │       │  Evaluates Lobbyist   │
                ▼                      │       └───────────────────────┘
    ┌───────────────────────┐          │                   │
    │  Develop &           │          │                   ▼
    │  Distribute RFP      │          │             ╱───────────╲    NO   ┌──────────────┐
    └───────────────────────┘          │            ╱ Lobbyist Meets╲──────▶│ Retire at End│
                │                      │            ╲ Expectations  ╱       │  of Session  │
                ▼                      │             ╲───────────╱          └──────────────┘
    ┌───────────────────────┐          │                   │ YES                  │
    │  Evaluate RFP        │          │                   ▼                      │
    │  Responses & Rank    │          │       ┌───────────────────────┐          │
    │  Candidates          │          │       │  Continue Working     │          │
    └───────────────────────┘          │       │  Relationship         │          │
                │                      │       └───────────────────────┘          │
                ▼                      │                   │                      │
    ┌───────────────────────┐          ▼                   ▼                      │
    │  Interview Top       │  ┌──────────────┐        Chapter 5 ◀────────────────┘
    │  Candidates          │─▶│ Select       │
    └───────────────────────┘  │ Lobbyist     │
                              └──────────────┘
```

CHAPTER 4

HIRING AND WORKING WITH CONTRACT LOBBYISTS

In your lobbying campaign, one of the most important decisions you will make is whether to hire a contract lobbyist. Lobbyists offering their services on a project-by-project basis may be referred to as "for-fee" or "contract" lobbyists. This distinguishes them from lobbyists who are employees of government, corporations, public interest groups, professional and industry associations, labor unions, or other organizations.

The right lobbyist can be a tremendous help to you and worth every penny. The wrong one will bring you financial and political losses. The following discussion will help you do a first-cut analysis of your need for a lobbyist and give you some idea of what will be involved in working with one.

If you conclude you need a lobbyist, then before going any further, I urge you to read *Insiders Talk: Winning with Lobbyists, Professional edition*. This best practices manual will guide you to becoming a sophisticated consumer of lobbying services getting more cost-effective and better lobbying results. Relative to a lobbyist's fees, the price of the book is negligible.

This chapter may lead you to conclude you don't need a lobbyist. If you are not going to engage one, then *Insiders Talk: Winning with Lobbyists, Readers edition* provides greater depth and insights into lobbying beyond that provided in this primer. It explains the psyches, motivators, and drivers of special interests, legislative and agency staffs, lawmakers, Governor's office, and lobbyists.

WHAT CAN A CONTRACT LOBBYIST DO FOR YOU?

A contract lobbyist's most fundamental job is to *help you do your job better*. This is your legislative campaign. You have a plan and infrastructure and teams to carry it out. You have the bill you want to move into law. "Your lobbyist can keep you in the game, but you have to put yourself over the goal line."[62]

While lobbyists can bring much to you, their greatest value is established relationships with and insights into persons inside and outside of the legislature who will affect the progress of your bill. They advise you on legislative strategy, tactics, and procedure, and help you maximize your returns on investments of time, money, and other resources. However, unless yours is a minor bill, don't expect a lone lobbyist to *move your bill into law*. This is because in moving a bill into law there are too many other players and too many moving parts.

However, *killing a bill* and to a lesser degree amending a bill in the last moments of the session are exceptions to the above principle. A lobbyist well connected to a committee chair can kill a bill by convincing the chair not to take up the bill in committee, facilitate poison-pill amendments, or other maneuvers. The same can be done by convincing the chamber leader not to call the bill to the floor or by parliamentary procedures.

A lobbyist may also be able to insert an amendment, especially a small one, into a bill in the last hours of the legislative session when chaos seems to rule and few really know what's happening. However, absent these exceptions, the lobbyist is there to help you do your job moving a bill to enactment using the standard route and process.

Finally, a lobbyist should give a client a sense of connection to the maneuverings within the legislature, such that amidst the capitol's seeming chaos the client sees itself as having an impact beyond its Chapter 2 political strength. Contractors' familiarity with process, knowledge of the players, and behind the scenes glimpses should boost client resolve to stay in the game as long as any chance of success remains.

CONTRACTOR KNOWLEDGE OF FORMAL LEGISLATIVE PROCEDURE - WHY IT MATTERS

Few lobbyists and fewer clients understand formal legislative procedure, that is, the prescribed processes by which a bill goes from an idea to a law. Chapter 6, *Navigating Legislative Procedure*, provides a general roadmap sufficient for most novices. However, sometimes detailed knowledge of legislative procedures can thwart an opponent or move to enactment an otherwise difficult bill.

Chris Micheli, Sacramento lobbyist and author of over 50 articles on lobbying, is an expert in California's legislative procedure. His principles below generally apply in all states. He advises,

> From my perspective, having been both an in-house trade association lobbyist, as well as a long-time contract lobbyist, I am always surprised by the number of individuals working in and around the state legislative process who do not understand or who do not know specific legislative rules that govern how the bill approval process actually works. This creates a situation where clients can be harmed because their lobbyist either doesn't know about or misunderstands some of the nuances of the legislative process.

> A successful contract lobbyist has three main attributes: strong working relationships with elected and appointed officials and their staff; subject matter experience; and, knowledge about the legislative process. You may ask, why is knowledge of the process important? The answer is, without this knowledge, a lobbyist can lose a bill at an important juncture of the process or not even realize that there was an opportunity to advance the bill forward.

Over the past two decades of state-level lobbying in Sacramento, I have numerous examples of how my knowledge of the rules has benefited me as a lobbyist which, in turn, benefited my clients. For example, knowing that the opposition to a client's major bill was gearing up for a Floor fight, we encouraged our author (ed. note, *sponsor*) to secure leadership's approval to waive the rules and have our bill taken up before it was on the Floor for the normal number of days. The other side's lobbyist wasn't even aware of this effort until the following day when his subscription services showed that our bill (i.e., the bill that he was opposing) had already passed the Floor and was headed over the other house.

While only the house parliamentarian may know all the rules, as well as their exceptions, successful lobbyists are familiar enough with them to not make mistakes that can embarrass themselves and their clients or prejudice their efforts. As a result, you should want a contract lobbyist who is knowledgeable about the inner workings of the legislative process to not only ensure that you comply with all of the requisite rules but also that you can take advantage of them to advance past your opposition.

The bottom line is that a contract lobbyist should be expected to have sufficient knowledge of the rules of the legislative process to secure passage or defeat of legislation on policy or fiscal grounds, rather than for failure to know or understand the relevant rules. And, a contract lobbyist should be expected to explain the process and walk his or her client through the different potential outcomes based upon knowledge of the rules.[63]

We discuss legislative procedure more in Chapter 6. For now, suffice to say that when: 1) neither side's contract lobbyist understands legislative procedure; 2) the bill is run-of-the-mill non-contentious; and, 3) enactment rates high, then detailed knowledge of legislative procedure may be unnecessary. However, when any of these three items are lacking, or if you really need your bill to become law, then for you the right contract lobbyist is one who understands the nuances of the enactment process.

FINDING THE RIGHT CONTRACT LOBBYIST

Stateside Associates[64] and MultiState Associates[65] are companies which in most U.S. jurisdictions can match clients of all sizes to lobbyists able to meet their needs. They can be especially helpful to small associations and clients who expect to have no further issues before the state legislature. These clients have relatively little leverage with lobbyists who, like most contractors, focus their attention on big clients or clients with subsequent or other issues. When companies like MultiState match clients with lobbyists, they help to level the client-contractor playing field because the lobbyist seeks to maintain a good relationship with them as sources of future client referrals.

However, since most contract lobbyists do not work through these companies, you may want to compile your own list of eligible lobbyists. Then investigate their interest in your organization as a client by sending them a *Request for Proposals to Provide Lobbying Services* (RFP), discussed below. It is important to manage the screening and hiring process carefully and professionally since candidates will likely tell other lobbyists and lawmakers about you.

Start your search at the state lobbyist registry. Annually published and updated, it lists all state-registered lobbyists, past and current clients, and sometimes their fees. You can obtain a copy from the Internet or state office that publishes the registry; often this is the ethics office, House Clerk, Senate Secretary, or Secretary of State. Your most effective lobbyist likely will be one who has represented interests similar to yours.

Absent some special exceptions, you likely will send RFPs to lobbyists whose clients have financial resources similar to yours. If you are of modest means, you will likely not become the client of firms representing General Motors, Goldman Sachs, or UPS. If you have assets to hire anyone you want, you likely will become the client of firms representing principals like General Motors, Goldman Sachs, or UPS. This is because the powerful like to associate with the powerful not the relatively powerless.

Special exceptions to this principle might include a charity or organization doing socially praiseworthy work. Such token groups on the client roster make the lobbying firm and by extension its clients look more sympathetic to the legislature and the public, and perhaps satisfy bar *pro bono publico* requirements for the firm's attorneys.

Ask associations, corporations, and state agencies involved in matters similar to yours to recommend lobbyists based upon their professional experiences. Large organizations have their own in-house legislative affairs departments staffed with lobbyists. When they need to lobby specific issues in states in which they have little presence or need extra help, they hire contract lobbyists in those states. Obtain recommendations from their staff lobbyists. However, DO NOT ASK LAWMAKERS for recommendations, as is explained below.

THINK TWICE BEFORE CONSIDERING SOME CANDIDATES

Some lobbyists bring with them potential complications that may make hiring them more trouble than they are worth. I'm not saying not to hire them, but rather for you to consider carefully the risks before you do. These lobbyists include: member-employee or contractors; lawmaker-recommended; and recent political leaders.

Member-employee or contractor. Any candidate who is an employee or contract lobbyist to one of your association's members is inherently conflicted. The lobbyist employed by an association member may later find him or herself in an unexpected conflict that would force a choice between the interests of the employer and those of the association. In a conflict, the lobbyist could choose the employer, either outright abandoning the association or overtly or subtly undermining association efforts.

Further, in an association comprised of competitors, suspicion the lobbyist is loyal only to the member-employer may undermine group cohesiveness. Other members of the association may fear their competitor's employee will use association representation as an opportunity to advance their employer's interests at the expense of other members.

Lawmaker-recommended. Do not ask a legislator to recommend or evaluate a lobbyist and delicately rebuff any unsolicited recommendations. Some lawmakers recommend certain lobbyists to accrue or pay back lawmaker-lobbyist political debts. If you ask and receive a recommendation but do not hire the lobbyist, you may cause the legislator to resent you, your issue, and the contract lobbyist you do select. The legislator may be upset by the perceived loss of political benefit or may be annoyed you wasted his or her time getting advice that was ignored. The lawmaker may be embarrassed if he or she had informed the lobbyist about making a recommendation and you do not follow through with interest or an offer.

On the other hand, a lawmaker's *recommendation* can in fact be a veiled *demand* that you hire a lobbyist friend. A regional government affairs manager for a household-name company says, "Lawmakers at times call me and recommend that my company hire a specific lobbyist. I have been forced to hire based upon the power of the requesting lawmaker." I have heard the same from other in-house lobbyists. In this case, you have to hire the lawmaker-*recommended* lobbyist.

Recent political leaders. Be cautious when considering as lobbyists recent former Governors, Senate Presidents, House Speakers, and other leaders of high offices. Those who have held the highest offices may be less willing or able to appeal for support to former opponents or less important legislators. This is especially true when they have to work with members of the opposing party. Former leaders may have made political enemies when they assigned to other lawmakers committees, offices, parking spaces, and staff. There may be lingering resentments over their choices for committee chairs, assignments of bills to committees, and other uses of power. *Of course, the inverse is possible* and they may be welcomed as old friends. And, former leaders who have grown comfortable with issuing orders to others may now find it difficult to follow *your* orders and may be very hard to work with, much less manage. The most suitable lawmaker turned lobbyist is usually drawn from rank-and-file legislators and staff.

Further, you have no reason to think recent former officials know anything about *doing lobbying*, such as coalition building, negotiating with special interests, implementing a grassroots campaign, or managing client expectations. They know about *being lobbied* and former lawmakers may have courtesy-based access with legislators, at least those of the same political party. In killing a bill that may be enough; but it won't normally be enough to move a bill to law.

These scenarios are not absolutes. Employees of member organizations have served associations well, lawmakers have made excellent suggestions about prospective lobbyists, and former leaders have been effective. The consequence of hiring the wrong lobbyist, however, is potentially disastrous. Because there are many lobbyists available, avoid taking unnecessary risks.

STEPS TO ENGAGING A LOBBYIST

The Management Team or Lobbying Team should begin searching for your lobbyist at least 6 to 9 months before the legislative session starts, and complete it within three months. This schedule provides an adequate amount of time to find your lobbyist, incorporate him or her into your plan, and begin pre-session lobbying of constituents, special interests, legislative and agency staff, perhaps the Governor's office, and lawmakers.

Once you have completed the list of acceptable candidates, recruitment and selection consists of five steps:

1. Developing and sending an RFP
2. Evaluating candidates' responses
3. Conducting personal interviews with the top two to four firms
4. Ranking candidates
5. Negotiating terms of the engagement and fees

1. *Developing and sending the RFP.* Your RFP must be complete, specific, well-written, and:

1. Provide a description of the association including its name, purpose, and a list of members and association staff.
2. Name other lobbying coalitions or groups to which your association belongs.
3. Explain what you want the lobbyist to do this session; for example, provide general legislative representation without specific outcomes or lobby for specific goals.
4. If specific goals, clearly state them and identify what you want the legislature to do. Do you want to enact or defeat a bill? Depending on enactment rates one may be harder to do than the other which will affect fees and availability to work your issues.
5. Clearly identify the role of your lobbyist in implementing your Chapter 3 lobbying plan. Identify the association's committees that will work with the lobbyist. It is very important to begin the lobbying relationship with a clear understanding of how he or she will work with your Management Team, Lobbying Team and Bill Manager, and Drafting Team and Historian.
6. Ask for a description of the expected theme(s) of the upcoming legislative session.
7. Within the context of the legislative theme, ask for a general description of how he or she would accomplish your goals and estimate the likelihood of success.
8. Ask for a written statement verifying no potential conflicts of interest between you and the lobbyist's other clients. By earlier reviewing the state's lobbyist registry you already disqualified lobbyists whose clients clearly would conflict with your interests. Unforeseen conflicts may yet arise, but you don't want to start off your relationship with predictable conflicts.
9. Ask the lobbyist what he or she does when the legislature is not in session and if he or she does executive agency lobbying. This will give you greater insight as to potential conflicts not gleaned from the legislature's lobbyist registry.
10. Ask for a description of his or her experience in state government, if any. Such experience suggests what level of hostility or professional courtesy and by whom may be shown to your lobbyist and by extension your bill. Was he or she ever a leg-

islator? If yes, which electoral district was represented and for what period of time? If the lobbyist was a staff member, state agency official, or worked for the legislature, ask for whom he or she worked, a description of the position, and number of years served. Recall from the previous chapter, such experience doesn't make a better lobbyist over all, but legislators' courtesy and access add value.

11. Ask how long he or she has been lobbying and determine if he or she has ever lobbied an issue similar to yours. If yes, what was the result?

12. Ask if he or she has appeared before the committee(s) having jurisdiction over the subject matter of your issue. If yes, for which clients and for what issues?

13. Ask for a description of his or her relationships with chamber leaders of both parties and chairs and members of *committees of referral.*

14. Ask the candidate to identify legislators he or she has supported in their election campaigns. Identify lawmakers' bills he or she supported, opposed, or stopped. The candidate's responses will enable you to identify the contacts and political relationships that might be leveraged in your favor or exist to your detriment.

15. Ask the candidate to explain his or her perception of the existing degree of partisanship in the legislature. The candidate's political party affiliation may be important, especially if the legislature is highly partisan. Unless you are hiring the lobbyist to work the minority party, when all other factors are equal, a lobbyist with the same party affiliation as the majority in the chamber is the better choice. Larger lobbying firms can provide lobbyists who are registered and active in each political party. A smaller firm will especially want to avoid a partisan label.

16. Ask for a description of the firm's lobbying practice. Ask about issues for which the firm has lobbied, issues they will lobby in the impending session, and a list of recent clients. You already know much of this from your research, but it's a good check for candor and opportunity to show your sophistication and wherewithal.

17. Ask who will represent you day-to-day. The person who brought in your business isn't necessarily going to lobby for you. Get the names and credentials of all the firm's members who could work on your project.

18. Determine how the work will be apportioned among junior and senior lobbyists and ask yourself if you are comfortable with assigning your project to associates.

19. Ask for an estimate of the amount of time the firm expects will be devoted to lobbying your issue. This predicts fees and level of service.

20. Ask for an estimate of time demands other clients and issues will make on the firm's availability to you.

21. Ask candidates to list their rates and costs to represent you. Some lobbyists will want to bill *dollar per hour* while others charge a *fixed-fee* for a project. They may at this point not want to talk fees preferring to wait until after your evaluation of all candidates. Fees are extensively discussed in *Insiders Talk: Winning with Lobbyists, Professional edition.*

22. Describe other legislative items important to your members or you, both in this session and in the to-be-determined future. If the lobbyist thinks you may become a long-term client expect greater interest in serving you.

23. Provide the date when the proposal will be due.

24. List your Bill Manager's name, telephone number, and email and mailing addresses as the contact person for the association.

A firm's willingness to respond to you is directly related to how much you bring to the firm in fees, name, and workload. When your association is small or is a one-time client with limited funds and offers little hope for future business, some lobbyists may not want to be part of your team. Smaller associations should expect their list of candidates will be drawn from a smaller pool of firms. A big-name potential client is so attractive lobbyists compete to add its name to the client roster expecting the big-name will attract more well-heeled principals thereby enhancing fees and expanding the firm's political power. Lobbyists may not find you attractive enough to talk to. Some will not respond to your request for proposal if, relative to your value as a client, it asks for too much information.

2. *Evaluation of candidates.* Carefully evaluate the responses to your RFP and rank your candidates based upon an item-by-item review of their answers to the questions above. Based upon responses to your RFP, identify those whom you think you can afford financially. Later, you will negotiate a final fee.

Select the top two to four respondents for personal interviews. Talk to them on the same day, if possible. Meet candidates in your office or rented conference room to avoid unconsciously skewing your evaluation in favor of the candidate having the nicest office and most attractive staff. Further, meeting on *your turf* conveys to lobbyists you intend to be the one steering your lobbying campaign. Client-lobbyist struggles for control of lobbying campaigns are frequent enough that you will be well served by establishing *your management role* before hiring.

Ask the lobbyist to bring to the interview the person who would be assigned to your account. Firms send to interviews their *rainmakers*, that is, their *salespersons*; but do not think they are the ones who will handle your account. You may like the rainmaker but dislike the colleague. Once a firm is hired and a notice of representation filed naming you as client, it's almost impossible to fire a lobbyist. I discuss this more below.

Be sure to look again at each lobbyist's list of clients to see if there appears to be any conflicts with your interests. Contact current and previous clients. After assuring confidentiality of their response, ask those who have employed each candidate to describe their experience and satisfaction with the lobbyist's work. Ask what the lobbyist did for them and ask them to be specific. Determine how the lobbying project was managed; did they direct the lobbyist and, if so, how well did he or she accept direction?

Send a letter of appreciation to all who responded to your RFP thanking them for their time and effort. You could find yourself working with some of them in the future. This, for example, could happen if a conflict arises between you and another of the lobbyist's more important clients, you have to fire your lobbyist, or you need future or additional current representation.

3. *Conducting personal interviews with the top two to four firms.* Personal interviews provide you with the opportunity to evaluate candidates' appearances, personalities, and communication skills. It enables you to determine with which candidates you are a good match. This is as much an *emotional* evaluation as a technical one. You are going to work closely with your lobbyist in a process that can be quite an ordeal, with many ups and downs, in a volatile context in which you must be able to trust each other. The more you emotionally connect with each other, the more you will trust each other, and the less likely adversities, which inevitably arise during most lobbying campaigns, will erode your partnership.

Prepare for your meeting with each candidate by again reviewing their responses to your RFP and checking online for ethical compliance and news stories. Based upon that review, formulate further questions to get answers to inadequate responses or where more information is needed.

Designate one person in your group to lead the interview. He or she will be responsible for pacing it, maintaining order, and assuring all of your questions are answered. In the personal interview:

- Request each candidate to describe his or her understanding of your issue.
- Ask for further clarification of vague or incomplete responses to the RFP.
- Evaluate his or her apparent credibility and honesty.
- Determine his or her interest in representing you.
- Ask about fees.

It is not uncommon for candidates to "puff" their relationships and accomplishments in an interview. Be skeptical of the contract lobbyist who claims to be every legislator's best friend. Depending upon political moment, lobbyists have different degrees of influence. Remember some contract lobbyists are closer to one political party than to the other, some work better on one issue than another, and some work more effectively with one committee or one chamber than another. Few bills become law solely from the work of one lobbyist. Beware of the lobbyist who claims too much.

Do not require your lobbyist to "look" like you. Organizations whose cultures demand uniformity are sometimes tempted to favor lobbyists who "look like them." In some states and for some issues, it can be a liability for the lobbyist to reflect the image of the client to lawmakers. Remember, your lobbyist should be acceptable to the legislators they hope to influence.

Finally, as noted above, make sure you are interviewing the person who is most likely to be assigned to your account. The rainmaker's job is to "wow" you to win your business. Once that's done you may have little or no future contact. For the session you will be living with the person assigned to your account, so make sure you are compatible!

4. *Ranking candidates.* Upon completing all interviews, your team should thoroughly discuss, compare, and rank them in order of attractiveness. You will negotiate terms of engagement and fees starting with your number one candidate.

5. *Negotiating terms of engagement and fees.* Having ranked firms in order of desirability, you now negotiate terms of engagement and fees. Your terms should clearly state the desired outcomes of your project, project duration, duties to be completed, schedule of payment, causes for termination, and requirements for reporting specific activities.

Fees charged by contract lobbyists vary and range from several thousand dollars to tens of thousands of dollars per legislative session. The amount a lobbyist charges depends on:

- State being lobbied
- Single issue or general representation
- Availability of lobbyists
- Competition among lobbyists
- Size and reputation of the lobbying firm
- Difficulty of lobbying the issue
- The fit of your issue within the theme(s) of the legislative session
- Expected amount of work to be done
- Your value as a client to the lobbyist

To reiterate, all states require lobbyists to report the names of their clients. You likely will hire a firm having clients similar to you. Many states report fees charged; from broad dollar ranges down to the very penny. These public records, available from the state agency that regulates lobbyists, can be used to obtain benchmarks for establishing appropriate fees. Keep in mind, *in most but not all* states, ethics office reports do not distinguish between lobbying for a single issue and providing general representation.

When lobbyists are widely available and there is competition among them for clients, fees will be less. In a very busy session, there may be a greater demand for lobbying services than in a less active session. Greater demand translates to higher fees.

Sometimes, wealthier organizations pay "conflict out" retainers to lobbyists whom they fear could impact negatively their legislative efforts. This creates conflicts of interest thereby making retained firms unavailable to opponents and driving fees higher for remaining firms.

Larger and more prestigious lobbying firms charge higher fees than smaller firms. A consumer of lobbying services shouldn't presume larger firms' lobbyists are any more competent or skilled than smaller firms' lobbyists. Further, "Few if any professional lobbyists have a significant degree of *personal political power.* They can, however, help maximize the power you have . . ."[66] (emphasis mine)

The key difference between larger and smaller firms is that larger firms also sell the aggregated gravitas of their big-name clients. Large firms' power is overt and subtle. Overt power flows from prestigious clients contributing to a kind of "joint power account" which is administered by the firm. A client borrows from the joint account via the lobbyist appearing on its behalf. "He represents those who have power, so he has power. Anybody with his lists of clients, and the resources and clout they bring with them would do well in the General Assembly."[67] For this reason, a lobbyist is no more powerful than the sum gravitas of his or her clients.

Subtle power comes when a staffer or lawmaker hoping to one day get a lobbying job behaves more favorably toward a firm. Large-firm influence may also flow from a staffer's or lawmaker's momentary feeling of importance from rubbing elbows with those who represent the powerful.

Household-name organizations may use their names in lieu of cash to pay part of their lobbying fees. Because big-name clients attract other big-name clients, these clients know their prestigious names on client rosters enhance firms' marketing and gravitas. To illustrate, a large population state contract lobbyist told his *Lobby School* class that his household-name client reduced his fee as a condition of his firm representing them. He said they further reduced his fee by another five percent for permission to use its name in his business promotions.

Unless you are a wealthy organization, do not use large firms or their rates to establish your benchmarks. Fees reported to the state lobbyist regulation office don't show the 25–30 percent discount given to these kinds of clients.

If your issue seems simple or if there is little work associated with it, it will cost less to lobby than one that is difficult. If it fits within the theme of the session, it will be easier and less costly to lobby.

Finally, a lobbyist may reduce fees to an association when he or she perceives individual members of the association may become future clients. You can leverage possible future business opportunities with members as an incentive to reduce prospective lobbyists' rates to your organization. Remember, lobbyists' fees are always negotiable.

METHODS OF PAYMENT

A *fixed-fee* contract incentivizes any consultant to finish work in a timely manner. Using this method of payment, the lobbyist works on your project for a predetermined fee, regardless of the amount of time or resources needed to complete it. A fixed-fee contract is a gamble for the lobbyist who may suffer financial loss if your task requires more time or resources than expected. However, he or she may also realize a good profit if the work is completed quickly. For the client, the fixed-fee is "safe" because all costs are established in advance of the project.

The lobbyist's preferred method of payment may be dollar per hour. In this fee arrangement, your lobbyist receives payment for the amount of time spent working on a project rather than for accomplishments. Avoid this method because for the lobbyist it makes productivity unprofitable and for the client difficult to contain costs and stay within a budget.

Be aware that work outside the scope of the terms of engagement may incur additional charges. If your lobbyist offers to you services not explicitly found within the four corners of the terms, ask if there will be added fees and amounts thereof. You should provide a reasonable budget for expenses such as calls, business meals, and photocopying.

Do not offer your lobbyist more than eighty percent of the total amount you have budgeted for lobbying services. Always keep some money in reserve to accommodate the unexpected. For example, you may need to hire an additional lobbyist for a one-time task because of an unforeseen situation with a legislator.

Sometimes, the amount of work required to move a bill exceeds all reasonable and foreseeable expectations. In a fixed-fee contract the entire overage falls upon your lobbyist. However, demanding a lobbyist work without appropriate compensation will diminish his or her quality of your representation and results. You should volunteer to offset some of the lobbyist's financial losses by providing additional compensation. (You will be glad you held back that twenty percent.)

Being fair with your lobbyist makes you a more attractive client with your lobbyist and the lobbying corps, from which you may hire in the future. Further, your all-important reputation for integrity will be enhanced in the capitol. Doing the right thing is its own reward.

Some lobbyists may ask you for a retainer. For the lobbyist, retainers are winners. But is it a winner for you? A retainer is payment of a fixed amount of money that ensures the lobbyist will be available to you for a specified number of hours each month. If you have specific regular repeating tasks for the firm, then a retainer may be appropriate. However, if you don't, then a retainer means you are paying your lobbyist for doing nothing.

This can be annoying because each month you are writing checks for 1/12 of the original engagement fee plus the retainer. All the while your lobbyist may be selling your unclaimed time to someone else.

Other lobbyists may ask for a retainer to let you know if any legislative action being contemplated could potentially affect your interests. This is a wholly unnecessary expense. Lobbyists knowing your interests will always be on watch for issues that can lead to more of your business. The moment they hear something they will be calling you to put them back on the payroll.

Lobbyists are hired to give their best efforts. Never suggest a bonus or additional payment is tied to successfully lobbying your issue. This is called a *contingency fee* which in 43 states is illegal in the offer and in the receipt.

LETTER OF ENGAGEMENT

Although some lobbyist-employers may insist upon formal contracts, a letter of engagement will suffice when hiring a lobbyist. Your letter should name the lobbyist who will complete the work and provide the name of your Bill Manager who will serve as the lobbyist's contact with the principal. Attach to your letter the RFP and terms of engagement.

WORKING WITH YOUR LOBBYIST

Once you have hired your lobbyist, never forget:

- No one understands or cares about your issue as much as you do.

- No one can explain the details of your issue as well as you can.
- Lawmakers want to hear from constituents and affected parties much more than they want to hear from contractors.
- You must manage your lobbying effort.
- "An association that relies on a lobbyist to do all the heavy lifting in a legislative campaign is its own worst enemy."[68] (James Leahy)

Few lobbyists can convey your technical details as well as you can. Few will be able to answer questions as well as you or convey your passion about the need for your legislation.

Although part of your Lobbying Team, your lobbyist has business interests that differ from and sometimes compete with yours. Lobbyists act first to protect their own long-term interests and wellbeing. Activity pursued on your behalf will be balanced against the contract lobbyist's own interests and those of other clients. Since the value of a lobbyist to current and prospective clients includes relationships with legislators, few will endanger a profit-making lobbyist-lawmaker friendship for any client, especially one not likely to need their services again.

Even the best contract lobbyist's relationship with a legislator is no match for strong home-folk involvement and their presentation of factual and political data related to an issue. Lawmakers want to hear from the parties who would have to live with the consequences of actions the legislature is considering. They least want to hear from contractors who have no real "skin in the game," are going to stay in business whether they succeed or not for any particular client, and who have little impact on a lawmaker staying in office.

Never allow the contract lobbyist to manage your legislative effort. This occasionally happens with weak clients. Although he or she is a valuable resource, only the client should make decisions critical to its interests. When a contract lobbyist controls the legislative activities of the client, or when he or she acts without direction from the client, the client's interests are unavoidably compromised.

Further, most lobbyists do not want to be responsible for making *your* decisions. It's your campaign, the lobbyist is your consultant, and you each have your own appropriate roles. If you, by default or intent, burden your lobbyist with making your decisions, you force him or her into an awkward position of being overly cautious or obtaining a bill you didn't really want. Only you can authoritatively declare what your principal can accept.

On the other hand, a few lobbyists don't want you involved, much less making decisions appropriately yours. The joke is told: A government affairs director (GAD) is interviewing a candidate contract lobbyist,

> GAD: How much would a retainer costs us?
> Lobbyist: $12,000.
> GAD: How much would you charge to lobby our bill?
> Lobbyist: $40,000.
> GAD: How much would you charge if we lobbied together?
> Lobbyist: $60,000.

Some lobbyists want to be left alone, undistracted by clients. They won't accept supervision, especially from novice clients. To advance their own interests they will try to control the lobbyist-client relationship. I was in a meeting being held by a Washington, D.C. association. Their prestigious lobbying firm said to them during the meeting, "It's our job to lobby and it's your job to write checks. And as long as you keep writing checks and stay out of lobbying, we'll do fine."

Avoid any lobbyist who would be willing to make your major decisions for you. Listen carefully to their advice and assistance. But remember you, the client, must be the final decision-maker. All lobbyists are inherently conflicted because every lobbyist balances each client's interests against his or her own interests, demands of lawmakers, and other clients – current and prospective.

Recall President Ronald Reagan in dealing with the Soviets used say, "Trust but verify." You should do the same when working with your lobbyist. *Trust but verify* to ensure your interests are being represented in the capitol. Don't presume; don't take for granted, make sure. A Rhode Island in-house lobbyist shared with me his brief conversation with a committee chair,

> Committee chair: "How come you don't have a presence here?"
> In-house lobbyist: "What do you mean? We have a lobbyist."
> Committee chair: "We never see him up here."
> In-house lobbyist: "Needless to say we fired our lobbyist."

But, while remaining in control of your overall lobbying effort, do not *micromanage* your contractor. They are professionals hired for their legislative expertise and political relationships, and they must be free to use their talents to implement the goals you assign. Micromanagement will frustrate you and your lobbyist. Once your lobbyist demonstrates he or she is part of your Lobbying Team, your relationship should be one of partnership rather than supervision.

EVALUATING PERFORMANCE

Most clients have no idea whether their lobbyist is doing a good job or not. You should evaluate the performance of your contract lobbyist at regular intervals. To help you do so, ask him or her to keep a log of activities completed on your behalf. Your lobbyist should provide weekly reports of progress in the early days of the session; and, in the last hours, reports may be delivered daily or hourly. These reports, oral or written, should describe activities completed and progress made on your behalf, and should provide updates about your bill's movement. As you evaluate your lobbyist's performance, consider these questions:

- Does the lobbyist contact you sufficiently in advance so you can plan for and attend critical meetings?
- Does the lobbyist refrain from making major decisions pending your approval?
- Are you included in all major deliberations related to your issue among the lobbyist, legislators, staff, and special interests?

- Has the lobbyist arranged meetings with *relevant* legislators and committee members? Check the relevance of each legislator prior to meeting with him or her.
- Has your lobbyist helped mitigate the effects of the opposition or have opponents gained strength?

Following the legislative session, your lobbyist should provide a detailed report of the effort. This report should describe the successes and failures, likely administrative agency actions to follow, specifically rulemaking, and expectations for the next legislative session.

You will measure the performance of your lobbyist by comparing your goals in the lobbying plan against results achieved. The simplest and most meaningful measure of overall success is achieving the desired legislative outcome. However, that a bill was not enacted in one legislative session does not mean you and your lobbyist have failed. You may have created momentum making enactment more likely in the next session. It often takes three or more years to enact new legislation. We discuss post-*committee of first referral* (CFR) and post-*sine die* activities in Chapter 9.

REPLACING YOUR LOBBYIST

Sometimes you may need to terminate a contract lobbyist. Termination prior to the end of the session, however, is a drastic step to be avoided, as much as possible. If you change your lobbyist mid-session, you may create the appearance you are unstable and lose the momentum your bill had gained.

You cannot terminate a lobbyist without it literally becoming public record. This is because upon being fired your contractor must file with the lobbyist registration office a *notice of termination of representation*. Absent a scandal, firing a lobbyist is hazardous for more than just you looking unstable.

An angry lobbyist can damage you and the success of your proposed legislation. He or she might tell others the termination of your relationship was due to your dishonesty, instability, or insincerity. If your reputation is damaged, it may be more difficult to find another lobbyist to work for you because the legislature may also believe you are dishonest and untrustworthy. These factors will greatly reduce your chances of legislative success.

When you must terminate your lobbyist *during the session*, relieve him or her of duties without letting anyone external to your association know about it. Expect you will have to keep the lobbyist on your payroll until the end of the contract period.

If you secured your lobbyist through a firm that matches lobbyists to clients, contact it before taking action. Because matching firms want to satisfy their clients, they may be able to motivate the lobbyist to serve you better. This is because the lobbyist is hoping for future client referrals from the matching firm.

The best approach to terminating services is simply to continue working together for the remainder of the contract period; then do not renew the relationship for next year. Negotiate a mutually satisfactory public explanation for not renewing the relationship. As possible, only communicate positive messages about your former lobbyist. Unless he or she has been involved in some scandal involving you, do not disparage him or her. Disparagement discredits not only your former lobbyist, but by association, you and your issue.

Finally, you must either hire a replacement contractor or you must lobby your issue yourself. Were you a full participant in a synergistic relationship with your contract lobbyist together following the lobbying plan you made in Chapter 3, then you may be able to carry on the lobbying yourself. However, were you an administrator of lobbying contracts rather than an advocate, as first mentioned in Chapter 1, then you will have to find a substitute which may prove to be quite difficult in terms of performance and fees.

LEGISLATIVE ETHICS

As you move through the lobbying process, your actions must accord with state ethics laws and rules, as well as your own sense of right and wrong. Ethics requirements are designed to make the *formal* legislative process as fair as possible by limiting influences unrelated to good law-making. Legislators, legislative staff, lobbyist-employers, and lobbyists are subject to state standards. You must read the state's statutes, administrative rules, joint rules of the legislature, rules of each chamber, and perhaps committee rules. Your lobbyist, law firm, or contractor such as *State & Federal Communications*[69] can advise you. Violation of formal rules can carry formal sanctions.

Although there is general consensus about the nature of certain unethical behaviors, as for example, cash in an envelope, states have their own unique ethics requirements. Therefore, state-specific statutes and rules should be studied prior to contacting legislators. For example, logrolling, that is, one lawmaker saying to another, "I'll support your bill if you support mine," may be ethical in one state but unethical in another. If you are on the losing end, you would want to know if their deal was legal or not.

Before taking legislative action, lawmakers must disclose all *unique* personal benefits that would come from proposed legislation. Following this disclosure, they may be legally prohibited from voting on a bill. Lawmakers may request to be excused from voting on an issue if there is a conflict of interest. The legislature's ethics counsel guides lawmakers wary of possible violations, including determining extraordinary personal benefit or conflict with the public good.

LOBBYIST-SPECIFIC ETHICS

State ethics requirements seek to limit to the merits of proposed legislation lobbyists' influence on lawmakers. This is accomplished by imposing legal limits on campaign contributions, gifts, honoraria, and similar favors that may be given to legislators and staff. It is enforced by mandatory reporting and carries sanctions for violation.

Do not assume, just because you are an honest person, you are in compliance with your state's ethics statutes and rules. While some ethics rules are moral common sense, others are not. For example, do not consider suggesting to a lawmaker that for a campaign contribution he or she *quid pro quo* "owes" you a vote. Your statement may be construed as attempted "bribe giving." Bribery is both a federal and state crime.

Some laws have little to do with moral common sense. For example, seeking to influence a covered official by communicating with the covered official's employer violates Colorado law.[70] Other conduct is regulated by joint rule rather than by statute or administrative agency rule such as a lobbyist may not, "Enter or use a legislator's or elected or appointed state official's or state employee's or legislative employee's office, phone, or parking space without explicit permission."[71]

These examples demonstrate ethics compliance is much more than being personally honest. You have to read, know, and abide by ethics laws and rules to avoid violation and punishment.

Although ethics requirements vary from state to state, your adherence to the following will keep you on the safe side of the law:

- Read the ethics statutes and rules, chambers' joint ethics rules, and each chamber's rules.
- Register if you are close to the statutory "trigger points" for mandatory lobbyist registration.
- Maintain careful records of your lobbying activities to ensure you meet the requirements for reporting.
- File your state-required reports on time and make sure they are accurate.
- Make no gifts or contributions to lawmakers or staff during the legislative session.
- Ensure all information given to the legislature by you, your representatives, and your contract lobbyist is correct.

Lobbyists are required by law to register with the state office of lobbyist regulation, usually based on the number of contacts with lawmakers, amount of client money received, or place where lobbying occurs. Your contract lobbyist must register. It is likely your Bill Manager and one or more of your company or association representatives also will be required to register as lobbyists or lobbyist-employers.

Because lobbyist registration requirements do not apply to the citizen having periodic, infrequent contact with his or her lawmaker, association members who accompany your lobbyist to visit their legislators may not have to register. However, once an advocate becomes a registered lobbyist and makes the legislature aware of his or her activities, then the rules applying to reporting, gift-giving, and influencing of the legislature are enforced, sometimes vigorously.

Keep a daily record of your lobbying activities and make sure to file periodic reports by their due dates since late reports become easy targets for enforcement. States differ in their requirements for reporting information. Usually, reports ask for the names of those represented by the lobbyist and fees received, but some states ask for more information. For example, a state may require lobbyists to submit a log of the time they spend working on each issue.

Gift-giving to lawmakers is not a recommended practice but, if you consider doing it, make sure you know the state's rules that regulate it. In some states, unacceptable personal enrichment includes receipt of campaign contributions, gifts of nominal value, food, and entertainment while the receipt of such things may be perfectly acceptable in other states.

Do not give unique gifts to select legislators. The mass distribution of low-cost tokens given to all lawmakers and staff is generally, but not always, acceptable. If you give gifts, give only as clearly allowed by the state's rules. To meet gift-giving rules, use the highest dollar value for your gift when estimating its worth. Then make sure the estimated value is less than the gift-giving limit. In some states, lobbyists may be required to identify the lawmakers and staff to whom they have given gifts. They may also need to report the value of those gifts if valued above some threshold amount.

If making campaign contributions, do so before the legislative session begins and after it ends. Most states prohibit contributions *during the session*.[72]

A lobbyist must ensure, to the best of his or her ability, the information presented to the legislature is correct. Sometimes explicit, and always implicit, are expectations lobbyists are truthful with lawmakers and staff. A violation of this trust leads to formal or informal penalties. If you inadvertently provide incorrect information, correct it as soon as possible, and before your opponents expose your error.

Your Bill Manager is responsible for ensuring the association and its lobbyists comply with ethics laws. He or she ensures an ethics violation does not undermine the effectiveness of the association or the lobbying project. Any hint of lawbreaking can make you and your lobbyist pariahs and empower your opponents' efforts to defeat your bill.

In addition to mandated ethics, you should abide by principles embodied in moral ideals, religion, and social teachings to establish and preserve your reputation for principle, integrity, and honesty. A reputation for principle enables lawmakers and others to predict your response to legislative proposals. Integrity communicates to others you will follow through on your commitments. A reputation for honesty makes your information believable so no need exists to investigate your every statement and question your representations. A reputation for being unprincipled, unreliable, or disingenuous will undermine your lobbyist and legislative campaign, and destroy your effectiveness as a lobbyist or lobbyist-employer.

Summary Chapter 4

A contract lobbyist can help you build momentum to move your issue forward. He or she is a professional with established relationships and skills useful to drawing the lawmakers' attention to your issue. Your lobbyist will assist you throughout the legislative process. At every step of the lobbying campaign, you must abide by commonly held and state-specified ethical requirements providing safeguards against potential conflicts of interest or impropriety.

At this point in the process you have established your legislative goals, developed the lobbying campaign, drafted your bill, and made the decision about hiring a contract lobbyist. As you prepare to meet the legislature, the next step will be approaching other interest groups to gain support for your issue or minimize opposition. To do this effectively, you will rely on negotiation skills discussed in our next chapter.

Chapter 5: Negotiating with Special Interests

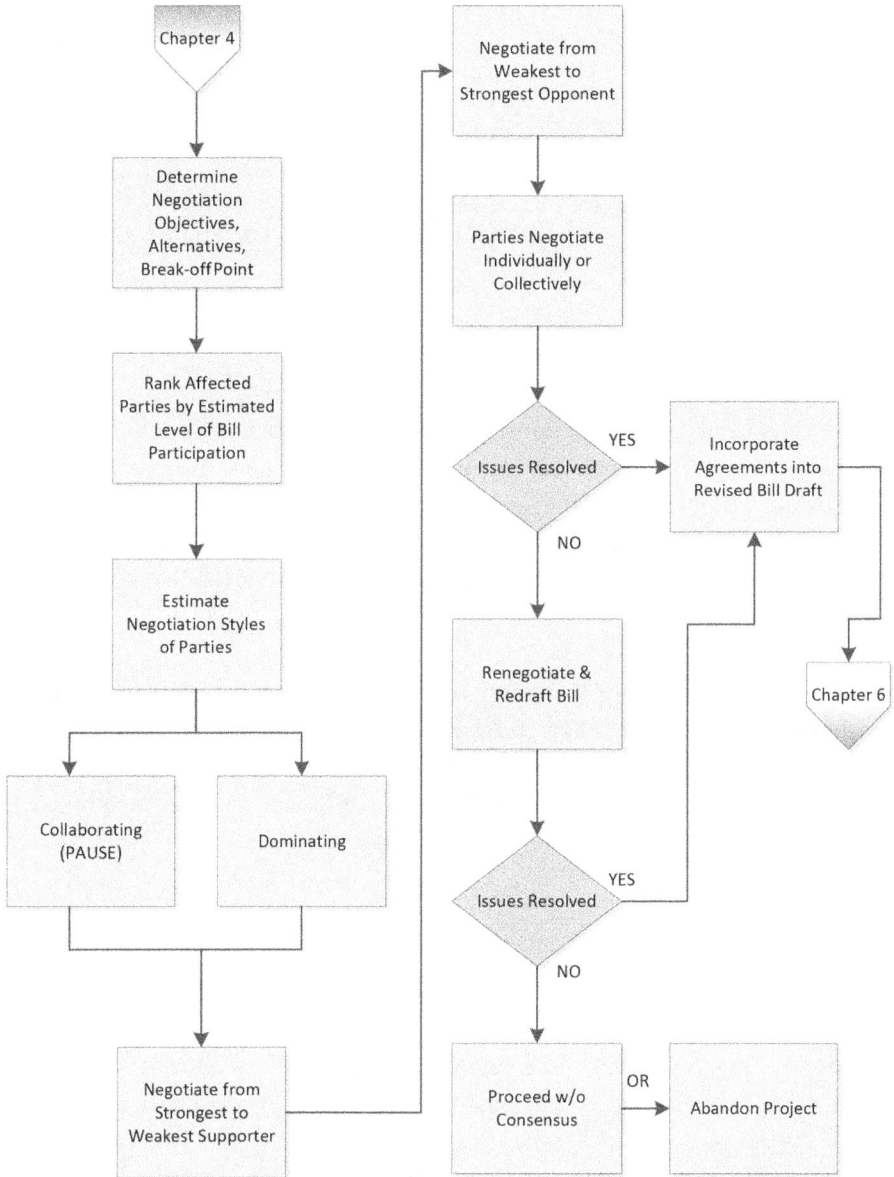

```
┌──────────────┐                              ┌──────────────────┐
│  Chapter 4   │                              │  Negotiate from  │
│              │                              │   Weakest to     │
└──────┬───────┘                   ┌─────────▶│Strongest Opponent│
       │                           │          └────────┬─────────┘
       ▼                           │                   │
┌──────────────┐                   │                   ▼
│  Determine   │                   │          ┌──────────────────┐
│  Negotiation │                   │          │ Parties Negotiate│
│  Objectives, │                   │          │  Individually or │
│ Alternatives,│                   │          │   Collectively   │
│Break-off Point│                  │          └────────┬─────────┘
└──────┬───────┘                   │                   │
       │                           │                   ▼
       ▼                           │               ◇ Issues ◇    YES    ┌────────────────┐
┌──────────────┐                   │            ◇  Resolved  ◇─────────▶│  Incorporate   │
│ Rank Affected│                   │               ◇       ◇            │Agreements into │
│  Parties by  │                   │                   │                │Revised Bill Draft│
│  Estimated   │                   │                  NO                └───────┬────────┘
│ Level of Bill│                   │                   │                        │
│ Participation│                   │                   ▼                        │
└──────┬───────┘                   │          ┌──────────────────┐              │
       │                           │          │  Renegotiate &   │              ▼
       ▼                           │          │  Redraft Bill    │       ┌──────────────┐
┌──────────────┐                   │          └────────┬─────────┘       │  Chapter 6   │
│   Estimate   │                   │                   │                 └──────────────┘
│ Negotiation  │                   │                   ▼
│Styles of Parties│                │               ◇ Issues ◇    YES
└──┬────────┬──┘                   │            ◇  Resolved  ◇──────┐
   │        │                      │               ◇       ◇       │
   ▼        ▼                      │                   │           │
┌──────┐ ┌──────────┐              │                  NO           │
│Collab│ │Dominating│              │                   │           │
│orating│ │          │             │                   ▼           │
│(PAUSE)│ │          │             │          ┌──────────────┐  OR  ┌──────────────┐
└───┬──┘ └────┬─────┘              │          │  Proceed w/o │─────▶│   Abandon    │
    │         │                    │          │  Consensus   │      │   Project    │
    └─────────┴──────┐             │          └──────────────┘      └──────────────┘
                     ▼             │
            ┌──────────────┐       │
            │ Negotiate from│──────┘
            │  Strongest to │
            │Weakest Supporter│
            └──────────────┘
```

CHAPTER 5

NEGOTIATING WITH SPECIAL INTERESTS

At some time in life, each of us has bargained with someone over the sales price of a house or a car, a new job's salary and perquisites, or when deciding upon a restaurant for dinner. The give and take surrounding this process of finding a mutually satisfactory agreement is called *negotiation* and you will have to do it throughout each stage of the lobbying process.

Negotiation is resolving human conflict using mutual agreement or compromise. Our use of the term describes the dynamic in which initially conflicting interests reach a consensus that can be published to the legislature. The strongest and most long-lasting agreements come from negotiations in which both sides enter *freely* and *give willingly* to reach resolution.

WHY NEGOTIATE?

You negotiate because in lobbying *consensus propels and controversy kills*. Legislators expect interest groups to reach as much consensus as possible *before* presenting them with a bill. Of course, as discussed below, in most states this expectation of consensus gives considerable help to those who for tactical advantage refuse to agree until they are forced to.

One of the first questions a lawmaker or staffer will ask a lobbyist is, "What does (interest group's name) think about your bill?" You must have a ready response based upon your communication with that group. It's easy to talk to your friends; not so much with opponents. Nevertheless, it's not optional. You have to communicate, even if it's tedious and at times unpleasant.

The obligation to communicate gives rise to a fundamental rule of lobbying etiquette, and that is, "*You have to talk to people you don't like and who don't like you.*" Should you respond to the above question with, "I haven't spoken to them," then you will be considered *ill-informed* as to good lobbying practice.[73] Being labeled ill-informed undermines the credibility and trust you need for lawmakers, staff, and other special interests to be willing to partner with you in your lobbying project.

Further, the legislature is more likely to enact bills enjoying broad support than bills burdened with controversy. Lawmakers avoid spending time on bills threatening to consume disproportionate amounts of legislative resources; resources which could be better spent on bills more likely to become law.

Unless the legislature considers your bill very important, which seldom happens, legislators will not spend more than a few moments negotiating it among themselves, much less with special interests. Therefore, before going to the legislature, you must for reasons of lobbying etiquette and good practice try to find as many points of agreement as possible with other groups interested in your bill. You may not reach complete agreement with all groups on each point, but by building as much agreement as possible, you improve chances your bill will become law; and, even more critically, you demonstrate you and your organization are professionals.

WITH WHOM WILL I NEGOTIATE?

After your association has written its bill, but before introduction into the legislature, you must negotiate with *all special interests* which could be affected, should your bill become law. These include persons or groups making up your organization, followed by those engaged in complimentary or similar activities such as those listed in The North American Industry Classification System. These we will call *internal actors*. Then you will negotiate with *external actors*, including competitors or opponents. Although you must achieve consensus among your own members and at least apparent consensus with internal actors, with external actors you will reach only varying degrees of agreement.

Internal actors. Negotiating begins when your association's members seek to define their common legislative problem, reach intra-association consensus, secure definite member commitment to the lobbying effort, organize the lobbying campaign, draft the bill, and possibly hire a contract lobbyist. As your bill continues to progress, you will negotiate internally to respond to amendments proposed by the legislature, opponents, opportunists, and friends.

You must have internal association consensus, because lawmakers hate getting involved in family quarrels. They know, like in a marital divorce, taking sides ensures if the divorce goes through one party will hate you; but if the couple reconciles both parties will hate you. A family quarrel is the surest way to defeat a legislative initiative. If you can't get true internal association consensus, then at least try to get your dissidents not to oppose you publicly.

Next, lawmakers hate "turf wars." When they see associations, who should be collaborating, fighting with each other, lawmakers will either table the bill or go forward with regard to neither. Conflicting associations who negate each other in an apparent turf war motivate lawmakers to ignore advice from both, which can have disastrous results.

To illustrate, preceding my bill was a bill to include pain management in the scope of practice of certain non-physician medical practitioners, especially advance practice nurses. Outside urban areas, anesthesiologists were generally absent in this large, mostly poor rural state. The committee saw the bill as solving a real medical need in underserved counties.

Doctors came from urban areas in white lab coats to tell the committee that non-physician prescribers of pain medication are hazardous to patient health, at times leading to patient deaths. Committee members saw this not just as one more doctor-nurse turf war but equally as an urban-rural divide of who gets pain relief and who doesn't.

In the end, the committee favorably reported the bill without regard to either doctors or non-physician prescribers. Had doctors and nurses, complimentary professions, worked together they could have influenced the committee. However, in their perceived turf war over pain killers, each negated the other, depriving the legislature of unified expert advice. The state has been trying to remediate and reverse the long-term damage to public health.[74]

External actors. Discover interest groups which might be concerned with your bill. The legislature's lobbyist registration office lists all lobbyists, their principals, and often bills they are lobbying now or have lobbied over time. Rank these potentially interested parties based upon your estimate of the importance of your bill relative to their other bills and interests. Then look outside of the legislature for other impacted interest groups. This brainstorming helps you initially outline the universe of those who will be likely friends and enemies in the legislature.

Their levels of interest and actions may be affected by many factors. For example, if a group with interest in your bill expects a busy legislative session to deal with matters more pressing than your bill, they may not give you much attention. Some groups will not have sufficient political resources to work on your bill in addition to their priority bills. On the other hand, if your bill impacts a group greatly, especially if they have few other legislative issues, they may be very interested and give your issue much attention.

As your bill advances though the legislative process, you may find yourself negotiating with persons you never considered. For example, with or without your consent, legislators may combine your bill with one or more similar bills to form one larger *omnibus* or *train bill*. Or opportunists may target your bill for amendment(s) seeing it as a vehicle to carry their bill(s) to enactment. In either case, you find yourself negotiating with unforeseen supporters and opponents.

Will I Negotiate with Agencies or Lawmakers?

Agencies for all practical purposes are technical staff to the legislature and the Governor. Their approval can skyrocket your chances of legislative success; their disapproval can sink any legislative campaign. And agency recommendations will greatly affect the Governor's disposition of your bill.

However, generally, you will not negotiate with lawmakers over your bill for two reasons. First, once your bill is introduced into the legislature, no longer is it *your bill*. It is the *legislature's bill* and they, not you, control it. Legislators look first to your sponsor and they may or may not consult with you during their negotiations. Second, lawmakers seldom engage in negotiations over most bills because they have too many of them and too little time.

In the *unlikely event* the legislature spends any time negotiating your bill, hopefully your sponsor will invite your assistance. With his or her direction, you will lobby for your bill, but keep in mind you make no agreements without first talking to your sponsor. Your sponsor's name is on the bill, not yours.

Sometimes an amendment sponsor may ask for your *consent* to his or her proposed changes to the bill. Your support increases the political acceptability of these changes. However, "Guess what, I'm changing your bill. What do you think?" is not a negotiation. The lawmaker is amending your bill to satisfy someone else, not you, and amendments will go forward whether you like them or not. Should this come up, speak to your sponsor before acting.

WHEN TO NEGOTIATE?

The time to start negotiations depends upon the themes of the forth-coming legislative session, the size and scope of your bill, and its impact upon affected parties. Small bills with limited impact that fit within the session's theme require much less negotiation than large bills affecting many or which do not fit the theme. Reduce as much conflict over your bill as possible *before it is introduced*. A committee chair may not call up a controversial bill he or she believes will consume a disproportionate amount of committee resources; therefore, you have until *first reading* to minimize to a few items the disputes over your bill. *Readings* are discussed in Chapter 6, Navigating Legislative Procedure.

BUILDING MOMENTUM THROUGH NEGOTIATION

A focused series of negotiations will be used to build momentum for your bill. Once you have identified and ranked groups from most to least supportive, starting with the most supportive, begin building agreement and minimizing opposition. Support will be *active* proportionate to the degree a group sees sufficient benefit to itself and has the political resources to invest.

Work systematically down your list until reaching groups that will support you, but *passively*. Support is passive because, although they agree with your goals, they have more important issues to lobby during the legislative session.

Move lastly to groups likely to oppose you, starting with those whose opposition is weakest. You complete negotiations by speaking with groups strongly opposing you. While you don't expect agreement with them, you have to at least try to get the answer to the lawmaker's question, "What does interest group X think about your bill?" You know from talking to them and you can explain to lawmakers why the group is wrong to oppose the bill.

Although most negotiation occurs before and in the early part of the legislative session, you may find yourself negotiating throughout the session to gain and keep support and minimize opposition. As you negotiate you will find two broad categories of negotiating styles, dominating and collaborating.

NEGOTIATING STYLES

Two frequently used negotiating styles are *dominating* and *collaborating*. Each style uses a very different dynamic of human interaction and each proceeds to reach agreement using different techniques. In practice, you may see one style used exclusively or you may see a mixture of both.

DOMINATING

The dominating style is encountered most frequently when one party has a disproportionate amount of power over other parties or is disproportionately important to the success of the negotiation. Possessing dominance, it nakedly demands its own way. For example, in an association of hospitals, one large regional hospital may threaten to withdraw from the hospital association unless the smaller community hospitals agree to accept the big hospital's legislative preferences. Smaller hospitals may bend to the demands of the bigger institution, as for example to keep the political power the large hospital brings to their association.

The dominating style produces fragile alliances because other parties are bullied into submission, rather than entering freely. A dominating negotiator may offer arguments but the reasons given to justify his or her position are really veiled ultimatums. Members and associations surrender to, rather than voluntarily partner with, the dominating style negotiator's positions or requests.

The dominating style of negotiation builds vulnerability, illegitimacy, and weakness in agreements reached. Were the dominating negotiator's tactics publicly exposed, the social distaste for bullying can free the weaker parties from the agreements they were forced to make.

Those who consider using the dominating style should ask themselves, "What would the public reaction be if their negotiating session were to be shown on the evening news or social media?" Because dominating negotiators rely on power rather than sound public policy or equity, public and legislative disapproval may greet the arguments advanced to support their position. The threat of public exposure can be used to reduce the effectiveness of this style.

COLLABORATING

The most frequently used negotiation style in lobbying is collaborating. Collaborative negotiations occur most often among parties who are independent of each other. Independence allows them to negotiate freely as peers.

Agreements forged through collaboration tend to be politically sturdier because parties reached voluntary agreements not influenced by forces unrelated to an issue. Legislators expect parties to adhere to their commitments when they freely enter into agreements with one another. In collaborating style negotiations, no party can withdraw from an agreement unless bad faith is discovered or unless provisions in the negotiated bill change considerably.

While I never personally participated in a collaborating negotiation (all mine were hostile dominating), the PAUSE model offers a good framework for implementing the collaborating style.

THE PAUSE MODEL

In *The Peacemaker*, Ken Sande proposes a collaborating style for reaching agreement.[75] His method is useful for persons of goodwill sincerely wanting to arrive at mutually beneficial compromises. In a sense it starts

113

out with a *win-win, equity and fairness* attitude as contrasted with the dominating style's *winner-take-all-just-because-I-can* approach.

Called PAUSE, the acronym stands for **P**repare, **A**ffirm Relationships, **U**nderstand Interests, **S**earch for Creative Solutions, and **E**valuate Options Objectively and Reasonably. Sande's approach embodies the collaborating style in which the principles and interests of all parties are balanced. Sande recommends using these steps to reach agreement:

Prepare. Get the facts, identify issues and interests, use ethical principles, develop options, anticipate reactions, plan an alternative to a negotiated agreement, select an appropriate time and place to meet, plan opening remarks, and seek counsel.

Affirm Relationships. Communicate in a courteous manner, spend time on personal issues before moving to material issues, respect the authority of leaders, earnestly seek to understand by asking sincere questions about what the other negotiators are thinking and feeling, discuss their responses, advance the public interest and interests of others by seeking solutions that really satisfy the needs and desires of all, confront in a gracious manner, allow face-saving, and give praise and thanks for valid points.

Understand Interests. Distinguish interests from positions. An interest is an identifiable and concrete question that must be addressed to reach agreement. A position is a desired outcome or definable perspective on an issue. To find ready resolution, focus on interests rather than positions.

Ask questions to determine how your interests and those of the other parties coincide or conflict. The more you understand the interests of others, the more persuasive and effective you will be when negotiating. Understand your own interests and use caution in revealing them.

Search for Creative Solutions. Spontaneously invent solutions by throwing out ideas that might satisfy needs. Try to "expand the pie" by bringing in additional interests which might be satisfied.

Evaluate Options Objectively and Reasonably. Keep an open and fair mind when negotiating and do not let the negotiation degenerate into a battle of wills. Use rules of reason, laws, ethics, or religious principles to evaluate options. Try to discover the hidden reasons behind objections and positions. Look for points you can give up easily, for matters on which you cannot bend, for issues your opponents can and cannot give up easily, and for points on which you can both agree.

SELECTING YOUR NEGOTIATOR

Negotiating is more art than science. Credentials, expertise, and titles, while valuable, cannot take the place of negotiating talents, training and, most of all, acting experience. One negotiator will be better at calm, collaborative, PAUSE-style negotiating. A collaborative negotiator generally is ill-suited for hard-ball, high-pressure, "slam the table and scream" dominating style negotiation often seen when large sums of money or power are at stake.

Use this checklist to *select* and *prepare* your representative(s) for a dominating style negotiation. Even if you expect a collaborating negotiation, even a PAUSE-style one, nevertheless be prepared for the dominating style. Ask, can my negotiator(s):

1. Not be broken by opponents' rudeness, disapproval, and demeaning techniques?
2. Handle rejection well? The most common response to their proposals will be "no." A negotiator who seeks personal approval from others may unconsciously sacrifice your position to avoid rejection by other negotiators.
3. Be likable and remain pleasant even in hostile circumstances? It is harder to be rude to a nice person than it is to an unpleasant one.
4. Pretend they need more than they actually do intending to settle for less?
5. Not equate failure with not getting all they want? Persons who fear failure will aim low and accept less to avoid feeling defeated.

6. Return again and again to a matter to which earlier answers were "no"? They must not stop at "no" and must be able to say "no" as often as needed.
7. Remain calm and not lose sight of their goals?
8. Creatively find common ground on which to reach agreement?
9. Even under pressure, keep their sense of integrity, honesty, and fairness? The more consistent and trustworthy your negotiator, the more credible he or she will be with other parties.
10. See and counter negotiating tricks? (Tricks are discussed below.)
11. Realize much negotiation is just play acting?

INCREASING YOUR RELATIVE STRENGTH AS A NEGOTIATOR

Your negotiator's effectiveness is first affected by the other parties' perception of your organization's political strength and secondly by your representative's personal strength relative to theirs. A stronger personality can compensate somewhat for an organization's weakness. While you cannot instantaneously increase your organization's political strength, by using some simple tactics, you can shift a dominating negotiator to become more collaborative. These will give you a stronger negotiating position:

- Hold the negotiating session within the view of the legislature. When forced to negotiate in the public eye, the dominating style will be greatly moderated or entirely replaced by the collaborating style. You can ask an important lawmaker or member of a key committee of referral to attend the meeting, send his or her staffer, express in writing or in person his or her interest in the conduct, outcome, and report of negotiation. This strategy undermines the dominating style.

- Ask your main sponsor to *delegate a measure* of his or her authority as a member of the legislature to you for the negotiating session. A lawmaker does this by telling your opponent he or she will do whatever you agree to in the negotiation. This will cause the other party to face the power your sponsor has delegated to you.

- As your bill appears ever more likely to become law, your negotiating strength will increase. So, although opponents still don't want your bill, in light of its increasing inevitability, they now will concede more to protect themselves from something worse in the future.

- As your bill continues to move forward, those who were previously uninterested in it may see it as a potential vehicle to carry their own stalled issues to enactment. If they amend their bill onto yours, they will become interested in working with you to see the bill carrying their amendment become law. Their support brings additional strength to your combined bills. Of course, the opposite can happen when their amendment sinks your bill.

- You can also become stronger by manufacturing controversy. Lawmakers want to spend time on bills more likely to become law and a bill burdened by controversy is less likely to become a statute. In defeating a bill the statistics are in favor of a bill's opponents because in most *but not all* states defeating a bill is easier than passing one. Of course, check your state's enactment rate but, as a national average, 25 percent of bills introduced become law, which means, 75 percent are killed.[76] When your opponents are trying to move a bill, your threat of burdening it with controversy should make them more willing to make concessions to you.

- You may also increase your negotiating strength by hiring strong or experienced negotiators to represent you. A good negotiator who represents a weaker association gains advantage over a poor negotiator representing a stronger one.

- Finally, you may be able to reduce your strength-disadvantage relative to your opponent's by bringing in a mediator. A northeastern state legislature pressured advance practice nurses and medical doctor specialists to try this. However, their mediation broke down and they continue to fight in nationwide "trench warfare." While mediation didn't work in this one instance, that doesn't mean it can't work in another.

DETERMINING ALTERNATIVE POSITIONS

In negotiation your starting gambit is your ideal bill. Your ending position is the point at which you cannot give any more. Between these two points are your alternative positions, that is, a series of decreasingly acceptable alternatives to your ideal bill.

You must clearly identify before going into a negotiating session at what point you say, "Thank you for your time. However, this negotiation has not provided the compromise for which we had hoped and so I'm going to excuse myself. I hope we can resume our discussions at a more opportune time after I consult with my principal." Then get up and leave with resolve. Negotiators who lack a clear point at which to walk away from negotiations may not know where to stop giving in to the other party's demands and may damage your lobbying effort.

Throughout the legislative process, you will be asked to make concessions, accept the "middle ground," choose among competing positions, add and delete bill language, and change bill provisions. With this in mind, try to identify and rank order all of your alternative positions before they are proposed by you or by another party. As you evaluate each alternative, identify its strengths and limitations. Then, when you or the other party proposes an alternative, you can maintain momentum in the negotiating session because you already know how you will handle ramifications of each one.

Alternative positions must not be viewed by your negotiator as equivalent. They are not. You earlier ranked them from most to least attractive. Have him or her memorize the rank ordering of acceptable alternatives and urge the negotiator to aim high, to "go for the gold" and not for the bronze medal. Inexperienced negotiators often seek the path of least resistance, and the outcome least difficult to achieve is often accomplished most.

Another strategy is to give your negotiator no alternatives. Sometimes negotiators work best when given no alternatives to the ideal bill since an "all-or-none" position forces them to make their greatest effort or risk failure. On the other hand, allowing your negotiator no alternative can lead to accomplishing nothing and loss of credibility. To illustrate, I found myself negotiating my principal's bill with a member of the committee of subject matter jurisdiction. Given my orders were all-or-none, I refused every one of his wholly reasonable amendments to the bill. He soon identified my intransigence as bad faith and began to insult and humiliate me. In the end, my principal's all-or-nothing instruction cost us credibility and perhaps wasted a year of lobbying.

PREPARING FOR THE NEGOTIATING SESSION

Regardless of negotiating style, collaborative or dominating, you must be ready for the actual meeting in which you will try to find agreement. Preparation increases the likelihood of achieving your goals. Thinking through these points beforehand will prepare you for a more successful negotiating session:

1. Know your association's lobbying goals and overall strategy. Commit them to memory so you can better focus the negotiation on what is important to the association.
2. Memorize how you want key sections from the bill to read at the conclusion of the negotiation.
3. Memorize your alternative position(s), if any.
4. Determine your political strength and the relative strength of the other parties because strength greatly affects their willingness to negotiate. If you are the stronger, you may have little reason to make concessions to the politically weaker. If you are the weaker, look for strategies to increase your political strength. (Chapters 2 and 5)

5. Estimate other parties' likely positions and supporting information. What do they want? How will they justify their positions? By identifying their needs and supporting rationale beforehand, you can identify ways to satisfy or counter their concerns.

6. Determine interests you share with the other parties. Shared interests may include relationships, legislative goals, social, economic, and environmental concerns. Shared interests promote harmony and a favorable disposition toward working together. Offering easy "yeses" brings a conciliatory tone to collaborative style negotiations.

7. Identify your low value interests which might be of higher value to the other parties and identify their low value interests that might be of higher value to you.

8. Learn as much as possible about the other negotiator(s). What are their reputations and experiences? Who are their other clients, association members, and allied interest groups?

9. Propose an agenda for the negotiation session to the other parties. Allocate time to discuss each issue. Include your draft bill as an early discussion item.

10. When scheduling the session, do not allow other parties to begin negotiations over the telephone. Tell them you do not have the authority to commit at the moment, but at the session you will.

11. Agree to record points of agreement on a flip chart or dry board in plain view for all to see. On separate flip charts or dry boards, record unresolved issues and those deferred for later discussion.

12. Agree to develop a consensus document from the negotiation and name one member from each party to draft it together.

13. Mutually decide to limit the number of participants to represent each party at the negotiation. Being outnumbered is a psychological handicap.

14. Ensure from the start and reconfirm at key moments that other negotiators have authority to reach the desired level of resolution.

15. Before going into the meeting, designate one person from your team to be the lead negotiator. Only he or she may commit you

to a position with the other parties.

16. Designate one member from your team to take notes.

17. Agree to tape or video record the negotiation, especially if dominating style negotiators will be present.

18. Agree upon a neutral location such as a hotel conference room to minimize meeting interruptions, distractions, and deny a "home field" advantage to any party.

19. If you think this will be a dominating style negotiation and you are the weaker party, tell the other teams you will request your lead sponsor or his or her staff to attend.

20. Practice your negotiation.

Dr. Chester Karrass offers numerous resources to grow into a more effective negotiator. He advises, "Understanding the basic negotiating terms and concepts is one way to prepare yourself for negotiations" and for this he provides a glossary.[77] Studying his materials and in particular his glossary is a great way to expand your understanding of the negotiating art and preparing to meet your opponents.

NOBODY IS YOUR FRIEND

Critical to preparing your mind to negotiate is realizing nobody has been sent to the negotiation to be your friend, no matter how beguiling they are. They are being paid to get the best deal for their principals, not yours. When negotiators are nice, assume it's a tactic to lull you into a false sense of security and into dropping your awareness *this is a competition* with winners and losers, either them or you.

For example, you are feeling good about another negotiator when suddenly and for you unexpectedly (not for them, it's been planned), you find yourself facing a "good cop-bad cop" hardball negotiating trick, one of many discussed below. Your supposed friend has allied with a clear opponent and together they are ready for the kill shot, that is, to win for their principals at your expense. Expect as skilled negotiators, they earlier cut side-bar deals to roll the naïve and unaware.

When anyone is pleasant, smile and reciprocate their congeniality but don't put too much stock in it. In any negotiation, especially when significant money or power is on the table, friendliness will be short lived.

THE NEGOTIATING SESSION

A dominating style negotiation, by design, creates a tense environment. For the unprepared, emotion can cloud judgment and impair performance. In a collaborating style negotiation, the inexperienced can be lulled into a false sense of trust to be exploited to their disadvantage by other negotiators. A wise negotiator realizes everyone in the room is an opponent out to get all they can at your expense. Use these guidelines to stay focused and emotionally defused when negotiating:

1. Negotiations begin the moment you greet your opponents. Much negotiation is a power-directing image game. Establish your persona by intentionally employing your every word, facial expression, and mannerism to project certainty. However, avoid discussing the bill and its details until the session formally convenes.

2. As parties arrive, establish the common humanity you share with other negotiators by discussing neutral topics, such as the weather and weekend activities. Have appropriate refreshments available. This may help you separate issues from personalities later in the meeting and the sharing of food creates commonality.

3. Ensure the numbers of participants from each party in the negotiation session are as agreed. Failure to abide by earlier agreements shows bad faith on the part of the violating party, another trick mentioned below.

4. Do not lose sight of your goals and acceptable alternatives to the ideal bill.

5. Keep in mind the point at which you will break off negotiations.

6. As a first item of business, review the agenda you and the other parties developed in advance to guide the negotiating session.

This will help you focus and adhere to the time allocated to each topic.

7. Identify the lead negotiator for each party and confirm he or she has authority to commit at the level of agreement desired. Cancel the session if there is inadequate authority; or state clearly because other parties do not have authority to commit, discussion may proceed but no agreements can be reached.

8. Use your draft bill as a template for discussion with the other parties and ask them to identify points of agreement. This may enable you initially to lead the meeting and affect its outcome.

9. Budget your use of "yes" and "no." Because reciprocity characterizes collaborating style negotiation, other parties expect a "yes" from you in exchange for each "yes" they give. Sometimes, they may expect you to give a "yes" on the basis of reciprocity rather than on the substance of their request. You must avoid feeling pressured to respond with a "yes" if the substance of their request is unacceptable.

10. Likewise, do not spend one of your "noes" on an outrageous suggestion. Ignore it, smile about it, or record it on the flip chart or dry board as an item for discussion at a later time.

11. In a dominating style negotiation, reciprocity is not expected so avoid making concessions to other parties just because they have made concessions to you. Give information or make concessions only when you receive benefit. You can never take back what has been given away. Doing so will destroy their trust in you.

12. Stay focused on issues and do not allow others to sidetrack discussions by "being difficult."

13. Remain politely skeptical of facts, figures, and conclusions presented by other parties. The interpretation of data may sometimes be skewed to yield conclusions not supported by objective analysis. Freely question data and supporting arguments.

14. Never hesitate to ask questions if you cannot understand exactly what somebody is talking about.

15. Remember you are tied to your spoken word. Give yourself time to process what is happening. Take breaks as needed.

16. Respond slowly to others and do not speak until you are ready. This prevents you from rushing into a bad decision.

17. In plain view of all parties, record on flip charts or dry boards points of agreement, areas of disagreement, and items deferred for later discussion.

18. Using the data recorded on the flip charts or dry boards, charge a team consisting of one representative from each party to draft a consensus document. If possible, distribute this draft and solicit comments from all participants during the meeting. If not possible, distribute it as soon as you are able.

19. With your sponsor or staffer attending, the lobbyist's duty of scrupulous honesty to lawmakers will make negotiators hesitant to deceive, by commission or omission. And the legislature's expectation that negotiating parties act in good faith with the goal of bringing the legislature solutions will shift negotiators to being more collaborating and less dominating.

20. At the conclusion of the session do not allow small talk with other parties to reopen negotiations. Remember every time you discuss your issue, you are re-negotiating it.

21. Depart promptly and amicably and do not linger with other parties. Until you are alone and well outside of the building, avoid conversation even among yourselves about the negotiation.

22. In private, review the events of the meeting with each person in your party and plan the next steps.

NEGOTIATING TRICKS AND TECHNIQUES TO COUNTER THEM

Here are some tricks and suggested techniques to help you counter them based, in part, upon the work of negotiating pioneer Chester Karrass. If your sponsor or his or her staffer is in the room, this behavior is much less likely.

1. *Intimidating environment.* A party may offer or even insist that you hold negotiations in his or her offices. Negotiating on the "home court" creates opportunity for your opponent to design an intimidating and often uncomfortable environment. You should insist that a neutral environment, such as a hotel conference room, be used for negotiations.

2. *Exceeding the agreed upon number of negotiators.* Insist on adherence to prior commitments that limit all parties to the agreed number of attendees or don't negotiate. Outnumbering you is a psychological technique to overpower you.

3. *Rudeness.* Rudeness is used to unnerve you into making concessions to escape opponents' hostility. Rudeness is an especially useful tool against collaborating negotiators. [78] Confront rudeness directly and ask if it is the negotiator's technique. If he or she continues, ignore it, complain to a higher authority about it, or tell the other party you will leave until such time as a civil negotiator is substituted for the rude one.

4. *Good cop-bad cop.* This is a version of the rudeness technique. While one of the other party's negotiators (bad cop) badgers you, his or her teammate (good cop) appears to constrain the bad cop and offers to mediate a reasonable agreement between you and the bad cop. If you will not yield on important points, the good cop says he or she will have no choice but to leave you to negotiate again with the uncivil teammate. Do not let the good cop-bad cop game start. At the first clear sign of rudeness, respond as in number three above.

5. *Disapproval.* Verbally and non-verbally, the other party sends a message of disapproval to shame, embarrass, or humiliate you for not agreeing to their "reasonable" demands. Counter disapproval by sending a negotiator to the session who does not equate success with personal approval from other parties.

6. *I'm your friend.* After the above unpleasantness you may be ready for some succor. Do not allow yourself to be seduced into giving away anything *material* in order to keep this fair-weather friend. He or she will be on good terms with you only as long as the illusion facilitates achieving their principal's objectives.

7. *I gave you "that" so you have to give me "this."* You don't have an obligation to give anything over a feigned sense of reciprocity. Give to get, not to appease.

8. *Wasting time.* To force last minute desperate concessions as time is running out, one party may refuse to follow the agenda and may consistently exceed time allocations. To counter this trick,

at first sign of time wasting insist on adherence to the original agenda and its allotted times.

9. *Introducing new demands.* A party may try to insert new demands or place a new item on the agenda. This can be avoided by establishing and adhering to the agenda. As the negotiation session begins, review the agenda to limit issues to be considered at the meeting.

10. *Making extreme demands.* A party may ask for more than is reasonable or make outrageous statements. Respond by appealing to fairness and remind him or her that your sponsor will not accept a bill with unfair agreements.

11. *No alternatives to the first offer.* This trick tries to force you into accepting a no-discussion, "take it or leave it" position. Counter by asking the other party to explain how it arrived at its position. Then look for weaknesses in reasoning as the rationale is explained.

12. *Threatening and bluffing.* This trick threatens to bring consequences unrelated to your bill. For example, a party may threaten to do an unrelated harm to you if your bill is enacted. Counter the threats by protesting and ask the party to reveal the facts supporting the statements.

13. *Sellout panic.* The other party may claim your allies are about to "sell you out" and urge you to protect your interests by reaching an agreement now. Avoid this trick by communicating regularly with your allies to confirm no conflicts exist.

14. *Suddenly no authority.* As a negotiating session concludes, a party's lead negotiator may unexpectedly announce his or her principal must approve the agreement for it to become effective. This causes the negotiated agreement to degrade into an offer that can later be accepted or rejected in part or in full by the other parties. Avoid this maneuver by asking all parties *before* negotiations begin to reveal their level of authority to bind their organizations.

15. *Ask for more and expect to settle for less.* Each side assumes the other is doing this, and each probably is.

Dr. Karrass suggests when you see a trick being used, ask the user what he or she thinks the gain will be. By demonstrating awareness, you may discourage further trickery.

Remember, you can always walk out of a negotiating session. The other parties are not going to physically restrain you. If other parties are trying to subvert the negotiation, let them know you will walk away if necessary and you will bring to the sponsor and legislature the facts that prompted your departure. The other parties may lose credibility if negotiations cease. Ask the offending party if exposing their maneuvers will cause the legislature to label them as acting in bad faith. If you have taped the negotiating session, you have the evidence. The threat of public exposure for unfairness or dishonesty and consequent legislative disapproval may sober them.

LET'S MEET HALFWAY

Because issues often remain unresolved as the negotiating session-clock concludes, the other parties may offer to meet you *halfway* to resolve them. Agreeing to a seemingly *fair* offer can get for you or the other parties fifty to one hundred percent of what could not be obtained earlier.

For quantitative items, such as money and time, a fifty-fifty split can be calculated easily. For qualitative issues, however, calculating the split is usually more difficult and may lead to, "I'll give you your way on this matter, if you give me my way on that other matter." Remember the reason an issue was not resolved earlier was because an acceptable agreement could not be reached within the allotted time. Splitting up the unresolved issues at the end of the session can be productive but dangerous. Be aware other parties may agree to give you a small issue and "in the spirit of reciprocity," demand you concede on a big one. Problems arise when negotiators focus on splitting items on a list rather than thinking about their relative importance.

WHAT IF YOU AND YOUR OPPONENTS CANNOT AGREE?

Good faith negotiators may not be able to agree on one or more provisions in a draft bill. When this happens, the two sides should clearly identify the points on which they do agree and those on which they do not. Legislators understand a few issues may remain unresolved following negotiation. As long as all parties have acted in good faith to resolve as many issues as possible, the process has worked as well as it can.

But keep in mind, if you don't solve your problems yourselves, the legislature will solve them; although in ways neither of you may like. This is why litigants settle on courthouse steps. Ensure something while you have control or risk losing everything when you both have none.

However, be on the lookout for the negotiator seeming to disagree for no solid reason. They may be strategically disagreeable because their job is to scuttle the negotiation. Their principal may not want your bill to go forward regardless of anything you agree to. In most states killing a bill is easier than moving one and by maintaining a burden of controversy and disagreement the legislature may not even take up your bill, much less pass it.

The value of consensus among special interests affected by your bill cannot be overemphasized. Consensus propels and controversy kills bills.

After negotiating, bring to your sponsor for his or her approval a revised version of the bill showing all of the agreed-upon amendments, as well as a list of those points on which consensus could not be reached. Your negotiated agreement ends up being of no avail if your sponsor refuses to carry a bill containing newly added but objectionable provisions.

Even with your sponsor's support, keep in mind the legislature's ratification of your negotiated agreement, while highly likely, is not certain. It's all a cost-benefit for legislators. That is, how much time and energy must they invest in your bill relative to how much benefit personally and collectively they get for enacting it. Unless you bill is important to key lawmakers, a bill that is just too much trouble won't become law.

SUMMARY CHAPTER 5

You start negotiating with other parties as soon as you gain consensus among your association members. Negotiating skills will be used when working with interest groups that support and oppose you. Throughout the lobbying campaign, you will negotiate repeatedly within your association and with interest groups.

Now that the fundamentals of preparing to meet the legislature have been addressed, you must give time and attention to learning legislative procedure. Your involvement with each procedural step will help your bill meet prescribed deadlines and may prevent it from being overlooked by the legislature. Familiarizing yourself with legislative procedure is your final step in preparing to meet the legislature, which is the topic of our next chapter.

Chapter 6: Navigating Legislative Procedure

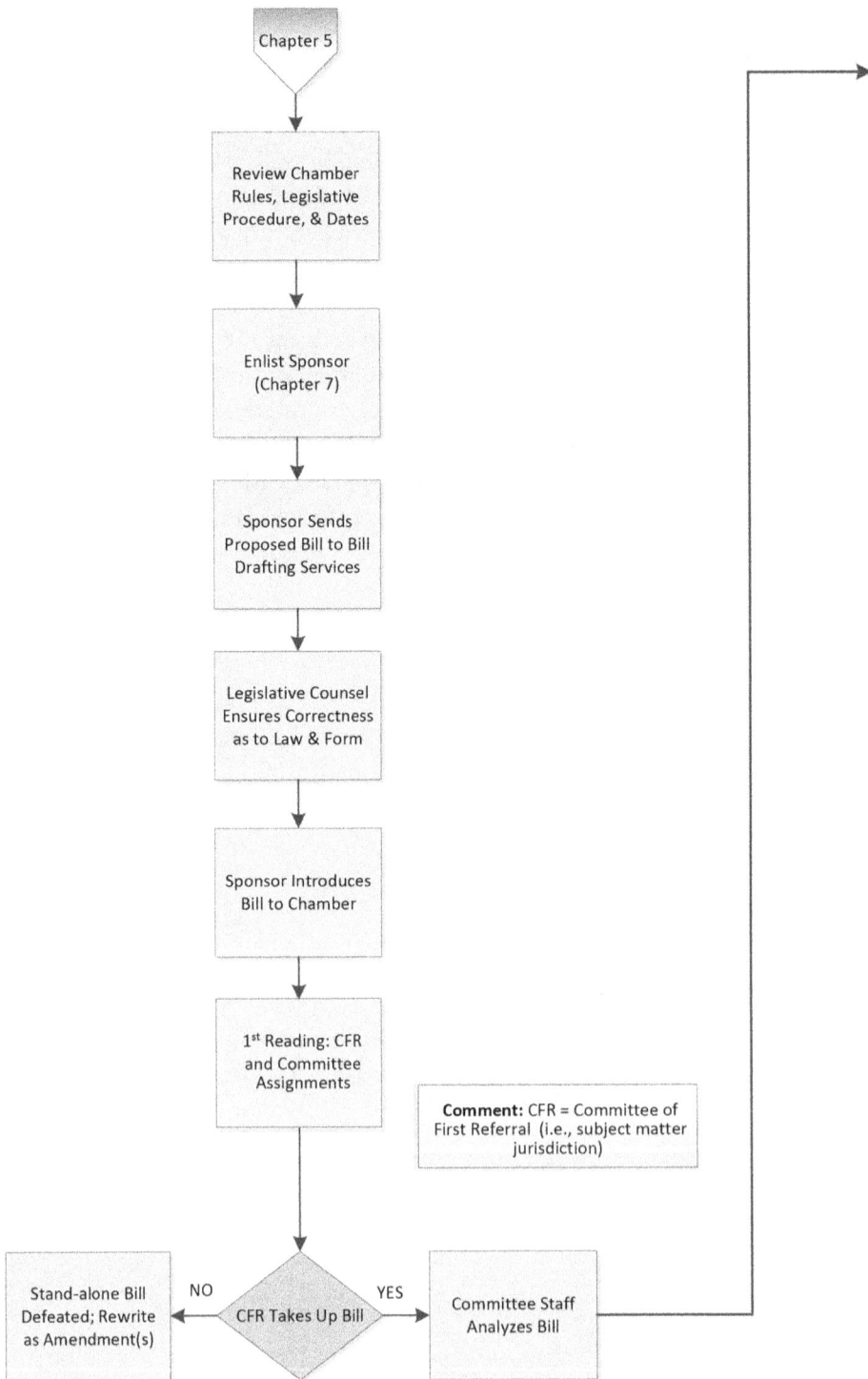

```
        ┌──────────┐
        │ Chapter 5 │
        └────┬─────┘
             │
             ▼
   ┌─────────────────────┐
   │   Review Chamber     │
   │  Rules, Legislative  │
   │  Procedure, & Dates  │
   └──────────┬──────────┘
             │
             ▼
   ┌─────────────────────┐
   │   Enlist Sponsor     │
   │    (Chapter 7)       │
   └──────────┬──────────┘
             │
             ▼
   ┌─────────────────────┐
   │   Sponsor Sends      │
   │ Proposed Bill to Bill│
   │  Drafting Services   │
   └──────────┬──────────┘
             │
             ▼
   ┌─────────────────────┐
   │ Legislative Counsel  │
   │ Ensures Correctness  │
   │  as to Law & Form    │
   └──────────┬──────────┘
             │
             ▼
   ┌─────────────────────┐
   │  Sponsor Introduces  │
   │   Bill to Chamber    │
   └──────────┬──────────┘
             │
             ▼
   ┌─────────────────────┐
   │ 1st Reading: CFR     │
   │  and Committee       │
   │  Assignments         │
   └──────────┬──────────┘
```

Comment: CFR = Committee of First Referral (i.e., subject matter jurisdiction)

```
┌──────────────────┐   NO        ◇          YES   ┌──────────────────┐
│ Stand-alone Bill │◄──────  CFR Takes Up Bill ──────►│ Committee Staff  │
│ Defeated; Rewrite│             ◇                 │  Analyzes Bill   │
│ as Amendment(s)  │                               └──────────────────┘
└──────────────────┘
```

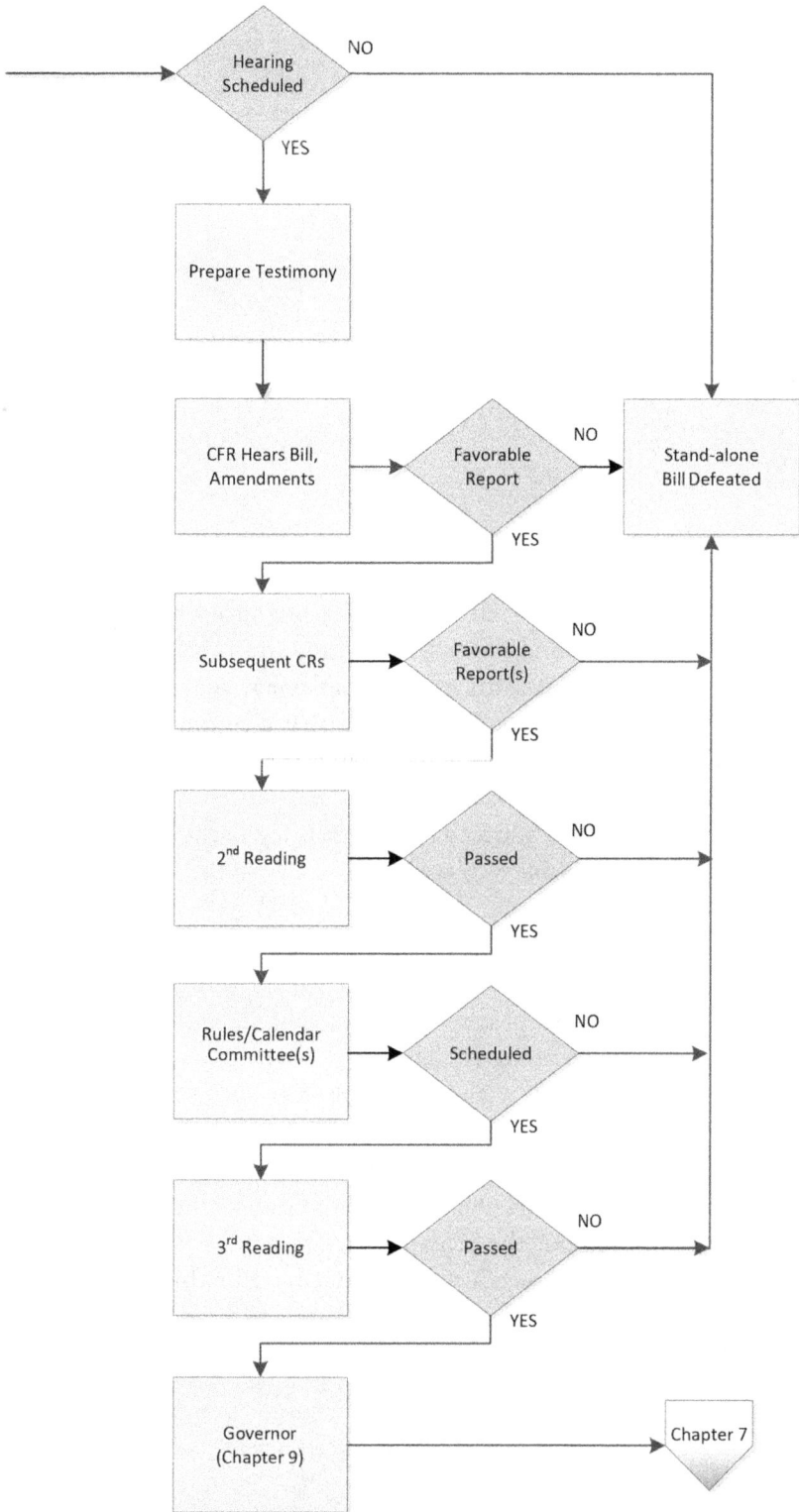

```
                    Hearing          NO
                    Scheduled ───────────────────────────┐
                        │                                 │
                      YES                                 │
                        │                                 │
                        ▼                                 │
                  Prepare Testimony                       │
                        │                                 │
                        ▼                                 ▼
              CFR Hears Bill,    Favorable   NO     Stand-alone
              Amendments    ───▶  Report    ───▶    Bill Defeated
                        │            │                    ▲
                      YES          YES                    │
                        │                                 │
                        ▼                                 │
              Subsequent CRs   Favorable    NO            │
                           ───▶ Report(s)  ───▶           │
                        │            │                    │
                      YES          YES                    │
                        ▼                                 │
              2nd Reading        Passed     NO            │
                           ───▶            ───▶           │
                        │            │                    │
                      YES          YES                    │
                        ▼                                 │
              Rules/Calendar     Scheduled  NO            │
              Committee(s)  ───▶            ───▶          │
                        │            │                    │
                      YES          YES                    │
                        ▼                                 │
              3rd Reading        Passed     NO            │
                           ───▶            ───▶───────────┘
                        │            │
                      YES          YES
                        ▼
              Governor
              (Chapter 9)  ─────────────▶  Chapter 7
```

CHAPTER 6

NAVIGATING LEGISLATIVE PROCEDURE

At this point you understand what lobbying is and the overall context in which you will work. You assessed your political strength, that is, your chances of succeeding. Deciding to go forward, you developed your lobbying campaign. The infrastructure to implement your campaign is built and ready to go. You determined whether a contract lobbyist would be useful and, if so, you have integrated him or her into your lobbying team. Knowing that *consensus propels and controversy kills*, you are equipped to negotiate with friend and foe to bring to the legislature the greatest consensus possible over your bill.

Your final step in preparing to go to the legislature is to generally understand the formal processes your bill has to traverse in order to go from idea to law. These processes collectively are called *legislative procedure* and differ among the states.[79, 80] Even if you followed the advice in Chapter 4, section *Contractor Knowledge of Legislative Process - Why It Matters*, and concluded you needed and hired a contractor fluent with legislative procedure, to ensure you responsibly manage your project you should become familiar with legislative procedure. Throughout the remainder of this book you will be referred back to specific procedural steps outlined in this chapter. And, in your lobbying practice, you will return again and again to this chapter.

This is because legislative procedure is your bill's roadmap through the legislature. The first step occurs when your sponsor files a bill drafting request and the last step is the Governor's approval, or veto and, perhaps, a veto override. The path in-between is filled with people, rules, and timelines that must be satisfied. A contract lobbyist can be invaluable helping you shepherd your bill through the procedural maze to the Governor's desk.

This chapter focuses on *formal* processes that occur in the public eye. At the same time, however, *informal* processes only insiders see are affecting your success or failure. These simultaneous and parallel processes are collectively called *politics*, which I will introduce at the end of this chapter and which are discussed in detail in the *Insiders Talk* series of books.

FORMAL LEGISLATIVE PROCEDURE

The goals of legislative procedure are to treat all persons and proposed bills impartially, require all bills follow the same sequence of steps, provide uniformity, predictability and order in the formal legislative process, and use the legislature's time and resources efficiently. It opens the process to public view and makes sure each interest group and lawmaker receives the same opportunity to argue the merits of his or her bill. The intended result of procedure is fairness and integrity in the legislative process.

"In the states, there are essentially five sources of rules: the state constitution; statutes; joint rules of both houses of the legislature; individual house rules; and, what we often refer to as the 'custom and practice' of the legislature (while these are unwritten rules, they are recognized as being 'this is the way we conduct business in the legislature')."[81] The rules in one chamber are not necessarily the same. Micheli writes,

> For example, each house of the legislature has its own set of rules on some matters. They may have different monetary thresholds for considering fiscal bills. In one house, your bill

will get a hearing. In the other house, the committee waives the hearing. In one instance, you need a witness to testify at the hearing, but no one needs to show at the other committee hearing. You certainly wouldn't want to embarrass yourself in front of your client by making the client attend a bill hearing that doesn't actually take place.

You need to be aware of what takes place next in the process so that you can plan accordingly. How far in advance does the next policy committee want letters of support or opposition? Do they want several copies? Are they submitted electronically or by hard copy? How are proposed amendments handled? Does the author (ed. note *sponsor*) of the bill have to sign them? Or can they simply be dropped off by staff? A lobbyist needs to know the answers to these questions, plus many more, and prepare for the work ahead.

While the entire body of legislative procedure can be very complex with parliamentary and chamber rules, the points that you need to know are straightforward. Should your bill find itself in the unusual circumstance of being subject to a complex parliamentary process, your sponsor and contract lobbyist will assist you. However, you need to know enough basic procedure to monitor and manage the progress of your bill, and to help your sponsor keep your bill from a fatal stumble or delay along the way, and to protect your credibility. Micheli again writes,

A lobbying coalition leader saw that the bill his coalition was opposing appeared on the Second Reading File. Assuming that later in the week the bill would thereafter be on the Third Reading File and eligible to be taken up on the floor, he quickly prepared a Floor Alert and had it hand-delivered to all members of the lower house.

Unfortunately, the bill was on the Second Reading File for just that day because it was being referred to the fiscal committee and wouldn't be on the Third Reading File for several more weeks. As a result, this lobbyist had "egg on his face" when he had to tell the coalition members that he had activated their floor lobbying and delivered dozens of floor alerts incorrectly because he simply did not understand that a bill lands on the Second Reading File when it moves from one committee to the next one.

PERSONNEL STRUCTURE

Your state's constitution establishes a legislature and two or more presiding officers. All legislatures have two legislative *chambers*, except Nebraska, which has only a Senate. One chamber in the legislature is called the Senate or "Upper House." Senators serve a four-year term in most states and a two-year term in a few. The other legislative chamber is called the House, Assembly, or "Lower House." House members, variously called Representatives, Delegates, or Assembly Members serve a two-year legislative term, except in five states having four-year terms. On average, a state legislature has two to three times as many lower house members as there are members of the upper house.

The legislature is a hierarchical institution with specific job functions at successive levels. Some positions are constitutionally established and others created for reasons of custom, convenience and efficient operations. Key personnel, elected and appointed, include:

- Presiding officers
- Majority and minority floor leaders
- Committee chairs and members
- Clerk of the House and Secretary of the Senate
- Sergeant at Arms
- Ethics offices
- Legislative services agencies (LSA)
- Committee and personal staffs

Presiding Officers. Each state's constitution establishes two presiding officers, one for each chamber. Lobbyists are interested in the presiding officers because among many other privileges, they:

135

- Appoint chairs, vice-chairs, and members of committees.
- Establish calendars for legislative activities.
- Often refer bills to or withdraw bills from committees.
- Chair chamber sessions.
- Authenticate all official acts of the chamber by their signatures.

The leader of the Senate is called the *President* except in Tennessee where the term *Speaker* is used. In most states, the upper chamber elects its President while in others, the Lieutenant Governor is constitutionally appointed as President. The President appoints or the chamber elects a *President pro tempore* to serve in the President's absence. The presiding officer in the lower chamber is called the *Speaker* and he or she is elected by the chamber. The *Speaker pro tempore* is appointed by the Speaker or elected by the chamber to serve in the Speaker's absence.

The legislature and political parties elect or appoint a number of offices not established by the state constitution but created by statute or chamber rules. [82] The legislature identifies and may change the positions, duties, and terms of office for non-constitutional officers.

Majority Leader or Majority Floor Leader. The majority political party elects its leader to represent it on the floor of the chamber. He or she may make parliamentary motions, points of order, or take actions from the floor that the President or Speaker, as the presiding officer, may not take. When the Lieutenant Governor is mainly a ceremonial Senate President, the Majority Leader is the de facto elected leader of the chamber.

Minority Leader or Minority Floor Leader. The Minority Leader is elected by the minority political party to serve as its leader on the floor. He or she works with the presiding officer, majority party leader, and majority party to ensure that the concerns of the minority party and its constituents are heard. When the Lieutenant Governor is President and a member of the minority party, the Minority Leader may take actions on the floor for the President.

Committee and Subcommittee Chairs. Chairs of committees have tremendous power to influence the progress of a bill. Except in states in which all bills are heard, chairs decide whether their committees will hear a bill, allow citizen testimony, and vote to report bills. In some states 75 percent of bills die in committee because chairs don't call them up for committee consideration. Committee members often won't oppose a powerful chair for fear they and their bills will be blackballed by the chair. Subcommittees, appointed by chairs as useful to full committees' deliberations, may have little legal significance but great procedural consequence.

Clerk of the House and Secretary of the Senate. The Clerk of the House and Secretary of the Senate are *non-lawmaker* chief executive officers responsible for the *non-political* good order and operation of their respective chambers. They are elected by each chamber or appointed by the Speaker or President to complete ministerial, technical, and clerical duties. Their professional staffs read and log-in bills, maintain the chamber journal, proofread amendments, track bill progress, engross bills, assist in parliamentary matters, and otherwise ensure smooth operation of the chamber. Their respective signatures are required to enroll and certify enactments for submittal to the Governor.

Sergeant at Arms. The Sergeant at Arms helps the President or Speaker maintain order in the chamber, bars unauthorized persons from the floor, announces and carries messages, and delivers orders issued by the chamber commanding attendance at official meetings. Assistant sergeants at arms, such as Doorkeepers, assist the Sergeant at Arms.

Ethics Offices.[83] This office is charged with enforcing ethics laws and rules for both lawmakers and lobbyists, including lobbyist registration and reporting requirements. Your, your representatives' or lobbyist's failure to comply with state ethics requirements can lead to punishment in the form of fines or loss of lobbying privileges. However, the worst fallout from an ethics violation is being labeled either an amateur or a criminal, both of whom are shunned.

Legislative Services Agencies (LSA). These non-partisan offices ensure bills meet requirements for legality, form, and style; certify that bills do not conflict with state or federal law; and produce analyses of fiscal, legal, social, environmental, and other impacts of proposed legislation.

Committee and Personal Staff. Staffing levels differ greatly among the states ranging from a couple of dozen permanent staff in a small state to thousands of staff in a large state, consisting of both permanent and session-only staffs. Expect the larger the state the more politically partisan are committee staffs. Committees in all states have clerical staffs and in larger states also technical staffs. Legislators in at least 61 of 99 state chambers have personal staff. Expect personal staffs to be as partisan as the lawmakers they serve.

JOINT, CHAMBER, AND COMMITTEE RULES

Each state constitution stipulates: basic rules of the legislature, terms and qualifications of legislators, dates and times allowed for legislative sessions, effective dates for laws, and other foundational provisions. State constitutions impose requirements on the legislature ranging from basic to detailed.

The legislature adopts its own rules by resolution at the beginning of each constitutionally prescribed session,[84] and broad changes to the rules may occur at the beginning of each new biennium or quadrennium. The Senate and House adopt *joint rules* to facilitate interactions between the chambers. Each chamber then adopts its own rules governing its organization and operation, establishes committees and officers, and regulates conduct of members, employees, lobbyists, and visitors. Committees may have their own rules beyond the joint and chamber rules. Rules may be suspended on a case-by-case basis "to give a deliberative body a way to expedite the consideration of business in emergency situations."[85]

Legislative procedures affecting lobbying and lobbyists are embedded within and scattered throughout joint and chamber rules. Do not expect to find a section within the rules entitled *Legislative Procedure*. From the entire body of rules, those impacting lobbying could fill several pages.

Although most chamber rules won't affect your lobbying effort, you should read all of them to gain a sense of how the chamber functions. Then, isolate and study those rules related to bill enactment and lobbyist behavior. If the legislature fails to follow the correct procedures, your bill may be prevented from further consideration. Although the legislature alone is charged with the responsibility to follow prescribed legislative procedures, your knowledge of procedure will enable you to identify and overcome problems related to your bill's progress.

Remember that your bill can get lost among the hundreds to thousands of other bills that the legislature faces in a session. Stay involved with your bill's progress as quality control for your sponsor. Work closely with him or her and with other legislators to ensure your bill meets all deadlines and follows required procedural steps.

Supplemental Legislative Procedures

In addition to formally adopted legislative procedures, other prescribed rules and informal traditions govern the operation of the chamber. When the state constitution, statutes, rules of the legislature, or chamber rules provide insufficient guidance for dealing with a particular situation, then standard *manuals of legislative or parliamentary procedure* may be consulted. These references include the most frequently used Mason's Manual of Legislative Procedure,[86] but also Jefferson's Manual of Parliamentary Procedure, and Robert's Rules of Order. The 50 state legislatures, and even the senate and house of a particular legislature, may use different manuals.

Special *temporary rules* are adopted by the Rules Committee or leadership to deal with specific matters, such as the amount of time allowed to debate a particular piece of legislation. Special rules improve the efficiency of the legislature because they enable it to individualize procedure for unusual situations. Special rules may affect your bill.

Legislative Language

"Political jargon can make state politics tough to navigate."[87] Understanding legislative concepts and the language expressing them is central to navigating the capitol, its rules, and achieving successful participation in the lawmaking process. "The Capitol, like any other highly specialized workplace, has its own jargon that outsiders may find puzzling if they attend legislative hearings but one that any true insider must know to communicate and function effectively."[88]

The National Conference of State Legislatures provides a good starting point for broadly used technical terms.[89] Obtain a state-specific glossary prior to lobbying a particular legislature. Such glossaries are commonly found on the Internet.

Insiders Talk: Glossary of Legislative Concepts and Representative Terms[90] lists common capitol concepts followed by various state-specific terms describing the same processes and players. For example, *lower house* of a bicameral legislature is the concept; *Assembly*, *House of Representatives*, and *House of Delegates* are state-specific synonyms. Understand concepts and you will quickly master procedures, processes, and methods regardless of permutations of vocabulary.

CRITICAL DATES

State constitutions and legislatures establish critical dates consonant with the prescribed steps for a bill becoming law. Because the time and scope of legislative sessions are limited, your bill must meet each deadline. Failure to meet even one of them may cost you your bill. Although, as with most all of its rules, the chamber can suspend or revise timeline requirements, you cannot rely on a suspension of timelines to save a bill that falls behind in meeting critical dates.

At this point you have written your bill and enlisted your main sponsor. You are familiar with chamber structure. Now it's time to discuss a generic path your bill must travel to become law, that is, the prescribed series of steps found in legislative procedure.

HOW A BILL BECOMES LAW – A GENERIC MODEL

Below is a procedural composite derived from practices of many states. It is a generic model to help you think through the process. A more complete description of each step in the model will follow. Of course, before lobbying, obtain your state's rules. Chapters 7–9 headings reference what steps are being mentioned in the particular chapter.

The steps are:

1. Lawmaker submits bill drafting request (BDR) to LSA-Bill Drafting Office (BDO).
2. BDO composes bill in accord with chamber bill drafting manual.
3. LSA-Legislative Counsel ensures bill is correct as to law and form.
4. Chamber clerk logs bill in and assigns bill tracking number.
5. First reading: clerk verbally announces bill and publication in journal.
6. Bill referred to committee(s) of jurisdiction.
7. Majority and minority caucuses analyze bill.
8. Committee of first referral (CFR) staff evaluates and reports on bill to committee.
9. CFR considers bill, amendments, and votes to report.
10. LSA attaches to reported bill its note on social, fiscal, other impacts.
11. Sequential committees of referral process select subsections of bill.
12. Committee(s) report(s) bill to chamber or Committee of the Whole.
13. Committee of the Whole debates bill, amends, reports to chamber.
14. Second reading: chamber debate, amendment, and vote.
15. Rules Committee or leadership schedules amended bill for third reading.
16. Third reading: perhaps limited debate, and vote.
17. Chamber of origin engrosses bill and messages it to second house.

18. Second house approves a version of the messaged bill and returns it to chamber of origin.
19. Versions are reconciled in conference and each chamber approves.
20. Bill is enrolled.
21. Legislature forwards enrolled bill to Governor for approval.
22. Governor approves bill making an enactment, vetoes bill, or does nothing with it.
23. Legislature overrides veto, sustains it, amends bill to meet Governor's demands, lets it die, or sues in court to overturn veto.
24. Bill enacted without Governor's signature.
25. Publication of enactment by the Secretary of State which upon specified date becomes an act, that is, a statute.

1. *Lawmaker submits bill drafting request (BDR) to LSA-Bill Drafting Office (BDO).* Lawmaker submits BDR to BDO, also variously called Bill Drafting Services, Office of Legislative Legal Services, or similar name. Sometimes BDRs are general descriptions of the problem with suggested resolutions. Other times attached to BDRs are bills perfect as to form, legality, and content.

2. *BDO composes bill in accord with chamber bill drafting manual.* Even if the BDO receives your perfectly drafted bill, it still ensures the bill meets the legislature's standards for use of terms, recitations, bill summaries, citing of statutes, and other requirements. The sponsor may ask the BDO to speak to you as to any questions it may have about the bill. The BDO attaches its bill summary to the bill.

3. *LSA-Legislative Counsel ensures the bill is correct as to law and form.* The Office of Legislative Counsel, Revisor of Statutes, Rules Committee, or similar agency approves the bill for form and legal sufficiency, including issuing a legal opinion.[91] The office may certify the bill does not conflict with constitutional or statutory requirements. Certification may be required for introduction. Office notes may accompany the bill, as introduced. (Once the bill passes out of the CFR, original notes may be revised or notes are drafted for the first time, the most indispensable of which is called the fiscal note.[92])

4. *Chamber clerk logs in bill and assigns bill tracking number.* The main sponsor in the *chamber of origin* submits the certified measure to the Bill Clerk. The Bill Clerk ensures that the bill is in accord with chamber rules, enters the bill into its logbook, and assigns a bill number. In some states the BDR number becomes the chamber bill tracking number. In general, only members of the chamber may introduce and sponsor or co-sponsor bills, which sponsorship is attested to by their signatures.

Identical bills often simultaneously introduced in each chamber are called *companion bills.* Concurrent consideration allows each chamber to evaluate a bill before expiration of key procedural dates. The first bill to be messaged to the receiving chamber becomes the final bill. Because enactment requires approval of an identical bill by both chambers, lobbyists and sponsors in each chamber must coordinate activities to keep the companion bills identical.

5. *First reading: clerk verbally announces bill and publication in journal.* A bill must be read and approved at least three times over three different days by the majority of each chamber before it can become a law. First reading may consist of the reading clerk announcing to the chamber the bill number and title, and perhaps a short description or summary of the bill, or printing the same in the journal.[93] However, any member may urge the chamber to reject the bill.[94]

6. *Bill referred to committee(s) of jurisdiction.* At first reading, in some states *before*, the chamber *refers* (sends) the bill to one or possibly more committees[95] for advice as to what the chamber should do with your bill. These are called *committees of referral.* The first committee to process the bill is called the *committee of subject matter jurisdiction, policy committee, standing committee,* or simply *committee of first referral* (CFR). Environmental bills go to the Environment Committee, agricultural bills to the Agricultural Committee, and so on. You will work most closely with the CFR without ignoring subsequent committees of referral.

Depending on the breadth and impact of your bill, it may be referred to additional committees that review it following the CFR.[96] You drafted your bill narrowly to minimize the number of referrals because each referral offers opportunities for unfavorable amendments, delay, or defeat.

Depending on leadership's intentions, your bill may have been passed or killed before the CFR or any committee considers it. This is mentioned in step 11 below and further discussed in Chapter 8, section *However, Most Committee Meetings Are Just Theatre*, and Chapter 9, section *Does Enough Time Remain to Reach the Governor's Desk?*, subsection 1.a "Leadership's intentions."

7. *Majority and minority caucuses analyze the bill.* Each party's caucus assesses your bill to determine how well it fits into the direction the caucus wants. However, the majority caucus decides whether your bill will pass, be amended, be killed, or left alone without direction to caucus members. Few bills are won and lost in committees or on the floor, as indispensable as these are. Their fates often are determined by the majority caucus, open or closed.[97] It may redirect your bill at any time.

8. *Committee of first referral (CFR) staff evaluates and reports on bill to committee.* Because few legislators are experts in all matters that come before their committees, most states employ professional staffs to advise them about technical matters. Committee staffs have great influence on the outcome of committee actions on your bill. Expect staff to request input from and defer to *technical* recommendations from the executive agency that would implement your bill.

9. *CFR considers bill, amendments, and votes to report.* Referral to a committee does not ensure action will be taken. Committees generally don't want to embarrass majority member sponsors, so disfavored bills are defeated by committee inaction or withdrawal by the sponsor. This is called a *soft kill*. On the other hand, as a courtesy to the sponsor, a chair may call up a bill with no chance of a favorable report. Bills are disfavored due to disinterest in the bill, dislike of the bill's sponsor, work overload, or other reasons.

On the other hand, the committee chair may hold a hearing on a *favored bill*, take testimony on it, consider amendments, and call a vote. With majority caucus and chair support, all the committee and staff work invested, and for reasons of professional courtesy, a *do not pass* report, called a *hard kill*, is unlikely. Local bills and non-controversial bills with full committee support are sent to the floor for unanimous consent.[98] Failure of your bill to pass through any committee of jurisdiction generally means it is defeated.

Infrequently, the CFR unanimously passes a bill without amendments making it eligible for the *consent calendar* thereby avoiding further committees, second reading, and chamber passage due to it being non-controversial. Normally, a bill reported favorably, but not unanimously, continues to one or more sequential committees, subject matter and gatekeeper.

10. *LSA attaches to reported bill its note on social, fiscal, and other impacts.* The LSA evaluates the committee-approved bill and estimates its likely impacts on the state should it become law. Areas studied for impact include economic, environmental, social, governmental, and state budgetary. An initial or revised LSA note is attached to the bill.

11. *Sequential committees of referral process selected subsections of bill.* After the CFR, your bill may have sequential or split referrals to other committees. For example, if your bill primarily impacts environment but secondarily touches upon agriculture, the chamber's Environment committee will be the committee of first referral after which the Agricultural Committee will review the bill's subject matter within its jurisdiction.

As the term sequential indicates, depending on how the bill is written and leadership's intentions, a series of committees may be given jurisdiction over your bill. There is any number of committees to which your bill could be referred, either to move it or kill it. Split referrals require committees meet together to consider your bill. Because committee agendas are very full, the likelihood of a joint meeting is small. Therefore, your bill may never be taken up.

A bill with several referrals may not have enough time remaining in the session to run the gauntlet of committees thereby missing deadlines and be defeated. Scheduling too many referrals may be a soft kill by leadership. Further, any committee may amend or negatively report its piece but much more likely simply refuse to take it up, thereby killing it.

After committees of subject matter jurisdiction, your bill faces *gate-keeper* committees which evaluate bills for financial impacts and procedural matters. These are fiscal committees such as *Budget and Tax*, *Ways and Means*, or similar names which evaluate the impacts of bills upon the state budget, and *Government Operations* which evaluates impacts on state agencies and local governments. The *Rules (and Calendar) Committee* assures the legality of all bills and schedules them for floor consideration. Finally, your bill may be sent to a kill committee which does just what its name suggests. This is discussed in Chapter 9.

12. *Committee(s) report(s) bill to chamber or Committee of the Whole.* The CFR report includes a record of hearings, testimony, committee votes, and LSA notes. It concludes with a recommendation for chamber action among them: do pass, do pass as amended, or do not pass. An unfavorable report, which seldom happens, usually defeats the bill while a favorable report provides momentum for continuation through the legislative process.[99]

In cases of multiple referrals, each committee reports on its portion of the bill. For second reading, the *primary committee*, likely the CFR, consolidates sequential committees' reports into a master document. In the alternative the *Committee of the Whole* consolidates the various committees' reports.

13. *Committee of the Whole debates bill, amends, reports to chamber.* Many but not all chambers use this committee which is comprised of all legislators in the chamber and operates under relaxed rules of procedure.[100] The Committee of the Whole considers your bill, proposed amendments, and report(s) of the committee(s) of first referral. It may debate the bill and propose additional amendments. The Committee votes upon the bill and proposed amendments and defeats or reports the bill with recommendations to the chamber for second reading.

14. *Second reading: chamber debate and amendment.* In second reading, the chamber considers the Committee of the Whole's report, including proposed amendments, and may debate the bill. After debate, a vote is taken. If the vote is favorable, the bill is sent to third reading. If the bill is extensively amended, it may be re-referred to a committee of referral with subject matter jurisdiction. If the vote at second reading is unfavorable, the bill is defeated.

15. *Rules Committee or leadership schedules amended bill for third reading.*[101] Before third reading, the legality of the second reading amended bill is reviewed by Legislative Counsel. Staff may prepare another bill analysis to inform the chamber of the meaning and consequences of the final bill, if enacted. The Rules Committee schedules (calendars) the bill for third reading.[102] If not calendared, the bill never reaches the floor, and is defeated.

16. *Third reading: perhaps limited debate, vote.* At third reading, the entire chamber considers your bill for the final time. Since the bill was debated on second reading, some states limit or disallow debate or amendment during third reading. At third reading, the bill is read and a vote taken. If passed, the bill is certified as having passed the chamber (engrossed). If the vote at third reading is unfavorable, the bill is defeated.

However, in practice few bills are killed on third reading. To avoid wasting time and needless controversy, leadership normally polls members as to the likelihood of favorable action before bringing up a bill for third reading. If the poll shows likely failure, then the bill will not be brought up.

17. *Chamber of origin engrosses bill and messages it to second house.* To become law, both chambers must approve the identical bill(s). The chamber of origin next sends (*messages*) the engrossed bill to the other chamber for consideration and vote.

18. *Second house approves a version of the messaged bill and returns it to chamber of origin.* The receiving chamber considers the messaged bill by repeating some or all of steps 5–13 above, or by sending it to third

reading and final chamber vote.[103] If the receiving chamber has considered an identical *companion bill*, then the process can be shortened considerably. If the receiving chamber approves it without amendments, it returns the bill to the chamber of origin to be enrolled. If amended by the receiving chamber, the bill is messaged back to the originating chamber for concurrence.

19. *Versions are reconciled in conference and each chamber approves.*[104] Although each chamber may approve a different version of the bill, agreement on the identical version is required for enactment. The bill's differences will be resolved by a conference of representatives from each chamber.[105] The bill as reported by the conference committee is voted upon by each chamber. It's an up-or-down vote, no amendments. If either chamber rejects the conference report, the bill is defeated.

20. *Bill is enrolled.* The Speaker, President, Clerk of the House, and Secretary of the Senate *certify* by their signatures the bill has passed in identical form in each chamber, thereby enrolling the bill.

21. *Legislature forwards enrolled bill to Governor for approval.*[106] The legislature sends the bill to the Governor for his or her action. The Governor approves or objects to the bill.

22. *Governor approves bill making an enactment, vetoes bill, or does nothing with it.* The Governor signs the enrolled bill making an enactment. If vetoed, the bill goes back to the legislature, normally accompanied by a veto message detailing the Governor's reasons for rejecting the bill. Vetoes can be partial, conditional, or complete. Partial means only sections of the bill are vetoed. Conditional means if the legislature fixes the problems identified in the veto message then the Governor will sign the amended bill. Complete means the Governor will consider no appeal, the bill is dead. The legislature may attempt to *override* the veto.

The Governor may take no action. Depending upon state, inaction either allows an enrolled bill to become an enactment without the Governor's signature or is the same as a veto. Expect the Governor to request from the implementing executive agency its recommendation as to disposition of your bill. If the agency urges a veto, then expect a veto. However, under the principle of *comity*[107] most Governors veto few bills.

23. Legislature overrides veto, sustains it, amends bill to meet Governor's demands, lets it die, or sues in court to overturn veto. Supermajorities (infrequently, merely a majority) in both chambers can override, that is, reverse the veto to enact the bill. Failure to gain a supermajority in either chamber sustains the veto and the enactment is defeated. The chamber may amend the bill to meet the Governor's demands or may be too afraid of the Governor to override. Or the legislature may do nothing letting the bill die. Infrequently a chamber may sue to have a court declare the veto unconstitutional.

In practice, vetoes seldom are overridden, especially when both the legislature and Governor are of the same party. However, when the opposing party in the legislature has a supermajority, especially when it wants to embarrass or punish the Governor, it may override most or all vetoes.[108]

24. Bill enacted without Governor's signature. If inaction constitutes approval or if the legislature overrides the Governor's veto, the bill becomes an enactment without his or her signature.

25. Publication of enactment by the Secretary of State which upon specified date becomes an act, that is, a statute. The enactment becomes an enforceable act, that is a law, when published by the Secretary of State and upon reaching the effective date, either the date established by the state constitution or as scheduled by the act itself.

By the time your bill completes the above steps and is signed into law, amendments may have made your bill considerably different from the one your sponsor attached to the BDR. You should be less concerned by the fact that your bill has been amended and focus instead on how the subsequent amendments improve or diminish the likelihood of your concept becoming law.

However, remember that, for all practical purposes, you don't have a law until the implementing agency tells you that you have a law; and you don't know what the law means until they tell you what it means. The agency does this through rule adoption and enforcement, as mentioned in Chapter 9.

WHO WILL CHANGE YOUR BILL? – AMENDMENTS

As your bill proceeds through the legislative process, different individuals will propose amendments. First, before introduction your main sponsor may require changes to your bill as a condition of sponsorship. It may also be changed by the LSA if found legally deficient. (They won't change the substance but only ensure form and legal sufficiency.)

Those interested in changing your bill will come from two broad groups. The first consists of the same opponents with whom you negotiated previously or new ones added along the way. Issues on which you failed to reach agreement earlier will be advanced again by your opponents' legislative allies. The second group consists of opportunists interested in your bill not because of its substance, but because they see it as a vehicle to carry their stalled bills to the Governor's desk. Do not think harshly of these opportunists because you may need to become an opportunist yourself.

Chamber leadership may amend your bill by combining it with any number of other bills, germane or not,[109] to form one large bill, called an *omnibus*, *Christmas tree*, or *train* bill. They may do this because dealing with one large omnibus bill may conserve legislative time and energy relative to dealing with several *stand-alone* bills. In an omnibus bill, leadership mixes bills likely to pass with bills unlikely to become law. Leadership wants the *good bills* to carry the *bad bills* to the Governor's desk. Leadership uses the omnibus bill to force each individual bill's lobbyist into a political "press-gang" of sorts to get their concepts into law.[110] Leadership in effect says to the press-gang, "You are going to hang together or you are going to hang separately."[111]

Remember, too, that if the other chamber amends your bill when received from the chamber of origin, the chamber of origin must approve the amended bill to enroll it. If your bill was amended unfavorably in committee, you may ask your main sponsor to amend it back to the original version and, if it has stalled, you may ask him or her to amend your concept to a bill that is moving forward. (See, now you've become an opportunist!) However, expect this parliamentary effort has a low probability of success.

TECHNICAL CONSIDERATIONS OF AMENDMENTS

The process of amending a bill varies somewhat among state legislatures. Three-fourths of the state legislative chambers have rules on germaneness of amendments or motions.[112] For an amendment to be germane, it must be relevant to the topic of the bill being amended.

Amendments may be proposed in written or oral form. When written and prior to a vote the amendment's sponsor must supply the committee secretary or chamber Clerk with a copy to be printed and distributed to the committee or chamber.

Requirements for oral amendments vary among the states. In some, the Clerk writes out the amendment before the committee or chamber considers it, while in others the amendment may be considered and voted upon when spoken.

In some states, the LSA or chamber Clerk drafts the amendment. If an amendment substantially changes a bill, then the staff, the committee of origin, LSA or all three may complete a revised bill analysis and notes, respectively. If enough time remains in the session, then substantially amended bills must often return to the committee(s) of referral for consideration and report. If amended in the last hours of the session, then action is solely at the chamber's discretion.

Amendments are proposed on a word-by-word basis and the amendment sponsor is responsible for proposing the amendment and leading

151

debate, if any. Each amendment must be adopted individually. Depending upon state, any member may propose amendments to a bill during the second or sometimes third reading. After all amendments to the bill have been accepted by the committee or chamber, the bill, as amended, is voted upon.

The phrase "amended in committee" is a technical misnomer but a practical reality in most states. Only the chamber, not committees, can amend bills. Committees recommend amendments to the chamber. Since ninety-five percent of committee recommendations are accepted, although technically incorrect, in practice a committee *amends* a bill.

Amendments of bills on third reading made in the last hours of the session amidst the weariness of all and the press of the clock, may pass with little discussion or debate, much less comprehension. Further, spoken amendments may be misinterpreted such that the amendment one thinks he or she heard may be very different from what appears in the engrossed bill. You won't know what the adopted bill says until you read it, and what you read may be very different from what you expected.

VARIATIONS OF TERMINOLOGY AND SEQUENCE AMONG STATES

Remember that state legislatures differ in terms used to describe the same legislative concept or activity. You should have a copy of your state's glossary as found on the legislature's website.

Also, the sequence of steps in the legislative process varies slightly from state to state. Despite minor variations, however, all states generally conform to the information related to the legislative process provided in this chapter. Most publish flowcharts broadly listing steps for a bill to become a law. These charts may be obtained from the Internet or chamber Clerk's or Secretary's offices. *To be an effective lobbyist, you must obtain the legislative procedures of your state and follow them.*

Having considered the overall process, certain key elements deserve a bit more discussion. These are how the chamber gives notice of upcoming and completed activities and time frames during which the chamber does business.

CALENDARING

The chamber gives public notice of its actions on its *calendar*. Each time a bill is to be considered, read, debated, or voted upon, it must be *calendared*. By following the calendar, you know when and where to invest political resources and lobby lawmakers and staff. Except by supermajority vote, a bill not calendared may not be considered by the chamber and is defeated.

Each chamber uses a number of different calendars. For example, the *daily calendar, four-day calendar,* and *advance journal and calendar* announce expected orders of business for a specific forthcoming legislative day. Calendars are distributed 24 to 96 hours before consideration of listed bills. Because much can change after publishing a calendar, a *supplemental daily calendar* identifies the current day's agenda. The supplemental daily calendar is prepared each morning and may be changed by supermajority vote of the chamber.

Of concern to lobbyists, the daily calendar provides notice of bills passed during the previous day and a variety of bills to be considered on the current day, including, but not limited to:

1. Bills for third reading
2. Bills for second reading
3. Bills carried over from the previous day
4. Postponed bills
5. Motions to recall tabled bills
6. Bills vetoed by the Governor that the chamber will try to override
7. Bills from the other chamber
8. Conference committee bills

A daily calendar may also list other chamber activities scheduled to occur. These include committee meetings, public hearings, resolutions, consideration of gubernatorial and judicial nominations (Senate), and other items of chamber business.

A *special orders calendar* allows the Rules Committee or by supermajority vote the chamber itself, to place an item on the calendar for consideration at a specific date and time. This consideration takes precedence over all other scheduled items. Some states use the *general orders* or *special orders calendar* to list bills for second reading and *special orders* or *bill calendar* listing bills for third reading.

The *consent calendar* or *consent orders* allows non-controversial and local bills to be enacted with the minimum expenditure of legislative energy. "Consent calendars are used in 35 state legislatures. In 21 states both chambers use them; in 14 states (including Nebraska) only one chamber uses them."[113] It requires unanimous consent of both the committees of referral and chamber. If an amendment is demanded or objection made, the bill is removed from the calendar and, with a favorable committee report, is sent to second reading. Bills passed on the consent calendar are engrossed and sent to the other chamber.

However, in the waning hours of the session, there is no time for notices. This means you must be physically present in the chamber regardless of the hour of the day to advocate for your bill as long as it still has a chance of enactment.

THE JOURNAL

Each chamber summarizes its floor activities in its *daily journal*. The daily journal enables lobbyists to know about chamber decisions regarding their bill and procedural plans of the legislature that affect it. At the end of the annual session, the daily journals are bound into the *annual journal* or simply *journal*.

PRE-SESSIONS

The pre-session is important to lobbyists because, although the entire chamber as one body will not meet, committees meet and bills are pre-filed. While prohibited from formal constitutional session and thereby from enacting legislation, the legislature uses the pre-session to prepare for the forthcoming regular session, such as by committees meeting to discuss pre-filed bills. You may obtain notices of pre-sessions from the legislature. If your state has pre-session activities, you need to be active in the capitol on behalf of your bill.

CONSTITUTIONAL SESSIONS

The term *session* refers to blocks of time during which the legislature may conduct official business. The term may also refer to the hours during which the legislature meets on a particular day. For example, the legislature will be *in session* from Tuesday 10 a.m. until 3 p.m. Some legislatures have customs indicating being in session, such as having the capitol's flag flying only at those times. It also refers to the length of time between the first day of the legislative session and the last day, that is, *sine die* adjournment. *Sine die* has its own customs, such as both chambers' Sergeants at Arms simultanously dropping handkerchiefs which, upon both touching the floor, ends the session *sine die.*

The state constitution may establish three kinds of sessions: organizational, regular, and special. *Organizational sessions* occur shortly after a general election when the legislature organizes itself by electing leaders and taking other administrative actions in anticipation of the pre-session and regular session. *Regular sessions* are established for conducting the normal business of the legislature.[114] Your bill and others will be considered for constitutional action during the regular session. By proclamation, a *special session* may be convened by the Governor or legislature itself.[115] During special sessions, topics for discussion are usually limited to those named in the proclamation.

MAKE SURE YOU ARE LOBBYING THE CURRENT VERSION OF YOUR BILL

Few actions discredit a lobbyist more than working in error from an out-of-date, like last night's, version of the bill. After each session in which the bill is considered and in advance of the next consideration, the chamber prints an engrossed version of the bill. The Bill Historian should contact the Bill Clerk, bill room, chamber printer, or other reliable source to assure that you have the current version of your bill. He or she should retain copies of each version of the bill, copies of amendments, and reasons for bill changes. Expect to find all on the legislature's webpage.

INFORMAL AND BEHIND THE SCENES PROCESSES

While this chapter discusses *formal* legislative processes, parallel and simultaneous to the formal, *informal* processes affecting your bill are taking place. These informal processes, largely taking place behind the scenes, are broadly called *politics*.

Observers of the formal processes see votes being cast but seldom do they know *why* lawmakers so voted. This is because effective lobbyists secured most votes in private out of sight of the public and media. They did this at fish fries, fundraisers, private dinners, retreats and conferences, and private moments on the golf links, hunting trips, and other venues. Other settings are lawmakers' offices in the capitol and legislative districts and in party caucuses, open or closed.

Lawmakers are *politicians*. They are not impartial judges, nor are they supposed to be. John Stuart Mill, influential in the political thought of the time, commented, "Parliament has an office . . . to be at once the nation's Committee of Grievances, and its Congress of Opinions."

Because political deal-making is difficult in the public eye, and especially when the media are in the vicinity, there is a tendency to resolve legislative issues in private, then have the formal processes we discussed in this chapter, ratify the out-of-sight deals. The cameras are on in the committee room, but not in the restrooms and hallways. Yes, there are "government in the sunshine" laws but there is also politics.

The relative control caucuses exert over their members varies greatly.[116] However, when the caucus has taken a position, votes in committees and on the floor merely ratify what the majority party had already agreed to do. That is, the votes you see were likely settled before the first lawmaker entered into the committee room or chamber. A lawmaker voting against instructions of party leadership will be punished by loss of committee assignments, financial and political support and, in extreme cases, expelled from the caucus. In our final three chapters we discuss the politics of lobbying, including motivating lawmakers to vote as you request.

SUMMARY CHAPTER 6

To become law, your bill must pass through a series of legislative steps prescribed by the state's constitution, statutes, joint rules, and individual chamber rules. The series of prescribed steps is designed to make transparent the formal part of lawmaking. You must understand procedure and its terminology to navigate your bill through the legislature's many administrative shoals.

Managing your bill includes drafting it to minimize the number of committee referrals, monitoring actions of potentially interested parties, and attending all sessions at which the bill may be amended. You should work with your sponsor to control amendments to your bill as much as possible.

You are now ready to enter the legislative arena. Here, you will find a main sponsor for your bill, secure co-sponsors, and learn to work with legislators, committees, and their staffs.

PART II. MEETING THE LEGISLATURE – IMPLEMENTING YOUR LOBBYING CAMPAIGN

Chapter 7: Making Successful Lobbying Visits (Steps 1-6)

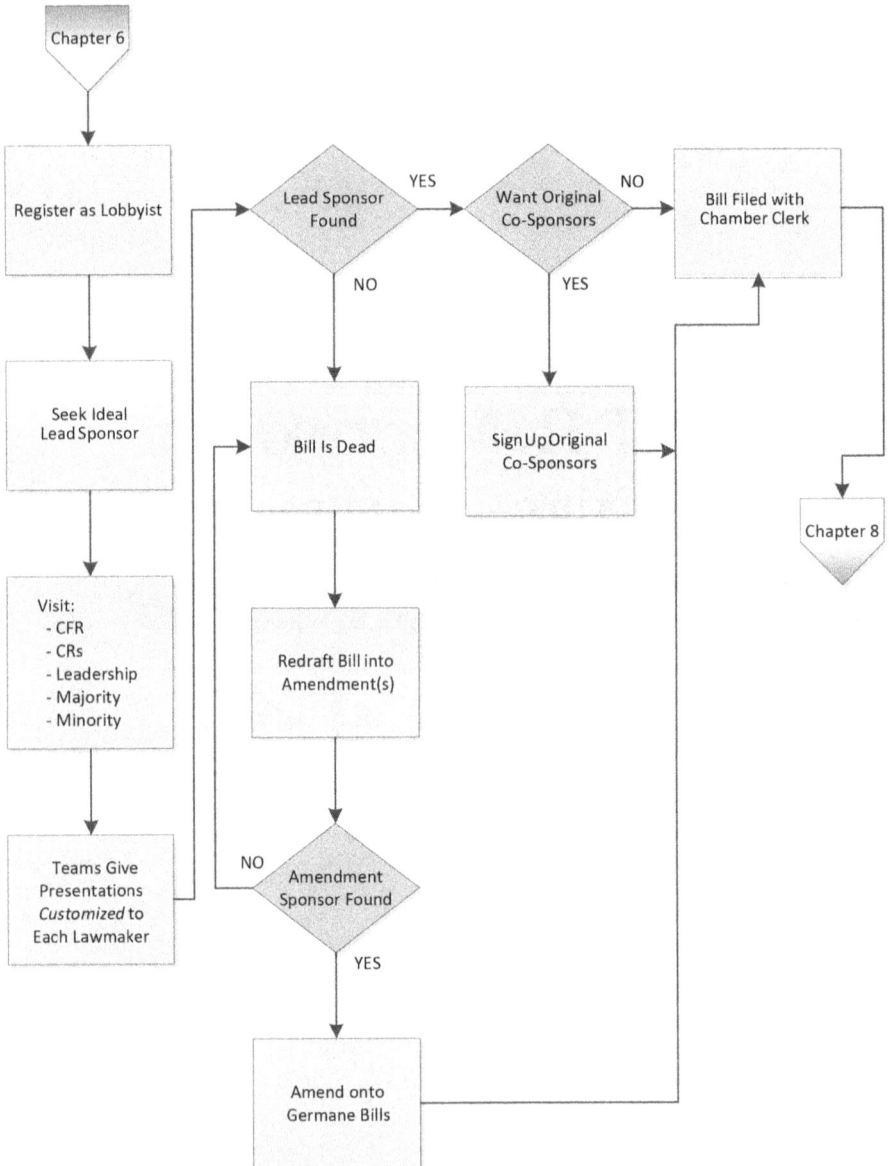

Chapter 6

Register as Lobbyist

Seek Ideal Lead Sponsor

Visit:
- CFR
- CRs
- Leadership
- Majority
- Minority

Teams Give Presentations *Customized* to Each Lawmaker

Lead Sponsor Found

YES

NO

Want Original Co-Sponsors

NO

YES

Bill Filed with Chamber Clerk

Bill Is Dead

Sign Up Original Co-Sponsors

Chapter 8

Redraft Bill into Amendment(s)

Amendment Sponsor Found

NO

YES

Amend onto Germane Bills

MAKING SUCCESSFUL LOBBYING VISITS (STEPS 1 – 6)

Now it's time to put all the pieces you've assembled to the test. You've negotiated with special interests reaching as much consensus as possible. Depending on state and bill, you have spoken with the executive agencies. Now it's time for the legislative lobbying visits.

The lobbying visits provide opportunity for the Lobbying Team to find your bill's main sponsor(s), add co-sponsor(s), and build legislative support. In these visits you cultivate relationships with lawmakers and staff, incline them against your opponents, and convince them it is in their best interests to support your bill. Each lobbying visit follows the same format and generally uses the same mechanics. But the details will vary depending upon the particular lawmaker, as you answer lobbying's threshold question, that is, *"Why would this lawmaker give me his or her vote?"*

But first, before going to the capitol you must determine whether per state law you are lobbying. If you are, do you need to register as a lobbyist? Failure to conform to registration requirements will embarrass you and your principal, damage your lobbying campaign, and may result in civil or criminal prosecutions.

AM I GOING TO BE LOBBYING?

Whether you are lobbying depends on your state's legal definition of lobbying. In one state, your conduct may be statutorily defined as lobbying whereas those same activities in another state would not. Self-serving assertions that you are not lobbying but rather *educating*, *informing*, or *just visiting* are immaterial when the law defines your conduct as *lobbying*. For now we will work with this generic definition, "States generally define lobbying as an attempt to influence government action through either written or oral communication."[117] If *educating*, *informing*, or *just visiting* could influence the legislature, then it's probably lobbying.

I AM LOBBYING. MUST I REGISTER AS A LOBBYIST?

Upon concluding your conduct is lobbying as defined by statute, you must answer the next question, "Must I register as a lobbyist?" That answer is found in the ethics requirements of each state. "The details of each state's lobbying laws differ markedly, so much so that nearly 50 different versions exist."[118] Generally, a person who lobbies must register as a lobbyist upon triggering a time, money, or place of lobbying threshold.

A body of laws regulates lobbyists with specific *do and don't* requirements found in:

- Statutes and administrative agency rules: public employee, election, and lobbyist
- Joint rules of the two chambers
- Rules of each chamber
- Ethics agency rules and opinions
- Procedures of the legislature's support services offices

These requirements are designed to enhance and protect the integrity of public officials, the legislative process, and your interactions with the legislature. Violation of an ethics requirement may result in criminal, civil, legislative, or administrative prosecution and punishment, as well as public humiliation. Even being accused of an ethics violation will result in loss of trust and credibility with lawmakers, legislative staff, and special interests.

In addition to lobbyist-specific requirements, you must abide by laws against corruption of public officials and the election code. For example, giving a lawmaker a gift or donation with your expressed expectation of legislative support could be found to be bribery, thereby violating the corruption statutes. Making a donation during the legislative session likely violates the elections code in a number of states.

Although lobbyist-specific ethics rules vary greatly from state to state, some rules are encountered frequently among the states. For example, in 43 states, an agreement to pay a *contingency fee*, that is, to pay your lobbyist depending on his or her success, is a crime in both the offer and the receipt. On the other hand, Delaware, Louisiana, Missouri, Montana, New Hampshire, West Virginia, Wyoming, and the District of Columbia allow contingency fees.

Other rules may be unique to a state. An example of a state-specific law is Arizona's requirement that each lobbyist must read the Arizona handbook for lobbyists and certify to the state he or she has read it.[119]

Before you or those in your group lobby the legislature, make certain you know and comply with your state's ethics requirements. Do not assume, do not guess you are in compliance - make certain you are. Further, *do not presume your contract lobbyist's registration makes your lobbying legal - it may or may not.*

Now that you are registered and in compliance with lobbying laws, you may proceed to influence legislative staff and lawmakers. You lobby both and at the same time. However, in smaller states you will mostly work with members. While the larger a state, the more you will work with staff rather than members.

Lobbying Legislative Staffs[120]

After special interests, Chapter 1 ranked legislative staff as the second greatest influence on your bill. This is because lawmakers trust their staffs. They rely on them and spend large amounts of time working closely with them. A lawmaker once said to me, "Win my staff and you win me."

Staffs manage lawmakers' personal offices and provide chamber support services. They give legal counsel, technical advice, and recommendations to lawmakers on a variety of possible legislative actions. Staffs have tremendous influence on the direction the legislature takes regarding your bill.

Staffs provide you with opportunities to help them affect the direction of your bill. For issues the legislator wishes to move forward, he or she asks staff to research the issue and provide supporting data needed to convince others to vote for a favored bill. For other bills, legislators ask their staffs to research the issue and advise them how to vote. Similarly, committees rely on staffs to provide subject matter expertise, legal counsel, and analyses of the economic, social, environmental, and other impacts of proposed legislation.

Staffs want to do a good job, but like legislators for whom they work, they suffer from the same excessive workloads, inadequate time during the session, and shortage of resources. This is where you come in. Offer, offer, offer them any help you can. They know you are a lobbyist advocating your own interests, but if they know you abide by the duty of trust mentioned in Chapter 1, they will listen. Because they are dedicated and highly motivated, they are interested in receiving trustworthy political and technical information about your bill. Educate them about your bill to help them make good recommendations to their legislators.

While both junior and senior staffers serve the legislature, senior staffers are more important to you because they serve in leadership positions. Their many years of experience within the legislature have given them technical knowledge, insights to fine points of chamber procedures, and institutional memory. They are the most influential staff members in the legislature. While you will work with different kinds of legislative staff, you will lobby three: personal, committee, and caucus.

Personal Staff. A lawmaker may have none or one or more personal staff. These aides help the lawmaker with his or her legislative duties. The lawmaker's district office staff focuses on communicating with constituents and meeting their needs. Capitol office staff conducts research, develops policy, provides technical analyses, and meets with capital players. A lawmaker may delegate to his or her personal staff authority to speak on the lawmaker's behalf.

Committee Staff. A committee may have its own staff comprised of clerical and technical persons. Clerical staffs record meetings, call the roll, keep minutes, receive written testimony and other submittals, distribute meeting packets, and provide general support functions. Technical staffs have expertise in the subject matter and legal considerations of topics within the committee's jurisdiction. Few lawmakers understand the technical fine points of bills they consider. Therefore, many rely heavily on staff's technical guidance.

Caucus Staff. 84 out of 99 state legislative chambers have party caucuses. For all practical purposes, bills are won or lost in the majority party caucus. Caucus staffs are more important than many rank-and-file legislators because caucus staffs draft bills, do legislative research, make policy and voting recommendations to caucus members, develop strategies to move legislation, and shepherd bills through the legislative process. They do the thinking necessary to inform and support caucus decisions. In limited circumstances, they may fulfill some legislators' duties such as requesting amendments.

Treat all staff with the greatest respect. There is no unimportant staff, including staffs you won't lobby, that is, chamber and LSA staffs.[121] Ask any lobbyist what he or she will do differently in the future having alienated the chamber doorkeeper who seems too occupied at the moment to bring a message to a lawmaker on the floor; or having spoken dismissively to the lawmaker's secretary now finding the lawmaker's schedule too crowded to fit in another appointment. You may not need a staffer's support but you cannot afford his or her opposition!

While per Chapter 1, lawmakers are quaternary in *political* importance, they are primary in *constitutional* importance. This is because they alone make enactments, the precursor to laws. Your first step is to secure a lawmaker to sponsor your bill.

LOBBYING TO FIND THE LEAD SPONSOR

You must secure the lead sponsor to file a bill drafting request (BDR), thereby initiating step one of the formal process of bill enactment described in Chapter 6, section *How a Bill Becomes a Law – a Generic Model*. And the relationship you build with him or her is the most important relationship you will have with a legislator.

Begin securing a lead sponsor by speaking with the CFR chair. If the chair opposes you such that he or she wouldn't consider your bill should it be referred, then getting a sponsor would be a waste of time for all concerned. In a sense you speak to the chair to get his or her *permission* to seek sponsors. With that permission, you can begin your search.

The lead sponsor must be selected carefully because you will work closely together. Sometimes called *patron, author,* or *main sponsor,* he or she is most responsible for your bill and managing its progress in the chamber. Other legislators will look to him or her for explanation, advocacy, and amendment of your bill.

Start talking to candidate sponsors before they make commitments to sponsor other bills. This is especially important in state chambers restricting the number of bills a lawmaker may sponsor during a session. Begin your search as early as you can; either once the chair has been appointed during the organizational session or a few months before following session(s), regular or special.

Although all members of the chamber may be candidates for your main sponsor, not all can be equally effective. An ideal main sponsor has these characteristics:

- Membership in the majority party in the chamber
- Membership on CFR or party leadership
- Respect of the chamber as a leader dealing with the subject matter of your bill
- Ability to learn your bill's subject matter
- Enthusiasm for you and your issue

In Chapter 3 you identified the electoral districts represented by members of committees likely to hear your bill, most importantly the committee of subject matter jurisdiction, which is the *committee of first referral*. If your bill is going to die, the CFR is most likely the place. A favorable report from the CFR skyrockets your bill's chances of enactment, as discussed in Chapter 9.

Having earlier identified your candidates, you connected with them on their social media sites and feeds. Now it's time to learn more detailed information which can be obtained from a number of sources including member data provided by the Clerk of the House or Secretary of the Senate, lobbyists, other legislators, and persons knowledgeable about state politics. Chapter 3, section *Conducting Legislative Research*, provided a number of information sources. A contract lobbyist can be invaluable winnowing potential sponsors and giving you insights and advice only capitol insiders would know.

Having developed profiles on your prospective sponsors, rank them in order of preference and probability they would sponsor your bill. Probabilities rest upon each lawmaker's cost-benefit ratio. High benefit-low cost for the lawmaker gets sponsors; low benefit-high cost does not. Then, personally interview them starting at the top of your rankings. As will be emphasized, lawmakers don't sponsor bills to be nice; they sponsor to achieve their own specific ends.

If you have strong relationships with lawmakers who are supportive but not on relevant committees, ask them to help you find a main sponsor. Not only can friendly lawmakers suggest candidate sponsors, but also they may be willing to speak favorably on your behalf to fellow lawmakers.

Bring evidence of support for your bill from within the prospective sponsor's district to show the lawmaker how his or her constituents and he or she will benefit from your bill. Bring important persons from the district, such as the mayor of a large city, to help reinforce the need for your bill. Finally, provide strong political arguments for your bill and have in your back pocket good technical support, just in case technical questions arise.

Invite a legislator to sponsor your bill if he or she has been ranked near the top of your list and appears supportive of you and your issue. If a candidate you interviewed is interested but unable to sponsor your bill, or if the lawmaker seems clearly disinterested, then express gratitude for the time spent with you. Ask the legislator to speak well of your bill to others and add you will provide updates when changes occur that could affect the lawmaker or his or her district.

As much as possible, avoid being turned down in your request for sponsorship; silence is better than a "no." A "no" following your invitation for sponsorship increases the likelihood the next member whom you ask will also refuse. Most lawmakers will ask you to disclose the names of chamber members whom you asked to sponsor your bill, and it is likely they will follow their leads. If your instincts hint you just might get a negative response, then it's best not to ask at all.

You don't want a "by request" sponsor. A lawmaker may agree to sponsor your bill *by request* (BR) which means he or she has little interest in working for the bill and is introducing it just to make a constituent happy. By request is "a phrase (or its initials 'br') used when a legislator introduces a bill or resolution as a courtesy to an executive agency or private organization or person who requests sponsorship of the proposed measure, but does not necessarily endorse the measure."[122]

If you develop unanimous CFR support for your bill, you might ask the chair to have the committee adopt your bill as a *committee bill*. If he or she agrees, the committee bill designation will move it quickly to second reading, and perhaps to the consent calendar.

Without a strong main sponsor, you must repackage your issue, accept a weaker main sponsor, or consider abandoning your project. If your bill is small, a sponsor not on the CFR or even one in the minority party may be able to carry it if he or she has close supporters on the committee. If you have a strong relationship with leadership and the bill will not be difficult to carry, you could ask the leader to assign a junior lawmaker to sponsor it and the chamber to pass it. With leadership's support for an easy bill, a junior legislator might welcome the opportunity for an easy win.

Without a main sponsor, a bill cannot move forward. But bills with bad sponsors usually are defeated, often without regard to the content of the bill. Avoid sponsors who are weak, unpopular or considered extreme by the majority of the chamber.

Avoid petulant, peevish, petty lawmakers – your lobbyist and capitol players can name them. A *Lobby School* participant told her class that for several years the sponsor for her association's bill couldn't move it. She was simply a bad sponsor. Her association then enlisted a different sponsor. The original sponsor, now scorned for another, killed the association's bill. If she couldn't sponsor the bill, then nobody could.

You and the main sponsor must work closely together to advance your bill. Consequently, communicate regularly with him or her to solve problems, review strategy, and otherwise keep your bill moving.

However, you must be prepared for your sponsor withdrawing from *active* participation with your bill because politics and party demand he or she refocus momentarily on more pressing matters. Even getting your sponsor to attend a committee discussion of your bill may become a challenge. Nevertheless, as long as your sponsor's name remains on the bill, you can continue to advance it. For the rest of this chapter I discuss lobbying presuming little active involvement from your sponsor.

LOBBYING FOR CO-SPONSORS

Each bill has one or more main sponsors but other legislators who wish to publicly support it but not take a leading role may become co-sponsors. Co-sponsors place their names on your bill. Generally, the more co-sponsors you have from each party, the greater the chance of bill enactment. Although any lawmaker can co-sponsor your bill, ideally, your co-sponsors will be drawn first from the committee(s) with jurisdiction over it.

Co-sponsors who add their names before the bill is introduced are called *original co-sponsors*. If they are added after the bill is introduced, they are simply called co-sponsors. Once original co-sponsors are secured, the main sponsor is ready to introduce your bill.

LOBBYING OTHER LEGISLATORS

Now that you have sponsors and co-sponsors, next lobby other lawmakers starting with remaining members of the CFR and likely subsequent committees of referral. Speak to majority members, followed by minority members.

Plan when and where you will visit, and decide who best to represent your association to each lawmaker, both lobbyist and constituents. You may have a different team for each lawmaker. Plan carefully to maximize effectiveness and minimize expenditures of time, money, and political capital.

Re-review the dossiers you earlier developed focusing on lawmakers' political philosophies, voting records, and your estimated lawmakers' cost-benefit ratios of supporting you. Appreciate the characteristics of their staffs, constituents and the districts they represent, and their most important concerns. Then, use these data to package and promote the relevant components of your issue to gain support for your bill.

Why Will Lawmakers Listen to Me?

Lawmakers want to hear from you for at least seven reasons. First, they were elected to serve and advance the wellbeing of their electoral districts and their residents. If your bill affects the welfare of people living and working in their districts, they want to hear from you.

Second, elected representatives want to know the views of their supporters, their voters, and constituents, that is, the people who put them in power and can remove them from power. Whenever possible, send constituents to visit their legislators to tell them why your bill benefits constituents and why they support it.

Third, lawmakers are elected on partisan political platforms and will promote laws and public policy consistent with them. A lawmaker's political philosophy predisposes him or her to join with either the supporters or opponents of your bill.

Fourth, a lawmaker will likely listen to you if an issue is at least neutral with regard to a legislator's philosophy and the caucus has not taken a position on your bill. That is, he or she has a *free vote* meaning the lawmaker may vote his or her own best interests. Do not lose hope if your bill is weakly at odds with a lawmaker's philosophy. He or she may be willing to put aside small reservations if it would help most of the people in the district or if it brings him or her some political advantage.

Fifth, lawmakers do their own cost-benefit self-interest analyses before acting. They consider whether supporting you will help or harm chances of reelection, potential campaign contributions, support from their caucuses, and opportunities to advance their political careers. To gain and then keep their support you must ensure that the benefits of supporting you well outweigh the costs.

Sixth, lawmakers need political and to a much lesser degree technical information to make good decisions about the issues they face. Because they cannot follow the politics of every bill, they need information about other lawmakers and organizations supporting and opposing you. They and their staffs appreciate facts, figures, and political information *upon which they can rely.*

Seventh, a record of success helps a lawmaker stay in power. If your bill would help a lawmaker demonstrate legislative skill and effectiveness to constituents and to the chamber, he or she will be interested in what you are selling.

WHOM TO VISIT?

Keep in mind 80 to 90 percent of lawmakers are largely irrelevant to your bill. This is because they are not on committees that will consider your bill. Their only vote is on the floor often as instructed by party leadership. Your focus will be on relevant lawmakers, that is, the 10 to 20 percent who matter, meaning those on committees of jurisdiction and perhaps leadership.

Relevant lawmakers fall into three broad and shifting groups: those who support you, those in opposition, and those who are undecided. Of these three, the largest group initially will be the undecided. To these you will direct the greatest amount of your lobbying time and energy. To move undecided lawmakers into becoming supporters you must build convincing political momentum.

Building political momentum rests upon this principle: a "yes" you get from a potential supporter makes more likely the next candidate you ask will give you a "yes." And a "no" makes more likely the next candidate will say "no." Especially, at the beginning of this momentum building process, you want lots of *yesses* and no *noes.*

Rank relevant lawmakers by likelihood of support. Begin approaching likely supporters. Supporters may be active or passive; active supporters champion your issue publicly through words and actions; whereas the passive vote for your bill but are more concerned about other issues. Spend more time courting the potentially active than passive supporters.

At the same time there is decorum and propriety to follow. Start lobbying the CFR's staff and chair's personal staff, if any exist. Lawmakers generally do as their staffs recommend and seldom go contrary to them.

Then lobby the committee chair. Expect staff already told the chair about you and your issues. Next lobby expected *supportive* CFR majority party members followed by *undecided* majority party members. Finally, from the minority party on the CFR lobby expected supporters followed by the undecided. Repeat this procedure for all remaining committees of referral, if any.

After lobbying committees of referral, lobby legislators who, although not appointed to committees of referral, may support you. They are more than a vote in caucus. They could help you greatly by lobbying fellow legislators and interest groups on your behalf.

If the opportunity to speak to chamber leaders arises, use it to advance your bill. However, since their focus is on administration and policy rather than the details of individual bills, their interest in your bill will likely be small unless it is very important to their particular constituents or the chamber.

Do not visit lawmakers whom you expect will *strongly* oppose you. Realize there are votes you will never get. Instead, send each one a letter clearly describing why your bill is good for the state and for their district and constituents. It's not likely they oppose you because they have some animosity toward you. It's more likely the special interests with whom you negotiated in Chapter 5 told their lawmakers they don't like your bill and have asked them to oppose you. Opposing lawmakers did their own cost-benefit analyses and opposing you provided more benefit than supporting you. It's just politics.

Finally, political momentum swings, ebbs, and flows. One moment you have a lawmaker's vote and the next you don't. It shifts by political winds. No one has any certainty as to the legislature until the bill is enrolled and certified. This can be a volatile process.

WHEN TO VISIT?

To build a critical mass of legislative support, start visiting lawmakers and their staffs as soon as you have ranked potential main sponsors. This should be well before the beginning of the annual session. In your initial planning you identified key lawmakers from among whom you expect to find your sponsor, did background research on each, and are now prepared to meet them. It will take time for you to explain your issue to legislators and staffs and then elicit their support. Your goal is to meet with them before your opposition has a chance to influence them. You also want to gain their support before other issues consume their attention.

Start early. Your most productive meetings will be in the calm of the off-session and back home in their districts. In unhurried moments, you have opportunity to develop relationships and gently introduce your issues. You will build on these visits during the pre-session and regular session. A major-league Mid-Atlantic lobbyist notes,

> For any major advocacy effort, i.e. "pushing a bill," I found that the vital and critical role of educating and winning support for the bill took place before the legislative session started. In fact, it starts the day after sine die. The schedule is so compact during the legislative session in most states that, it leaves little time for educating legislators during the actual legislative session. When the bell rings on opening day, you need to be ready for your hearings and maintaining a near daily vote count and pushing for an early hearing and a quick vote. From my personal experience and observations, that's the winning strategy.[123]

However, just because you seem to have support pre-session doesn't mean you will have it when the committee votes. You have to cultivate lawmakers with the consistency and attentiveness of growing a garden because politics and opponents can take away your supporters at any moment. A saying from Florida is, "September isn't April." The 60-calendar day Florida session, as of this writing, starts approximately

March 1 and ends April 30. Just because you had a lawmaker's support the previous September doesn't mean you'll have it for the April vote. Be attentive and take nothing for granted. September isn't April.

During session, legislative calendars show when legislators are available for lobbying in their home districts or in the capital. The calendars also show when lawmakers are in committee, in full session, or in their offices. However, if you haven't built good relationships well before the session, then influencing distracted lawmakers during the hectic session while they are being pulled in all directions will be difficult. You and your issue may get lost among their distractions of making laws, politicking, and dealing with lobbyists, home-folk, and the caucus.

WHERE TO VISIT?

Visit lawmakers in places where you can get their attention: in their home districts, capital, social gatherings, conventions, and capitol hallways. The most common and appropriate places to meet with lawmakers are in their legislative offices at the state capital, capitol, or in their legislative districts.

Lawmakers welcome contacts from their supporters, voters, and to a lesser extent people who just happen to live in the district. However, when they are in their districts to meet with their home-folk, some may view appointments with non-constituents as unwelcome distractions. Consequently, if you have no constituent presence, inquire about a lawmaker's preference in meeting with non-constituents while in the district before you schedule a visit.

Some issues are important enough for lawmakers to travel outside of their electoral districts to visit with non-constituents. Important issues may be defined as those with widespread economic, social, or environmental impact upon the state or specific groups within the state. If your issue has statewide significance, invite lawmakers to your convention, place of business, or other location related to your issue. Inform lawmakers representing your district you have invited the guest lawmaker.

Not every place is the right place to lobby. Allow a sense of propriety and decorum to make your contacts tasteful. A Missouri lobbyist writes,

> Basically, I was lobbying against a bill regarding mandatory sentencing for certain crimes and the bill sponsor was drawing little attention to her bill—just pushing it through committee without any fanfare. Our group began bringing attention to the bill to the other committee members and that caused them to rally against the bill. The sponsor got really annoyed with us as she just thought she could slip her bill through without much discussion. She was bad mouthing us around the building and so we wanted to talk to her and explain why we were fighting against her bill. She refused to see us, but, later, I saw her going into the bathroom. I followed her in and tried talking to her at the sink and she let loose, yelling at me about privacy and respect. Really, she was correct and I had overstepped my boundaries. At the time, I was mortified and apologetic and I learned a huge lesson about being effective in my meetings, not just having meetings.

MAKING APPOINTMENTS

Schedule appointments with lawmakers before session, early in the session, or when there is a lull in the session. Schedule as many different ten-minute visits as possible for each day spaced at thirty to sixty-minute intervals. Provide each legislator's secretary with your lobbyists' and accompanying constituents' names, affiliation, and reason for the visit. A few days before the appointment, confirm the meeting time, and briefly reiterate what you plan to discuss.

Although scheduled appointments are preferred, during the session it is acceptable to simply "drop in" on legislators and staff during office hours and ask for a brief moment to talk. Lawmakers and staff are in their offices to do the people's business and meeting with the citizenry is one important component. Whether in or out of session, lawmakers and staff will try to make at least a few minutes available to you, as they have time.

However, do not presume a lawmaker will be on time, much less keep the appointment. Duties of lawmaking supersede meetings with lobbyists. Extended committee meetings, emergency caucuses, or sudden crises lead to delays or canceled appointments. Lobbyists learn to be good at waiting patiently and gracious about lawmakers being unable to stay on schedule; he or she will make it up to you. Any hint of complaint to staff or the lawmaker or hint that you don't understand that these things happen will demonstrate the advocate is a rude amateur, undermining future opportunities with the lawmaker and staff.

CHOOSING YOUR REPRESENTATIVES

Visit lawmakers and staffs as teams. Bring two to four of the legislator's constituents for the lobbying visit; ideally members of your association. Although any resident of the electoral district can establish the lawmaker-constituent link, the most effective representatives are lawmakers' supporters and voters. If you can't get either of these, then any constituent who has a *positive* relationship with him or her would be useful. Select representatives who share as many characteristics as possible in common with the lawmaker, as mentioned in Chapter 1. Appoint an articulate and credentialed member to serve as the spokesperson. In my own practice, when lacking a constituent spokesperson, I have taken that role after ensuring I was backed up by constituents whom I had coached to play their roles.

Your representatives should dress appropriately, but that does not necessarily mean formally. If your attire would send a positive message, such as distinctive work clothes or uniforms, then one of more of you should wear them.

If you hire a contract lobbyist, include him or her in the visit if he or she has a good relationship with the lawmaker. If no relationship exists, bring a constituent rather than the lobbyist. Exclude anyone, association member or contract lobbyist, from your meeting having a poor relationship with the lawmaker's office.

177

If a committee chair, chamber leader, or *swing vote* member's support will be critical for your bill, bring the most prestigious person you can draft from the district. That is, after you make sure there is a positive or neutral relationship with the lawmaker. Consider leaders of important companies, public interest groups, unions, or local government. The presence of a liked, or at least neutral, community leader communicates the importance of your issue, the district's need for the lawmaker's support, and suggests a likely political benefit to the lawmaker.

If you cannot locate an available constituent for the particular visit, inform the lawmaker that, although not present, his or her constituents are part of your group and many have been supporters (donors). Following careful research to ensure the lawmaker has no negative relationships with any of them, mention their names and affiliations. If no constituents are part of your association, try to find some or as a last resort, visit without them.

YOUR FORMAL PRESENTATION

Plan each word. Your case will be won or lost within three minutes of meeting.[124] Your presentation should be concise and ten minutes or less. The final seven minutes either builds upon the success of the first three minutes or tries to redeem a poor first impression. The six most important elements of the presentation are:

1. Your likeability as a person and, by extension, your bill
2. Names of the main sponsor, co-sponsors, and legislators who support it
3. Names of constituents, important persons, and associations who support it
4. Why it is good for the district and state and by extension the lawmaker
5. Why your opponents are wrong
6. Factual bases

First, in lobbying, that is, legislative sales, *likeability is job one*. If they like you they will listen to you and if they listen, then they just may be convinced. When they like you they will want to give you what you are asking for.

On the other hand, if they don't like you, then, at best they won't hear a word you say and at worst refuse to speak to you at all. Your degree of likeability directly affects the attractiveness of your bill. On the other hand, if the lawmaker doesn't like your organization, then, despite you being a delightful person, you may not be welcome.

Second, mention lawmakers who support you. A lawmaker's support is less based on technical facts than upon consensus among like-minded fellow lawmakers. If you are just beginning the process and don't yet have lawmaker support, then rely on constituents. But in time you have to build a momentum of lawmaker support.

Every chamber usually has a member respected for expertise in an area of knowledge. Make a special effort to gain his or her support. Legislators look to fellow legislators for guidance. Commonly, a lawmaker may conclude, "If Legislator X supports the bill, then I can be sure it is a good bill."

Third, bring home-folk with you, ideally those known and liked by the lawmaker and staff. Provide a handout listing supporters, starting with lawmakers who share his or her philosophy or party affiliation. Then, list the names of organizations, interest groups, influential constituents, and other individuals who support your bill. This political information will be central to helping the lawmaker decide his or her position on your bill. See Appendix 2, *Suggested Lobbying Visit Leave-Behind*.

Fourth, a bill benefitting the district helps the lawmaker stay in voters' good graces. *Lawmaking is campaigning*. Every decision a lawmaker makes, every bill he or she supports, the lawmaker considers how that decision will affect his or her next election. A bill that benefits a lawmaker's chances of winning the next election will be well received.

Even better is a bill benefitting the whole state because, by helping district and state, the lawmaker gains broader political benefit and support, such as campaign donations across a broader spectrum. Anticipate the lawmaker's interests and position on your bill. Determine how you will reinforce favorable views, rebut opposing positions, and answer the questions he or she might ask.

Fifth, disclose contacts you have had with bill opponents. Chapter 5 introduced a fundamental rule of lobbying which is, *you have to talk to people you don't like and who don't like you.* By this time, you have met with every party having a legitimate interest in your bill. So you know what your opponents think about your bill and why they are wrong to oppose it.

Disclosures, pro and con, affirm to lawmakers and staffs that you are competent, honest, and trustworthy. They provide important political information. However, do not speak negatively about opponents, even if your comments are true. Speak only that which is absolutely necessary and germane to the moment. Gratuitous negative comments undermine you as well as the one being attacked.

If your opponents lobbied the lawmaker before you, be ready for the lawmaker's or staff's pushback. The following from a contract lobbyist demonstrates pushback and talking points:

> One of the biggest challenges I had to overcome as a new lobbyist was realizing legislators are not experts on everything. This was difficult for me, especially after listening to them debate issues in committee, where they always seemed to have the "perfect talking points" to address every question or opposing argument that was put before them.
>
> I would say at first it prevented me from scheduling appointments with legislators I needed to talk to simply because I never felt I knew enough to talk intelligently about an issue, especially if it was the bill sponsor, and if the group I was working for opposed the legislation.

However, that all changed in one meeting. In 2012, I was working as a lobbyist during the legislative session for the Florida League of Cities. Partnered with another member of their legislative team, we were working on an issue that had the potential of costing local governments millions of dollars in increased construction costs and eliminate jobs for some of their city staff.

The proponents of the legislation, a statewide association, had convinced lawmakers to sponsor a bill they thought would benefit their members by removing local regulations requiring a portion of government contracts to be awarded to local companies (within their municipal boundaries).

They had prepared a talk sheet for their members who wanted to advocate on behalf of the bill. We were fortunate enough to get a copy. After reviewing their key points, we prepared our opposing argument, and then scheduled a meeting with the bill's sponsor.

During the conversation, the lawmaker countered our position by quoting the talking points he had been given by the bill's proponents. These were the same arguments we had reviewed. Suddenly, I realized he wasn't the expert I originally thought. He was simply sharing the information they had given him.

That was the day I understood lawmakers were not and could not be experts on every issue.

Now that I knew this, I knew what I had to do. It started by being prepared. That included: going deeper than just researching the issue, but also the individuals or organizations supporting the legislation (and why), if they had made campaign contributions to the sponsoring legislator, and the political affiliation of the lawmaker. And it also included understanding the legislative process and the key "players." That meant knowing if the sponsor was in a leadership position in their respective chamber which could affect the likelihood of the bill's passage, and actually understanding how much they really cared about the issue.

But I also had to be prepared with a solid, legitimate argument that would present an opportunity to amend legislation that would affect the impact for my client.

Today I own a government relations and advocacy consulting firm. For my clients that experience this same challenge, I offer the following advice. Ensure you are ready to share the actual (never exaggerated) fiscal impact of a bill and a compelling, personal story that illustrates that impact. They can do that better than anyone, especially if they are a constituent in the legislator's district.

Lastly, I encourage them to have language ready to present the lawmaker that offers a compromise, minimizing that impact. If the legislator or their staff have to come up with an alternative on their own . . . they are much less likely to do so!

Finally, if time remains, mention briefly the factual basis of your bill. If the politics are good, then technical facts mean little as long as you have sufficient technical backup to protect the lawmaker from opponents' fact-based attacks. Technical facts are for agencies, not for legislators. Further, most lawmakers and staff are lay persons who likely know little about your issue, much less its technical details.

While you shouldn't start off with technical facts, every so often you might get a lawmaker or staffer who is interested. You must be prepared to answer their technical questions. Have in reserve a simple presentation, especially if the issue is highly technical or complex. As non-experts, technical subtleties and explanations can be very difficult for legislators and their staffs to understand. Use visual aids, exhibits, storytelling, and analogies to engage the listeners. Make the presentation interesting and relevant to the lawmaker's philosophy, cost-benefit analysis, and district.

If they want to hear more, they will ask you to stay longer to discuss your bill. You can stay longer because your schedule was set to have your next appointment thirty to sixty minutes from this one. Make sure, however, you call your next appointment and adjust the meeting time if you are going to be late.

You only requested ten minutes during which to make your case. Do not irritate your listeners by taking too much time. Practice until you are comfortable and can convey the merits of your bill with confidence within the planned meeting time.

GETTING INTO THE RIGHT FRAME OF MIND FOR YOUR LOBBYING VISIT

Getting into the right frame of mind to have a successful lobbying visit begins with realizing you are a petitioner requesting help from people having full, unfettered freedom to listen to you or throw you out of their offices. You are not in the driver's seat; lawmakers and their staffs are. A Florida House staffer interviewed for this book commented, "They bring in their CEOs and high-priced lobbyists but they forget for 60 days each year I'm the one in control." 60 calendar days is the length of his state's legislative session.

Further, before walking into their office you must have already answered the threshold question of lobbying, that is, *why would this lawmaker give me his or her vote?* Until you can answer that most basic question you won't likely be getting their support. And immediately dismiss any thought they will help you "just to be nice." They will be nice. But lobbying is a business resting upon the legal and ethical exchange of mutual benefits, that is, politics.

Recall from Chapter 1, "Nobody cares what you want until you make them care and you do that first by catering to their self-interests. Once their self-interests are taken care of then you can move on to yours." Unless you offer them something they want, they have no reason to give you their attention, much less a vote. A partial menu of what lawmakers want includes:

- Advancing the wellbeing of their constituents, district, and state overall
- Succeeding in office
- Staying true to their personal politics
- Following caucus directions
- Promoting self-interests

Of course, each item listed has a series of sub-activities within the menu choices.

Expending their time, energy, and political capital to give you what you want diminishes resources they could dedicate to other possibly more productive matters. To get their vote or support, you must offer them a positive cost-benefit ratio. That is, what they get from you is more valuable to them than the value of what they expend. Follow the advice in Chapter 4, section *Legislative Ethics*, as you formulate the elements you will use in your cost-benefit calculations.

Just as there are steps to do in your lobbying visit, there are things you don't do, among them, never:

- Expect lawmakers and especially staffs are there *for your convenience.*
- Forget likeability is job-one in selling and lobbying.
- Appear uncompromising.
- Lie or mislead.
- Be terse or rude.
- Suggest political consequences
- Promise to give or withhold financial or other forms of support.

The last two "don'ts" can have legal and political consequences. Never offer the lawmaker your opinions as to what his or her support or opposition to your bill will mean *politically.* Any suggestion that his or her support will harm or help at election time is wholly out of order. If taken as a threat, your suggestion may violate ethics laws. Lawmakers calculate the political consequences of their actions. They seldom want or need advocates doing their political calculus for them.

Do not hint that campaign contributions, monetary or political, are linked to the lawmaker doing what you want. Let everything you do to influence the legislature relate solely to sound public policy, constituent interest, and facts supporting your position.

THE LOBBYING VISIT

Upon meeting the lawmaker or staff, and after the initial introductions have been made, you should express gratitude for their willingness to meet with you. If you have constituents with you, coach them to say thanks and say something about the district. For example, "Senator, isn't it great our high school won the district football championship?" Then, begin the prepared formal presentation.

Be sensitive to when the legislator or staff wants to speak. At regular intervals, pause for their input and comments. Team members should listen closely to what the legislator or staff says, observe how the message is received, take notes about the visit, and provide supporting comments, as appropriate.

In sales calls, the vibe, feel, and mood are critical. Be sensitive to the moment. You are selling yourself first and then your likeability sells your product. Your product has to be a good product, that is, it provides a positive cost-benefit for the lawmaker, but it is you making the sale.

If the mood of the visit is good, ask the legislator for sponsorship or, if you already have a sponsor, then ask if you can count on his or her vote. If strong support is expressed, ask him or her to recommend your bill to undecided party members who serve on the committee(s) of referral and in caucus. A lawmaker who speaks on your behalf to a fellow legislator on a committee of referral might gain support for your bill that for you would be otherwise unattainable.

If the legislator does not commit or just seems disinterested, state you understand more facts or time may be needed to enable a decision about your bill. Communicate your interest in assisting the legislator and his or her staff with information. As the visit concludes, give the legislator or staffer your Appendix 2 Leave-Behind.

Depending upon capitol culture, gift-giving is not recommended. However, some states allow inexpensive tokens such as pens, coffee mugs, T-shirts, or other low-cost items representing your issue and given to all legislators and staffs. These tokens may help them recall your bill. However, before you leave these physical reminders make sure you comply with the legislature's gift rules on what you may offer or what the legislator may accept. It's the lobbyist's job to protect lawmakers from your ethical errors.

Be sure to thank the legislator or staff person for the visit and follow up with a written thank you letter to the lawmaker. Send a photocopy of the letter to the individual staff members and be sure to include a handwritten note of personal thanks to each of them.

Try to build future contacts into the visit because you are competing with hundreds of others for the lawmaker's attention. Offer to send additional information and, after sending it, call to ensure that it has been received. During the call, ask if the legislator or staff have additional questions about your issue. The more satisfying contacts they have with you and constituent lobbyists, the more you reinforce the appeal of your bill.

FOLLOW-UP VISITS

Short follow-up visits should be made to supportive and still undecided legislators in order to keep your face and issue before them. The legislative session is hectic and attention spans are short. In light of all the legislature has to do, your bill is just background noise unless you make it rise above the commotion.

Part of rising above the noise is keeping your face before the legislature. If they don't see you regularly, they will presume you don't care and your opponents will be emboldened. A former *Lobby School* participant, now an Illinois association government affairs director, writes,

Never miss a session day if you can avoid it. Sick day? Funeral? Negotiations all day? My old boss told me always take one lap around the capitol and carry a binder, people will think you're working and people will remember seeing you at the capitol that day. When I needed to miss a session day for a board meeting, the opposition used the opportunity to try to sabotage/highjack my bill and I caught them in the process. People are less likely to do these things if they think you're in the building. After that I learned to never reveal my own schedule-business trips out of town, plans to attend the organization's conference, plans for public speaking were all confidential so that absences from the capitol building would not be well known. Once I took a sick day and a top government staffer called my hotel room and told me to get to work. I said, I don't have a bill in committee or up for a vote right now. She said, "Lobbyists don't get sick days."

Your every contact ideally should add value to the lawmaker and staff. Dropping by with an updated Appendix 2, *Suggested Lobbying Visit Leave-Behind* should always be welcomed. These visits, along with grass roots involvement, help preserve supportive lawmakers' commitments to you and help the undecided resist your opponents.

Although passage of your bill by the committee(s) of referral is critical to your bill's success, do not forget the entire chamber votes on your bill one or more times. Most lawmakers in chamber are going to vote as instructed by the caucus. Ideally, you met with caucus staff before bill introduction and upon your bill being reported by the CFR.

The CFR and other committee report(s) make more predictable the consequences of the law thereby allowing the LSA to initially draft or redraft its fiscal and other notes. At this point, it becomes timely for the caucuses to take their respective positions.

When the full chamber is about to consider your bill, lobby those legislators whom you believe might be willing to speak from the floor on your behalf, even those not on committees that considered your bill.

These may be members of committee(s) of referral or members whose districts will be positively affected by your bill becoming law.

DOS AND DON'TS

The following dos and don'ts will help you stay on the right track.

Do at the start tell your lobbyist(s) and representatives they have no authority to commit your organization to anything. Lawmakers may ask you to amend the bill. Answer that while you cannot commit your association, their request will be timely acted upon by your principals. When you bring back the association's *prompt reply*, you inspire confidence in yourself and your organization.

Don't be an annoyance. Follow up visits adding value, such as updates affecting lawmakers and districts, are important. But simply dropping by to chat with nothing to add distracts lawmakers and staff from doing their jobs.

Do keep your face in front of the legislature every day it is in session, as mentioned above.

Don't think that you can be an advocate over the Internet. Yes, social media can be a useful tool as mentioned in Chapter 3, but it doesn't substitute for the human connection, especially with supporters and voters.

Do attend fundraisers, conferences, and social events where you can meet advocates, share gossip, and gather intelligence.

Don't fret if a lawmaker does not support you. A lawmaker's lack of support may result from forces wholly unrelated to your bill. Remember you only need the votes from the majority of lawmakers. You neither need nor should you expect them all.

Do be grateful to speak to a lawmaker's staffer, when the legislator doesn't meet with you. The fact he or she sends a staff person to meet with you should be taken as a sign of interest. Treat the staffer with the same respect and deference you would show the legislator.

Don't presume you have a vote until the roll has been called. Occasionally, despite a commitment to you, a lawmaker may withdraw support. Remember neither you nor your opponents truly have a lawmaker's vote until it is cast. This is why you must remain in contact with supportive and undecided lawmakers. Lobbying is a volatile process.

Do keep to your lobbying plan, that's why you created it.

Don't write off a lawmaker until he or she is a clear "no." You may find a lawmaker who seems inclined to support you but just won't commit. This does not mean he or she opposes you; rather, some lawmakers keep their options open and are silent for political reasons until the vote is called. A few do not come to a decision until the moment they vote. Keep working on them.

Do remain gracious throughout the lobbying process. You want to leave legislators with a good impression of you and your association.

Do not forget, you may be back next year.

A Maryland lobbyist offers her practical experience for some Dos and Don'ts. She writes,

> My first year out I inherited a difficult and controversial bill that had already failed in my state for at least a decade, but was very important to my nonprofit.
>
> My strategy was to meet with all the traditional opponents (members of our state's powerful health and education lobbies) and hash out as much as we could before session. This worked very well, and by the time the hearings came there was almost no public (and less private) opposition from those groups. The bill also had plenty of legislative support, but the bill still failed because 2 key and very senior members of the committee just

could not be budged, no matter what - even though their constituents testified on the bill.

The recent election has reconfigured that committee this session, and one of the new leaders there reached out to me to resurrect this bill this session.

This time around (my second session) I am also spending more time working with established allies from professional organizations, not well-meaning citizen wildcards. Last session, it did not help matters that I had reached out to a wide variety of unaffiliated individuals to support the bill, but they ended up testifying AGAINST the bill and our organization because they felt it represented too much compromise. In fairness, the position they wanted was the one we had wanted 10 years ago but simply could not fit in to our state's current powerful leadership and legal scheme. Individual activists' passion and enthusiasm is helpful in that it shows the importance of the issue to recalcitrant legislators but ultimately has not been persuasive enough to move the needle. If it were, this bill would have passed years ago.

On a final note, I am ushering another bill through this session that is nowhere near as controversial and I am using one of my *Lobby School* rules all the time:

Don't go near the legislative office without one of their constituents with you. Don't even ask for an appointment without the name of a constituent. Better yet, have them ask for the meeting.

It takes a lot more time and work that way, but the payoff is HUGE. Just about every meeting has yielded an offer to cosponsor and invitation to keep talking about the issues that we are experts in. I am also very careful to make sure that my partners are as diverse as the clients we serve - intersectionality is key.

Summary Chapter 7

Your lobbying visits secure sponsors and co-sponsors, and committee, caucus, and floor votes. To get their votes you answer the most fundamental question of lobbying, *"Why would that lawmaker give me his or her vote?"* Until you can answer that question, you're not likely to get the vote.

Most affected legislators and staffs are interested in learning about your issue and will listen carefully to your presentations. A concise and politically powerful presentation helps you secure a main sponsor, add co-sponsors, and persuade other legislators to support you. Once you have gained sufficient support, you must maintain it throughout the voting process. By working with staff, you can capitalize on major opportunities to gain support for your bill.

Gaining a favorable recommendation from the committee of first referral and other committees of referral, if any, are the next critical steps in securing the success of your bill. In Chapter 8 we discuss working with legislative committees, most importantly getting a favorable report from the CFR. Chapter 9 shows you what to do after the favorable CFR report and how to maintain momentum after the session concludes *sine die.*

In our next chapter we consider committees. They have been called, "the factory floor of the legislative process" because they accomplish most of the legislature's work. And it is at the committee level where you will do most of your work.

Chapter 8: Working with Legislative Committees (Steps 7-9)

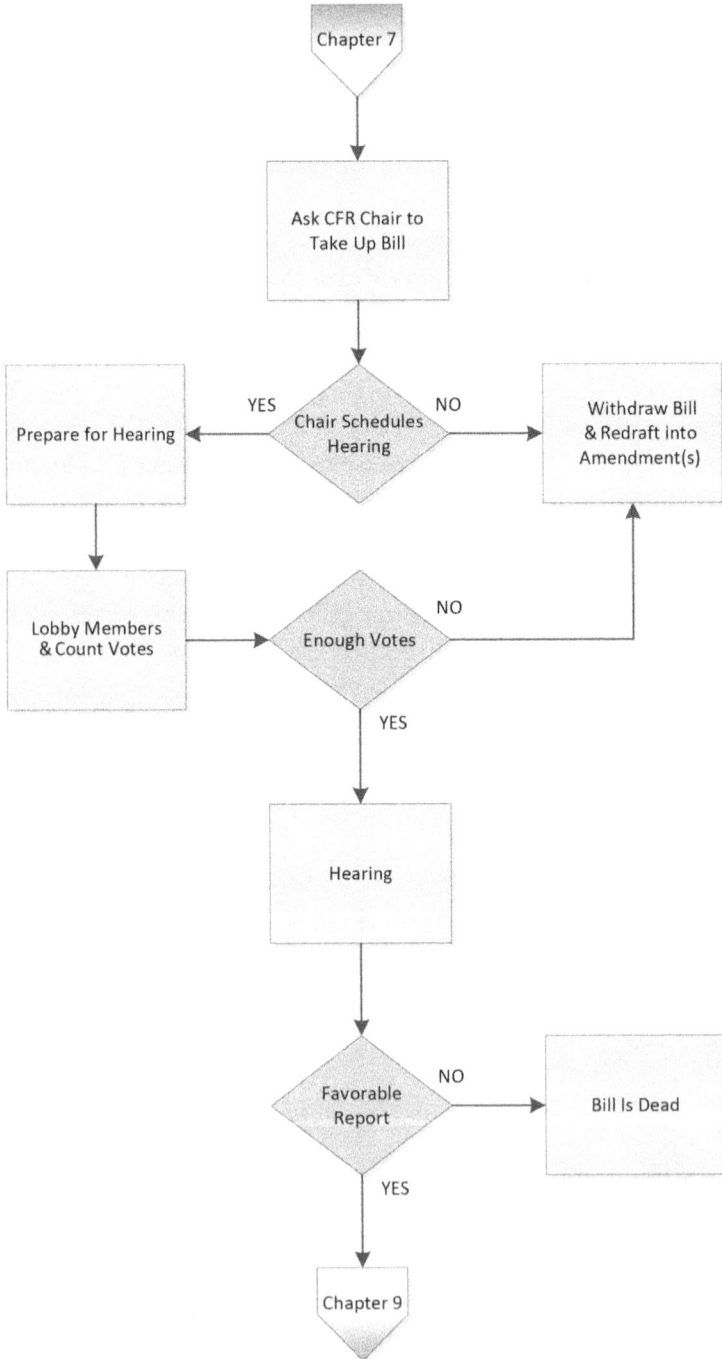

```
        ┌──────────┐
        │ Chapter 7│
        └────┬─────┘
             │
             ▼
    ┌──────────────────┐
    │  Ask CFR Chair to│
    │   Take Up Bill   │
    └────────┬─────────┘
             │
             ▼
```

| Prepare for Hearing | ◄── YES ── Chair Schedules Hearing ── NO ──► | Withdraw Bill & Redraft into Amendment(s) |

| Lobby Members & Count Votes | ──► Enough Votes ── NO ──► (Withdraw Bill & Redraft into Amendment(s)) |

Enough Votes — YES ──►

Hearing

Favorable Report ── NO ──► Bill Is Dead

Favorable Report — YES ──► Chapter 9

CHAPTER 8

WORKING WITH LEGISLATIVE COMMITTEES (STEPS 7 – 9)

Hundreds to thousands of bills are proposed each year depending upon legislative chamber. Numbers range from mid-hundreds in small-population states like Alaska, South Dakota, and Wyoming to over ten thousand in others. For example, in one session there were 11,721 in Texas, 13,712 in Illinois and 18,123 bills in New York.[125] While the average session is 120 days,[126] session durations are as short as 20 days in Wyoming's short-session to no intra-session time limits in Illinois and New York. To manage workload, legislatures form committees and divide among them bills for processing. Each committee has its exclusive areas of subject matter jurisdiction.

A chamber may have more than one dozen committees and each committee, in turn, may have one or more subcommittees. The scopes of committees in the respective chambers overlap, although names and full areas of jurisdiction may differ. For example, the Senate Natural Resources Committee and the House Environment and Public Works Committee both have jurisdiction in environmental law, although they do not intersect in other areas.

COMMITTEE STRUCTURE

The membership of committees is roughly proportional to party membership in each chamber. Lawmakers choose committees on which they would like to serve and request their caucuses nominate them thereto. Nominations are forwarded to the Senate President, House Speaker, or chamber's Committee on Committees. The appointing authority *for its best interests* assigns members to committees. A lawmaker may or may not receive his or her desired committee assignment.

Lawmakers' requests flow from their policy, financial, and political interests. Policy, because the lawmaker has a special interest or expertise in an area of legislation, as, for example, a medical professional may seek appointment to the chamber's health care committee. Financial, because lawmakers know some committees attract more campaign donations than do others. More and wealthier groups want to influence, and consequently donate to, a member of the transportation committee responsible for hundreds of millions of dollars in infrastructure appropriations than want to influence the ethics committee. Politically, because by moving bills, especially bills they sponsor through their committees, lawmakers build their reputations and advance their political careers.

Generally, committee chairs are majority party lawmakers, although occasionally philosophically kindred spirits from the opposing party may be appointed. The committee chair generally decides the direction of each bill assigned to the committee. This may include whether it will be brought up in committee; if brought up, whether to consider it in a committee meeting or to hold a formal public hearing with invited testimony; and, whether to assign it to a subcommittee.

COMMITTEE STAFFS

Chapter 7, section *Lobbying Legislative Staffs*, briefly mentioned committee staffs. In this section we go into more detail because committee staffs heavily influence their chairs and committee members.

Depending on state, committee staffs are either nonpartisan or partisan. Smaller states' staffs are few, nonpartisan, providing professional, clerical, administrative, and legal support, primarily through the non-partisan legislative services agencies. Larger states' committee staffs are several, partisan, professional, providing clerical, administrative, legal, and technical support. Partisan committee staffs generally advance the interests of the majority party. In the interests of a well-functioning committee, they also assist the committee minority.

Most committee votes advance caucus political decisions. In smaller states without committee staff, party caucus specialists provide committee members with partisan technical support, talking points, and advice. For example, "Republican and Democratic caucuses in both chambers utilize research staffs. The caucus staffs consist of directors, legislative research analysts, and secretaries and provide legislators with policy research, issue and bill analysis, and constituent services."[127] The Democratic and Republican members of a committee each rely on technical directions from their party caucus staff assigned to advise them on subject matter of their particular committee.

Staffs evaluate the technical elements of bills; partisan staffers also consider politics. Both translate technical input from agencies and special interests into forms useful to their committee members. They are useful conduits of your information to committee members and from the committee to you. They also protect legislators from being technically and politically tricked.

You woo both partisan and nonpartisan staff with good technical information and entice partisan staff with good political intelligence. Appendix 2, *Suggested Lobbying Visit Leave-Behind* is primarily intended to enable staff to justify and explain the political decision their member made to support your bill.

HOW BILLS ARE REFERRED TO COMMITTEES AND COMMITTEES' SCOPES OF REVIEW

"In two-thirds of the legislative assemblies, the presiding officer (that is, the president of the Senate or speaker of the House) makes the final bill referrals. Eighteen chambers have another leader set the assignment.

Nine legislative assemblies use a committee and, in Virginia, the chamber clerk makes this determination. In Maine, the full Senate or House sets the final referrals."[128]

The committee of first referral (CFR) is a bill's first critical test because it must pass through the CFR to proceed to subsequent committees, if any, and to votes by the full chamber. The CFR recommendation that the floor pass, amend, or defeat your bill determines, in large part, its probability of enactment. This is because chambers usually implement committee recommendations. A favorable report skyrockets your bill's chances of enactment. So, your first challenge is to gain favorable CFR committee action on your bill.

Subsequent committees of referral limit their considerations to aspects of the bill within their authority. They do not review recommendations of other committees of referral. However, any committee with jurisdiction over your bill, within the committee's scope of authority, may harmfully amend it, report it unfavorably, or refuse to consider it at all. In states with low enactment rates expect up to 90 percent of bills die in committees by inaction rather than by negative reports.

WILL THE CHAIR TAKE UP MY BILL?

The Lobbying Team must understand the practice of the legislature and its committees regarding consideration of bills. You must know whether all bills are referred automatically to committees and, if not, how you will ensure your bill will be referred. Usually all but a few bills are at least referred. However, just because your bill is referred doesn't mean the committee will do anything with it. In smaller states, committees automatically consider all referred bills; while in larger states, this is the decision of the chair.

The chair may not call up your bill for several possible reasons: it might consume excessive amounts of committee time; may be unlikely to pass; may be unimportant relative to other bills; the implementing executive agency might oppose it; or there may be political reasons, such as denying the opposing party legislative success, or the sponsor is weak or "blackballed." By doing well the 70 percent of the work that takes place before bill introduction, you may mitigate some countervailing forces.

When calling up a bill is at the chair's discretion, you should lobby committee staff and perhaps the chair's personal staff to take it up even before your bill is referred to the expected committee of first referral. Staffs working for the chairs largely set committee agendas including which bills will be considered.

However, before asking a committee chair to take up your bill, you and your sponsor must discuss the advisability of requesting a *formal public hearing*, also called a committee hearing. If a public hearing is at the chair's discretion, you may ask for one at the same time you ask the chair to take up your bill. Although the committee must in public meeting consider your bill for it to become law, you do not necessarily need, much less want, formal public testimony. A formal public hearing is a great way to put momentum behind your bill. On the other hand, a formal public hearing may bring to your bill unwanted attention, avoidable controversy, and scrutiny of details.

PUBLIC HEARING

The chair may choose to consider a bill with: formal testimony but no citizen comment; formal testimony followed by citizen comment; or no formal testimony but allow citizen comment. The chair also decides when to hear the bill, length of time for testimony, and whether to have the full committee or a subcommittee consider it.

The chair may opt for a *formal public hearing* if your bill is important enough as, for example, upon becoming law it would impact state government, the general public, state policy, or is controversial enough such that the committee could benefit from perspectives on all sides of the issue. On the other hand, if your bill appears to have wide committee support, the chair may conclude a formal public hearing would divert committee resources from more pressing issues.

In *formal testimony*, the chair invites the sponsor, implementing state agency, and a few persons pro and con closely identified with and knowledgeable of the bill or its subject matter to give their views. Formal testimony usually occurs in the CFR. Since each chamber has its own CFR, each chamber could hold a public hearing on your bill or they could meet jointly, as is done in some smaller states. However, in practice, if one chamber holds a formal hearing the other normally does not duplicate efforts by holding its own hearing, unless each party controls one chamber in a highly partisan legislature.[129] Further, a subsequent committee of referral may take citizen comment on that portion of the bill over which it has jurisdiction; and, if testimony is given to a subcommittee, it will not likely be repeated to the full committee.

The chair may invite the public to provide citizen comment which may be the only opportunity supporters and opponents have to present to the committee their positions on your bill. In one state public comment is a citizen right, by rule or by custom. In another state, committees have no obligation to take public comment and a committee suspends formal session to receive citizens' remarks. Of course, the public may lobby individual lawmakers outside the committee hearing. Normally, public comments are limited to a very short time, such as two minutes per speaker.

Because you may appear before a legislative committee or subcommittee, you should communicate with your bill's sponsor, committee and subcommittee chairs, and staffs. You had told them before the bill was referred that you would like to testify if a hearing is held. Once the hearing has been scheduled, immediately remind the chair, committee secretary, or chief committee staffer you would like to testify.

Notice of Committee Hearing

Most public hearings take place during pre-session or early in the session, especially in part-time legislatures. They are announced well in advance on the legislature's webpage, on social media, and hard copy postings.

A committee chair or staffer keeps a planning calendar showing when certain bills might be heard. Contact committee staff regularly to request your bill be heard and inquire when it might be. Once any committee schedules your bill, zealously *protect its time slot*. Your opponents will try to convince the scheduler that other bills are more pressing and that your bill should be put into the committee's inactive file. Most bills that are lost die in committee, largely because they are never called up.

As a matter of courtesy in some states, and as a matter of course in others, the committee notifies a bill's main sponsor in advance of a hearing. Thus, you should ask your sponsor to notify you about a hearing as soon as the scheduler gives notice. However, at times neither the sponsor nor you will know about the hearing until a few days before it is scheduled. For this reason, continuously stay in contact with the scheduler and update your testimony and be ready to give it at any time and on short notice.

PREPARING FOR THE
COMMITTEE MEETING AND HEARING

Prior to the committee meeting, go to the committee's video archives to get a feel for committee meetings and hearings. The legislative librarian can direct you to previous videos and exhibits for you to use as templates.

You should have met with all committee members and staffs expected to support you or who could be convinced to support you. You already know the "no" votes from your Chapter 7 lobbying visits and, other than a note to opposing lawmakers stating you hope the committee hearing will be useful to them, you need say little more.

If several days have elapsed since your last hopeful contacts, meet briefly with committee members or their staffs to update them about the progress of your bill. Remember, obstacles just normal to the process and your opponents are working to defeat your bill. Starting a few days before the committee meeting, ask constituents of each committee member to send letters, email, make social media posts, or call urging a favorable vote on your bill.

For formal testimony, update and revise the written and oral committee testimony developed by the Drafting Team prior to bill introduction. In addition to being factual, informative, and well researched, your testimony should convey the message that your goal is to help legislators reach a good decision on a good idea, that is, your proposed bill. Your presentation must be succinct and focused. Use a bit of human interest to say why you, or your witness if it's not you testifying, care and why lawmakers should care.

In written formal testimony, include legislative developments that have occurred since bill introduction, information about similar bills and proposed executive agency rules, names of co-sponsors, the other chamber's response to your bill, amendments, current estimates of fiscal and other impacts, and names of new supporters. Inform the committee of any positions taken by executive agencies, such as the Governor's office or administrative departments, on your bill and briefly mention those who oppose you. Mention similar actions in other states and emphasize actions by bellwether or precedent setting legislatures. Condense the formal testimony into much shorter oral testimony and prepare a succinct written summary of your oral comments.

As much as they will let you, coordinate your testimony with committee staff. Especially avoid duplicating their work. If you disagree with something you expect staff to report to the committee, try to resolve it with them beforehand and in private. Lawmakers are much more likely to believe staff than they are to believe you. Your ideal testimony adds to staff's report neither duplicating nor contradicting it. Of course, if you must contradict them, then do so, but let staff know beforehand of your differing view. *Surprises make bad politics.*

Before the hearing, ask committee staff how many copies of written testimony and summary of oral testimony to provide. Expect to give one copy to each committee member and the committee secretary and distribute additional copies to staff. Find out when your materials should be delivered and before the committee meeting provide the committee secretary with the correct number of copies of written testimony and summary of the oral presentation. Ask if exhibits may be brought to the public hearing and ask if a helper may accompany you to aid your presentation.

Discover the conventions for testifying before the committee. For example, how are committee members to be addressed? In some states, the address is quite formal with seemingly every paragraph preceded by, "Honorable Chair X and members of the Committee on Y." Other states are less formal.

Determine for informal citizen testimony if witness registration must be submitted prior to speaking. Registration is either by filling out paper forms or electronic registration. The registration form, hard copy or digital, asks the speaker's name, affiliation, pro or con position on the bill, and affirmation of truthfulness, under penalty of law. Ensure that you and your speakers comply with ethics laws if there is any chance that their testimony could trigger lobbyist registration requirements for citizen speakers.

Ask staff to estimate the total amount of committee time that will be allocated to your issue; amount to be given to formal testimony, yours and others; time to allow for questions; and if your witnesses will speak, time for citizen comments. Usually, time allocated for formal testimony is short and ranges from five minutes per speaker in the committee of first referral to a minute or so in successive committees.

Ask staff for the names of others invited to testify about your bill and learn whether committee members will ask questions. Anticipate the objections of your opponents as you update your testimony and consider talking to them again to resolve what you can. Ask for the names of other bills likely to be considered at the same meeting, estimate the time to be given to these other bills, and determine if any of them are controversial. Ask for your bill to be considered early on the agenda so you will not lose time to other bills that may require more time than expected.

In preparation for the committee meeting, committee staff prepares its report consisting of bill analyses, fact sheets, and other technical documents for committee members and the public. You ideally earlier offered to staff your suggested versions of these materials hoping they would use some or all. The LSA may additionally provide analyses of economic, environmental, social, and state budget impacts. Amendments may have been filed with the committee secretary.

The agenda for the public hearing, staff-prepared materials, copies of bills to be considered, and proposed amendments are all available prior to the meeting. The agenda will include a list of bills to be considered, sequence of consideration, and perhaps time allocated for bill deliberation. Ask staff to direct you to conventions for formatting (such as, binding, number of leaves, single- or double-sided, line spacing, font face, etc.), timing for delivery of documents, and to whom.

Use all the time you have been allocated for your oral presentation. Plan every moment of your time before the committee. Remember your bill will likely be one of several considered during a meeting. Depending on where your bill is scheduled on the agenda and how well the chair manages time, even a well-prepared presentation may find itself in a race with time. Prepare a shortened version of your testimony in case your time is unexpectedly cut short.

As soon as the agenda for the meeting is published, study it to assess the appropriateness of your planned presentation and testimony. Locate the room in which the hearing will be held and note the room number and seating capacity. Because anyone may attend a committee meeting, you can make your presence more strongly known by filling the committee room with your supporters. If the room is small, prepare to have your supporters arrive early to ensure their seating. Instruct them about decorum, coordinate what each might say, and if citizen comments are to be taken, the appropriate way to speak to the committee, registration requirements, and forms (digital or hardcopy). Ensure they do not say the same thing using the same words. Excessive repetition risks arousing committee hostility and peevishly negative votes against your bill.

Because your bill's sponsor will also testify at the hearing, coordinate your two testimonies. They must be harmonious presentations supporting each other and not present conflicting messages. Reinforce one another from different perspectives to appeal to the broad audience of legislators.

MOST COMMITTEE MEETINGS ARE JUST THEATRE

Finally, while your presentation is important for the *formal process*, politics may have made the hearing little more than just theatre. Much of the time, before the chair gaveled the meeting into order the outcome of the vote had been determined by:

Caucus. Chapter 6, section *How a Bill becomes a Law – a Generic Model*, "Step 7. Majority and minority caucuses review the bill," advises, "However, it is the majority caucus that decides whether your bill will pass, be amended, or killed. Bills are not won and lost in committees or on the floor, as indispensable as these are. Their fates are determined by the majority caucus."

Leadership. Leadership may have sealed the outcome of your bill before committee members took their seats, as for example having earlier instructed the committee chair to kill the bill. This was first mentioned in Chapter 6 and is discussed in greater detail in Chapter 9, section *Does Enough Time Remain to Reach the Governor's Desk?*, subsection 1.a., "Leadership's intentions."

Earlier vote count. However, while neither caucus nor leadership may have given instructions to members regarding your bill (*free vote*), you already have a good idea as to the committee's likely vote. Before the meeting you visited members or their staffs to confirm their expected votes. Either you know you have the votes or a couple of members are uncertain. If your vote count found you don't have a majority, your sponsor withdrew your bill from committee consideration as discussed in Chapter 6, section *How a Bill becomes Law - a Generic Model,* "Step 11. Sequential committees of referral process selected subsections of bill." Vote counting is discussed below.

Even if the vote is predetermined, many lawmakers know they are playing a theatrical role for those who matter. I recall just as the chair was to call the meeting to order, a lawmaker turned on her microphone loudly announcing, "I want to see my constituents." She wanted *her* audience.

It's when you don't know beforehand the outcome of a vote that the committee becomes exciting. This hearing isn't theatre; it's a live-action sporting event on which you have chosen to gamble the fate of your bill. Like it was yesterday, the committee secretary was calling the roll; tied, one vote uncast, the room silent. The member with whom I had worked for three years paused, linked his hands behind his head, looked up to the ceiling, and quietly said, "aye." It was the thrill of victory, adrenaline rush of winning a vote 3–2, that we lobbyists never forget.

SELECTING YOUR REPRESENTATIVES

Your representative giving formal testimony should be able to speak well, understand the issues, and calmly and succinctly answer legislators' questions, even hostile ones. Ideally, your lead speaker will have an impressive title and credentials such as president or officer of your organization or recognized expert on the topic. If your representative does not have the ideal credentials or needs technical assistance, with committee permission, ask a member of your association or consultant who is credentialed to accompany him or her.

Your representatives, including those making citizen comments, must be prepared to answer any challenges to their compliance with state lobbying laws, especially registration. Failure to conform to state lobbyist registration requirements can lead to a variety of actions ranging from public embarrassment, to being forced to sit down and, although unlikely, enforcement action by the state.

You should now authorize your representative to bind your organization if moved by an offer or forced into one that seems beneficial to your principal. This is the opposite of earlier instruction where you intentionally denied to your lobbyists authority to commit. Now at this moment, *if your representative can't commit*, he or she becomes irrelevant to the amendment process which will go forward without your input.

COUNT THE VOTES BEFOREHAND

Shortly before the hearing, you should talk to all lawmakers and staffs to estimate the number of votes to be cast for and against your bill. There may be one or two votes that are not known, but you must have a good idea as to whether or not the committee will vote to support your bill. If any committee reports your bill unfavorably or does not report it at all, the likelihood of enactment is greatly reduced.

An unfavorable report kills your bill because chambers generally do as recommended by their committees. To avoid a negative report you count the votes before each committee action on your bill. If you don't have the votes, your sponsor withdraws the bill *if allowed by the rules.*[130,] [131] If rules don't allow the bill to be withdrawn or you have chosen in desperation to take the chance hoping in a "Hail Mary pass"[132] kind of way to get a favorable outcome, you risk your bill being unfavorably reported.

For a full-time legislature, your sponsor might request the committee chair postpone consideration of your bill. Although delay is bad, defeat is far, far worse. However, for a part-time legislature any postponement, even a motion to *temporarily pass*, usually kills a bill.

DECORUM STARTS BEFORE YOU BEGIN

Yes, the capitol building is the people's house, but lawmakers are its current occupants. You are a guest in their house and should behave as one honored to be there. Be respectful and show it, as for example dressing appropriately. "Jeans and/or t-shirts are not permitted . . . All persons with access to the Senate chamber pursuant to section 1 shall, on all legislative days, wear appropriate business attire, e.g., no denim, tank tops, halter tops, or shorts shall be worn. Males must wear a coat and tie at all times when the Senate is in session . . ."[133] Dress like most everyone else in the capitol and you will show your respect.

For committee room behavior, a Montana lobbyist further advises,[134]

> Before you enter the committee room, TURN OFF YOUR CELL PHONE or pager. If your phone rings while the committee is in session, it is hugely embarrassing for you (everybody stares at you and smirks) AND you become obligated to buy delivered donuts for the whole committee. Get into the committee room early and stake out a seat. You can reserve a seat by putting your briefcase or coat on it. Minimize conversation inside the hearing room. After the committee session starts (committee "comes to order"), there should be NO conversation at all inside the hearing room above the softest whisper. This is a respect thing for legislators and others attending the hearing. If you MUST talk with somebody, leave the hearing room quietly and have your conversation outside in the hallway. Even then, keep the volume down. Loud conversation in the hallway tends to interfere with business in the committee room. (emphasis in original)

Keep in mind from Chapter 1, if lawmakers like you as a person, they may listen to you; and if they listen to you, they may do what you want. But if they don't like you as a person, they won't heed a word you say and they may vote against you out of spite. Be respectful at all times.

COMMITTEE MEETING AND PUBLIC HEARING

When upon review of the meeting agenda, you conclude that your bill is so far down that the committee will be pressed for time, ask your sponsor to request the chair move your bill to earlier in the meeting. If your sponsor has an honest conflict with another legislative duty such that earlier is the better time for him or her to testify, the chair may accommodate the request. The chair may also move it up for reasons of professional courtesy, especially if your sponsor can demonstrate that your bill can be disposed of quickly. If staff agrees with you, despite expected push back from other parties as to the change, you might get a better time slot.

As the committee meeting is about to begin, you may find the lack of a quorum threatens the meeting and, therefore, committee consideration of your bill. Rather than lose your opportunity, ask the chair to designate those members in attendance as a special temporary subcommittee. This subcommittee would have its required quorum and could proceed as a subcommittee meeting, take testimony, make recommendations for amendments, and issue a report to the full committee. If the chair agrees, the subcommittee meeting and your public hearing will proceed.

Of course, lawmakers on their own could choose to stay in the room and listen, but they also have much to do and likely would leave for more pressing matters. Having the special subcommittee structure makes more likely they will stay for the rest of the hearing.

Bill consideration normally begins with staff discussion of the materials prepared by the LSA and committee staffs. The materials include an explanation of the bill and expected fiscal and other impacts.

Next, the sponsor of the bill testifies using your talking points. However, many sponsors do not know the content of their own bills. I have with fear watched my sponsor testify knowing his familiarity with our bill was insufficient to answer even the most basic question. He was carrying our bill to satisfy an important supporter and that was all he needed to know. However, committee members' professional courtesy allowed him to read our script fearing no questions. They knew that on another day, in another committee meeting, they too will be in the same spot, and also appreciate being spared the public embarrassment of not knowing the first thing about their own bills.

Formal testimony from invited persons follows the sponsor's presentation. One or more panels of advocates and opponents, often including representatives of affected government agencies, speak to the bill. Each makes his or her short presentation until all invited speakers have spoken.

As you begin, inform the committee your written testimony has been given to the secretary and you will refer to it during your presentation. They likely have it before them. If you bring an expert to assist you, announce the name and credentials of that person and state he or she is there to answer members' technical questions. Stay within the allotted time for your oral testimony and you will be allowed to complete it without interruption.

However, don't be surprised during your presentation that committee members appear distracted, few are paying attention, some have left the room, and only a couple seem to have read the bill before them, much less have looked at your supporting materials. If you and your lobbyists have done your jobs well, they don't need to. They already know how they're going to vote.

Expect several members have zero interest in either you or your bill. Those who speak are most likely reading questions and answers provided to them earlier by lobbyists – either you or your opponents - or are being fed information by the lobbyist in the back of the room or who is watching the meeting on the Internet.

Further, don't take their rudeness to heart. Be respectful even in light of ludicrous statements, grandstanding, or rhetorical questions. Seldom is it personal as much as it is theatrical. They are playing to their voters and supporters in the room, watching online, and who will read about it tomorrow.

When you finish your testimony, thank the chair and the committee for allowing you to speak. The chair may allow committee members to question you about the bill and your statements or will ask them to hold their questions until later.

At the conclusion of formal presentations, the chair may invite informal citizen comments on your bill. Before speaking, make sure your supporters have met the speaker registration requirements, if any. Some states won't recognize a person wishing to speak to a bill unless, prior to the meeting, he or she had registered with the committee.

Except for adherence to time limits, and perhaps a requirement for speaker registration, the comment period is open to all relevant remarks. Several formats may be used. The most common is one in which citizens simply go to the microphone, state their names, indicate whom they represent, and disclose their views about a bill (in two minutes or less). An alternate format is for the chair to call persons to address the committee in the order in which they submitted their requests. The chair may also separate proponents from opponents and ask the proponents to speak first. If comments become redundant, the chair may ask subsequent speakers to limit their comments to providing new information.

After formal testimony and during informal citizen comment, the chair may allow committee members to ask questions. Normal decorum requires you to direct your answer to the committee chair when responding to a member's question.

If you do not know the answer to a question, just say so, promise to find the answer, and get back to the committee member and other members promptly. This presents another lobbying opportunity. However, in most legislatures, there isn't enough committee time remaining to get back to them; the process is moving too fast. But by getting back to them, you may influence their caucus and floor votes.

Never respond with hostility to unfriendly questions from committee members because they are seldom personal attacks. You should always maintain composure and diplomacy. If you show disrespect to a member, you show it to the entire committee and legislature itself. In that case, members will vote against you in solidarity with each other.

Finally, your lobbyist is almost never the one to commit your organization, as wonderful and indispensable as he or she is. It's your bill and your organization's and members' fates, it's your money on the line. As I've said repeatedly, contract lobbyists are often conflicted by other clients' bills, relationships with friendly lawmakers, and their own business interests. This is just the normal state of being a consultant. Your lobbyist is an adviser, guide, counselor but he or she is never a substitute for you. It's your bill, so you make the final decisions.

After closing the public hearing, but before calling for the vote, the chair invites committee discussion during which time amendments may be proposed and voted on individually. Finally, the chair asks the committee what it wants to do with the bill. Your CFR sponsor or ally calls for adoption of the bill, as amended. If your bill is sent to subsequent committees of referral or if your sponsor is not on the CFR, you must find for each committee a supportive member to champion your bill. You can be sure competent opponents have lined up their committee supporters to kill your bill by not reporting it or by unacceptable amendments. And while unlikely, you may yet see a "do not pass" report.

DEALING WITH PROPOSED COMMITTEE AMENDMENTS

Expect amendments to your bill to be proposed during committee consideration. Opponents will try to amend your bill unfavorably, hoping to defeat it by making it repugnant. Some committee members may propose amendments to make the bill more acceptable or better. Others, including those previously uninterested in your bill, may try to amend their stalled issues onto your bill to keep them moving forward. It is in such a moment your Chapter 2 political strength will be most tested.

Occasionally a committee member may ask you for your support before proposing an amendment to your bill. Your agreement or opposition may greatly affect the likelihood of committee adoption of both the amendment and your bill. If the amendment sponsor states that you agree with the proposed changes, your supporters on the committee will likely vote for the amendment. On the other hand, when you oppose the amendment, your supporters are more likely to oppose it. However, amendments will be proposed whether you agree to them or not. They are being proposed to help someone else, not you.

During the committee meeting a legislator may pressure you to agree to changes. He or she may state the bill has a significant problem that must be resolved by the involved parties before the committee vote is taken. You may find yourself negotiating amendments with special interests in the hallway during a short committee recess.

Your ability to negotiate successfully in the hallway greatly depends on your political strength, including the committee's attitude currently being displayed toward you. Your opponents have picked up on that, too. Whichever of you is the weaker knows this is the last chance to get a somewhat more favorable bill.

During my testimony, amidst much opposition, the chair called a recess saying, "Industry, the department, and environmentalists are going to go into the hallway and in ten minutes bring a solution back to the committee." Like settling on the courthouse steps, that's what we did rather than leave our individual well-beings in the unpredictable hands of politicians. When faced with the similar:

You should *agree* to a proposed amendment if it:

1. Is reasonable.
2. Does not harm your goals.
3. Increases probability of bill passage.
4. Is sponsored by a powerful committee member.
5. Receives your sponsor's support.
6. Will not be defeated by a majority of votes in committee.

You should *disagree* with a proposed amendment if it:

1. Is unreasonable.
2. Would harm your goals.
3. Would decrease likelihood of bill passage.

4. Is sponsored by a group not supported by a majority of the committee.
5. Is championed by a weak amendment sponsor.
6. Is opposed by your sponsor.
7. Will be defeated by a majority of votes in committee.

COMMITTEE ACTION

Each amendment is voted on individually by voice vote. After all amendments have been processed, the chair ends discussion and calls for a vote on the bill, as amended or not. This is normally by *roll call* taken by the committee secretary. A committee may take one of several actions:

1. Report a bill favorably.
2. Report an amended bill favorably.
3. Report a bill amended so extensively by the committee that it becomes a substitute for the original bill. In some jurisdictions the substitute bill may be called a committee substitute (CS) for the original bill, for example CS/HB 123. Other jurisdictions do not indicate when substitutions occur. In that case, the bill may have to be re-referred as a new bill to committees of jurisdiction.
4. Take no action, for example, it dies for lack of a second.
5. Vote not to report a bill.
6. Take some intermediate action, such as temporarily passing or tabling the bill, effectively defeating it.
7. Report the bill without recommendation.
8. Report an amended bill without recommendation.
9. Report the bill, but recommend it be referred to a different committee.
10. Report the bill unfavorably.

The first action is good for your bill because committee approval will help move it toward passage. The second action is good for the amended bill and hopefully will not adversely affect your needs or lead to losing the bill in second reading. The third action may indicate another bill has replaced your bill and your bill is defeated. When actions one, two, or three occur by unanimous committee vote, the bill may be sent to the consent calendar for final vote by the chamber. The other actions probably indicate your bill is defeated.

You cannot afford a negative committee report. It will kill your bill because chambers respect committee recommendations. When the committee reports your bill *do not pass*, it's not going to pass. And it's not likely to become an amendment. For this reason, your sponsor upon your count finding you don't have the votes for passage, if allowed under chamber rules, will withdraw the bill from committee consideration. By avoiding a negative committee report, the essence of the bill can become an amendment to a bill that's moving. Again, better to withdraw a bill from committee consideration than risk being doomed by a negative committee report.

After the committee meeting, thank each committee member for giving consideration to your bill, whether he or she voted for or against it. If the vote was favorable, you now need to prepare for consideration by subsequent committees of referral, if any, or for the Committee of the Whole, if any, and second reading.

Or you may have taken the risk and lost by getting a negative report. Parliamentary procedures can revive an unfavorably reported bill. However, given the limited amount of time and chambers' deference to committee recommendations, in practice most rescue actions fail. Your sponsor or lobbyist will advise you of the chances for a successful rescue of your bill. You may need to hire an expert on legislative procedure to find and navigate that glimmer of hope.

Subsequent committees of referral, if any, will consider it in a much more limited sense falling within the committee's jurisdiction. Ideally, you wrote the bill so narrowly there are no further committees of subject matter jurisdiction. Procedural committees await. If your bill is going to cost the state money, then it will go to a fiscal committee such as Ways and Means, Budget or similar financial committee. It has to go to the floor for second and third readings as scheduled by the Calendar committee, Rules committee or similar scheduling arm of the chamber.

In any of these committees, your bill may stall and thereby be lost. It may be amended in policy and fiscal committees. While unlikely that you will give formal testimony again, you must communicate with all committees and attend all committee meetings in which your bill is considered. Leave nothing to fate or chance!

THE COMMITTEE REPORT AND SECOND READING

The reports of the CFR and sequential committees of referral may include a listing of vote(s), detailed bill analysis, memorandum explaining the committee's view of the bill and its recommendations, and general background information such as testimony. The clerk, secretary, or chamber legal counsel uses these reports to prepare a revised bill for distribution at second reading, a revised LSA note, and caucus consideration.

As discussed in Chapter 6 many states use the *Committee of the Whole* which considers the report of the committee of first referral or combinations of all committees' reports. It will usually adopt their recommendations as it debates the bill and issues its own report to the chamber. With a favorable report, the chamber will likely pass the bill at second reading, amended or not, calendar it and move it to third reading. However, passage is not certain even with a favorable report. You must attend the readings to deal with proposed amendments, votes on your bill, or excessive delay.

SUMMARY CHAPTER 8

To become law your bill must secure approvals from all committees considering it. Approval by the committee of first referral gives a huge boost to your bill as it moves through a chamber. However, if other committees consider your bill, you must ensure they favorably report it, too. Your opponents have as many chances to kill your bill as votes yet untaken. Any sequential committee can kill your bill by either unfavorable amendments or negative report. However, the most common way to kill it is by inaction. As long as you don't get a negative com-mittee report, you may yet be able to rescue your issue by amending its essence onto a bill that is likely to become law. After policy, fiscal, and calendaring committees have processed the bill, it will be read on the floor two more times. If your state has the Committee of the Whole, the bill will be considered there and then reported for second reading or, if it does not have the Committee of the Whole, then the bill goes to second reading, debate, and amendment. On third reading normally no amendments are taken or debate permitted; it's an *up-or-down* vote.

Getting your bill through the committees' gauntlet is an accomplish-ment in most states. After the committee meeting(s), you must prepare for the second and third readings and floor votes. These will be followed by the other chamber's actions on your bill and, hopefully, enrollment. Most states offer explanations of their enactment processes which you should review prior to beginning your lobbying. In our final chapter, we discuss post-CFR and post-session activities.

Chapter 9: Post-CFR and Post-Session Follow-Through (Steps 10-25)

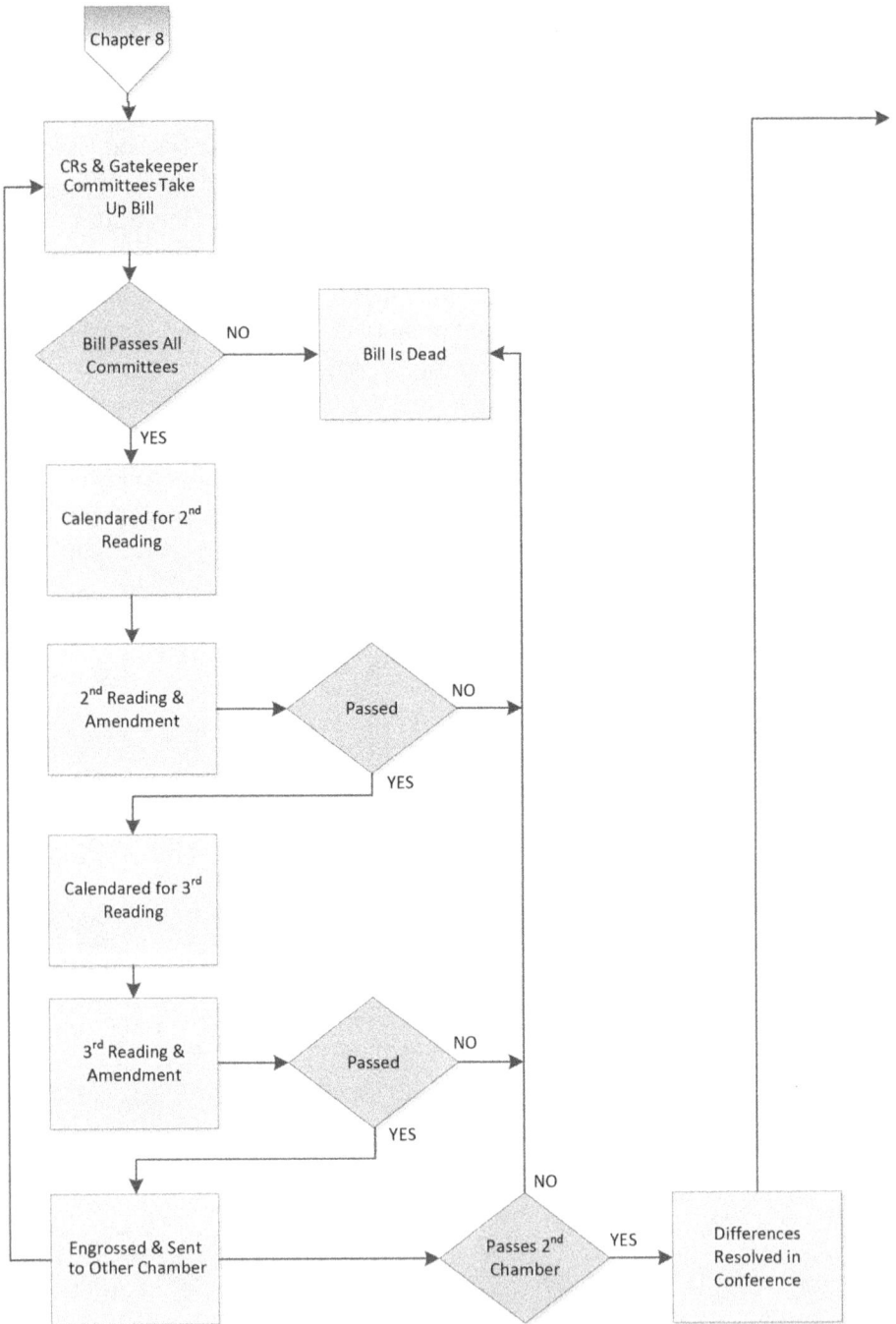

```
                    ┌─────────┐
                    │Chapter 8│
                    └────┬────┘
                         │
                         ▼
         ┌──────────────────────┐
         │   CRs & Gatekeeper   │
         │  Committees Take     │
         │      Up Bill         │
         └──────────┬───────────┘
                    │
                    ▼
             ╱─────────────╲      NO    ┌──────────────┐
            ╱ Bill Passes All╲─────────▶│  Bill Is Dead│
            ╲  Committees    ╱          └──────────────┘
             ╲─────────────╱
                    │ YES
                    ▼
         ┌──────────────────────┐
         │ Calendared for 2nd   │
         │      Reading         │
         └──────────┬───────────┘
                    │
                    ▼
         ┌──────────────┐          ╱────────╲   NO
         │ 2nd Reading &│─────────▶╱ Passed  ╲──────▶
         │  Amendment   │          ╲         ╱
         └──────────────┘           ╲───────╱
                                        │ YES
                                        │
                    ▼
         ┌──────────────────────┐
         │ Calendared for 3rd   │
         │      Reading         │
         └──────────┬───────────┘
                    │
                    ▼
         ┌──────────────┐          ╱────────╲   NO
         │ 3rd Reading &│─────────▶╱ Passed  ╲──────▶
         │  Amendment   │          ╲         ╱
         └──────────────┘           ╲───────╱
                                        │ YES
                                        │
                    ▼                        NO
         ┌──────────────────┐   ╱────────────╲      ┌──────────────┐
         │ Engrossed & Sent │──▶╱ Passes 2nd   ╲ YES │ Differences  │
         │ to Other Chamber │   ╲  Chamber     ╱────▶│ Resolved in  │
         └──────────────────┘    ╲────────────╱      │ Conference   │
                                                     └──────────────┘
```

CRs & Gatekeeper Committees Take Up Bill

Bill Passes All Committees — NO → Bill Is Dead

YES

Calendared for 2nd Reading

2nd Reading & Amendment → Passed — NO →

YES

Calendared for 3rd Reading

3rd Reading & Amendment → Passed — NO →

YES

Engrossed & Sent to Other Chamber → Passes 2nd Chamber — YES → Differences Resolved in Conference

NO

```
                                              NO
┌─────────────┐      ◇ Passes ◇      ┌─────────────┐
│ Conference  │ ───▶ ◇  Both  ◇ ───▶ │ Bill Is Dead│
│ Bill        │      ◇        ◇      │             │
│ Reported to │                      │             │
│ Chambers    │          │           └─────────────┘
└─────────────┘         YES               ▲
                                          │
┌─────────────┐                           │
│ Bill        │                          NO
│ Enrolled -  │                           │
│ Becomes     │                    ◇ Legislature ◇
│ Enactment   │                    ◇ Overrides   ◇
└─────────────┘        NO          ◇    Veto     ◇
                 ◇ Approved ◇ ───▶
┌─────────────┐                           │
│ Sent to     │ ───▶                     YES
│ Govenor     │          │
└─────────────┘         YES
```

Passes Both — NO → **Bill Is Dead**; YES → **Bill Enrolled - Becomes Enactment**

Bill Enrolled - Becomes Enactment → **Sent to Govenor**

Approved — NO → **Legislature Overrides Veto**; YES → **Enactment Becomes Act, Secretary of State Chapters**

Legislature Overrides Veto — NO → **Bill Is Dead**; YES → **Enactment Becomes Act, Secretary of State Chapters**

Enactment Becomes Act, Secretary of State Chapters → **Effective Date per Constitution or Bill, Becomes Law** → **Agency Rulemaking** → **End**

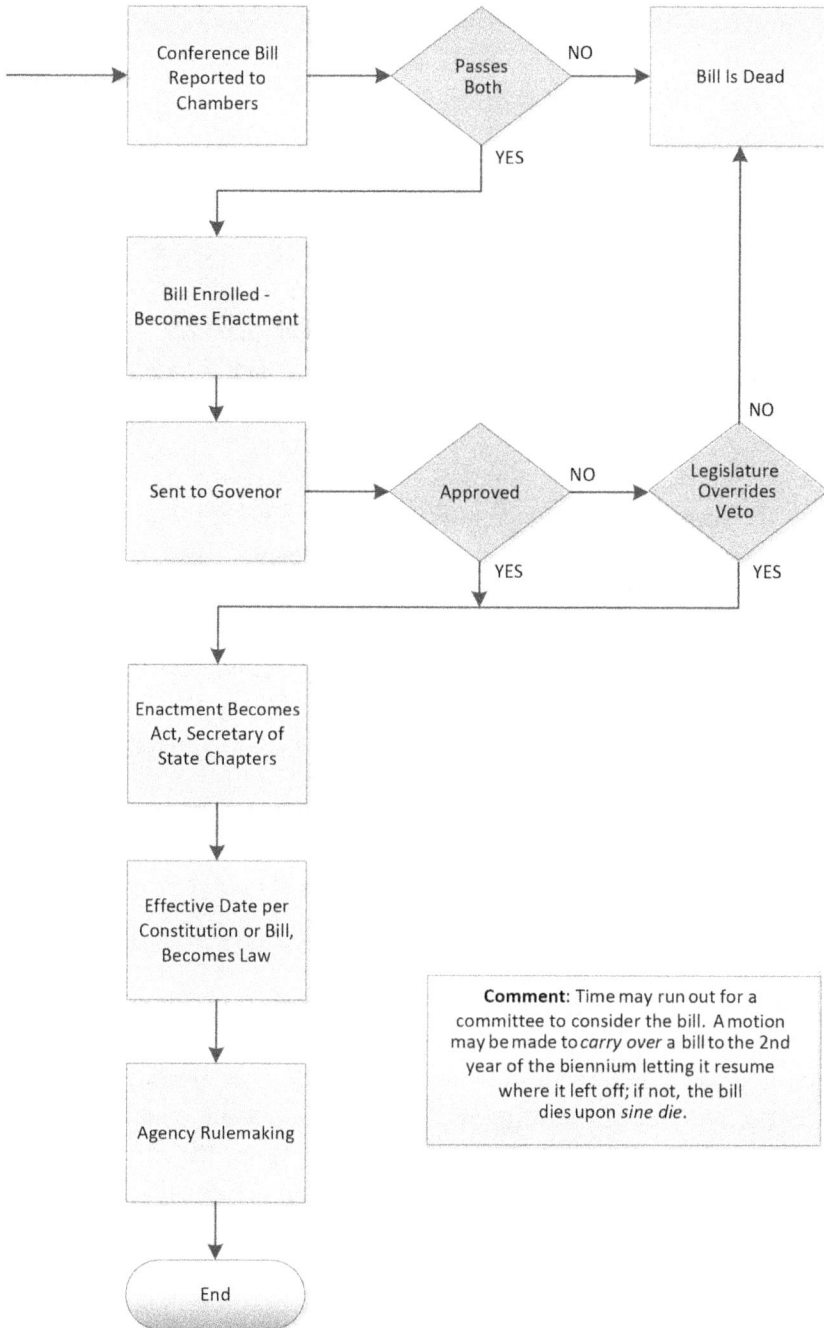

Comment: Time may run out for a committee to consider the bill. A motion may be made to *carry over* a bill to the 2nd year of the biennium letting it resume where it left off; if not, the bill dies upon *sine die*.

CHAPTER 9

POST-CFR AND POST-SESSION FOLLOW-THROUGH (STEPS 10 – 25)

When the committee of first referral favorably reported your bill, it gained considerable momentum towards enactment. However, your bill faces several more hurdles to reach the Governor's desk before the session ends *sine die*. And once the session ends *sine die*, you have post-session activities: either celebrating your win and preparing for agency implementation via rulemaking or, having not gotten your bill, capitalizing on this year's momentum in order to try again next session.

DOES ENOUGH TIME REMAIN TO REACH THE GOVERNOR'S DESK?

Four main factors determine whether sufficient time remains for your bill to move through the remaining legislative steps. The first factor is leadership's intentions as to your bill. The second is the number of sequential committees of referral, policy and gatekeeper. The third is companion legislation speeding up your bill. The fourth factor is amendments which can either speed up or slow down your progress.

LEADERSHIP'S INTENTIONS

Leadership may have no interest in your bill or it may have great interest, either to pass it or to kill it. However, at any time leadership can intervene to tilt the process to increase a bill's chances of enactment by referring it to committees few and favorable, joining it to a must-pass bill, and instructing a committee or even the chamber to pass it. On the other hand, leadership may kill a bill by doing the opposite.

Referrals. The fewer the number of referrals, the fewer delays your bill will have in reaching second reading. Further, the fewer referrals the less opportunity your opponents have to do mischief with your bill. And sending your bill to more favorable committees of jurisdiction improves its chances. The negative reciprocals of these are discussed below.

Joining it to a must-pass omnibus bill. We mentioned this in Chapter 6 but, in review, leadership may join bills with little chance of enactment to bills likely to pass. The strategy is to force several bills' sponsors, co-sponsors, supporters, and lobbyists to work together to enact the omnibus bill in which the good bills carry bad bills to enrollment.

Instructing the chamber to pass it. In a solidly leadership-driven legislature, the speaker, president, or majority leader can simply instruct the chamber to pass the bill. To illustrate, while it was set in the Senate, our bill in the House of Delegates couldn't even get a sponsor. Our in-house and contract lobbyists approached the Speaker, accompanied by one of the state's most important constituents. Wanting to keep the constituent in the state, the Speaker said, "I will assign Delegate X to sponsor the bill and instruct the chamber to pass it." That was all it took and our bill became law.

On the other hand, leadership may want to kill the bill. Occasionally, you will see a *hard kill* in the legislature but overwhelmingly leadership prefers the *soft kill*. We discussed soft and hard kills in Chapter 6, section *How a Bill Becomes Law - a Generic Model*, Step 9. "CFR considers bill, amendments, and votes to report."

Bills are almost never killed *by vote* on the chamber floor, especially to majority party lawmakers, because they:

- Openly pit the CFR against opponents on the floor. *Openly* is the operative word here.
- Discredit bill sponsors in the eyes of the special interest for which they are carrying the bill.
- Tell lawmakers, lobbying corps, lawmakers' supporters, voters, constituents, and donors that sponsors are ineffective or on leadership's bad side.
- Undermine party unity thereby threatening majority party chamber control.
- Needlessly antagonize the opposing party and perhaps the Governor.
- May reflect negatively on leadership's bill management.

Leadership's normal way to kill bills is *quiet neglect*. Keep in mind during session, chambers process from several hundred bills in a part-time legislature to 10,000 + bills in a full-time one. In larger states, there is insufficient time for committees to take up more than 25–30 percent of referred bills. For this reason, nationally 75 percent of introduced bills die and in Chapter 8 you faced the question, *will the chair take up my bill?*

Death by neglect avoids the problems mentioned above. It is especially useful for killing bills introduced *by request* for constituents or which have no chance of success. This saves the sponsor from embarrassment, lets the sponsor partially satisfy the party for whom the bill is being introduced, and keeps the chamber from wasting time and political capital on bills going nowhere.

While permutations of the above are many, all ensure a bill won't progress. Once it is clear the bill is languishing, its sponsors might seek a *motion to discharge* or remove the bill from the committee in which the bill is stalled. The bill would then without report be brought to the floor for chamber action. In some states a discharge petition may succeed with a minority[135] of lawmakers while in other states a supermajority[136] is required.

However, majority party members would hesitate to embarrass their leadership by overruling them; and, depending on how capable leadership is for retribution, going against leadership could be bad for rebelling lawmakers' careers. Do not expect a motion to discharge to succeed. And, in the unlikely event discharge succeeds, the floor still has to vote on the reported bill.

Sequential Committees of Referral

The number of sequential committees depends upon the chamber leader's intentions regarding your bill and how well it was drafted to avoid needless additional committee referrals. As noted above, leadership may refer your bill to committees few and favorable or kill it.

On the other hand, leadership may refer a bill to so many committees that it can't possibly get past them all before *sine die*. Or a bill may receive a *concurrent referral* to committees that won't have time to meet jointly. Infrequently, a bill is referred to a *kill committee*.[137] A kill committee doesn't have subject matter jurisdiction and therefore the chair has no reason to take up the bill. Most directly leadership or the caucus just tells the sponsors to wait to next year, as for example when the bill doesn't fit the legislative theme or may consume time that could be given to more important bills. Finally, a committee chair may refuse to take up a bill for reasons of vengeance or sincere concern.

A bill drafted in accord with Chapter 3, section *Drafting Your Conceptual Bill* will reduce your bill *appropriately receiving* multiple referrals. As I've noted before, the more referrals the more opportunity opponents have to kill or unfavorably amend your bill.

Companion Legislation

Companion legislation can speed up your bill's progress. The term *companion legislation* has several meanings, such as, one law cannot take effect unless something happens in another law. However, we are using the term in the Chapter 6 sense, that is, companion means identical bills introduced at the same time in each chamber of origin – two bills, two chambers, and two processes, hopefully simultaneous.

Chambers ideally coordinate with each other to ensure both bills remain identical, as amended. The first chamber of origin to pass its bill sends its engrossed version to the receiving chamber which can move it to second or third reading, pass it, and return it unamended to the chamber of origin. This saves time by allowing one chamber to fall behind in the process without slowing down the overall progress of the proposed law to enactment.

Of course, the whole purpose of companion legislation can be thwarted along the way. Either chamber can refuse to act on the other chamber's companion, insist on its own version of the bill, or otherwise disagree, leading to a conference. In some states few bills go to conference and those that do affect appropriations.[138] In states in which few bills are sent to a conference committee, this means the bill likely is dead. Further, in states allowing a *free conference*[139] a bill can be reported having little resemblance to either of the bills in dispute.

In states demanding companion legislation, the lack of a companion in the other chamber indicates a bill is in deep trouble. If, after a few weeks of session, a bill still has no companion its chances of enactment are nil and leadership may instruct chairs to discontinue work on the bill, thereby killing it.

Amendments

Amendments can stop, slow, or speed up your bill's progress. Reprising Chapter 6, opportunists will amend their bill onto yours seeing your bill as a vehicle to carry their stalled bill to enactment. I once lobbied for a solid waste bill to fix an unintended statutory impediment to recycling. With great support from the environmental agency and the legislature, the bill was on a fast track to enactment. However, its high probability of enactment attracted an amendment exempting a class of air polluters from state clean air regulations. While these opportunists had the Chapter 2 political strength to burden my bill with their amendment, the weight of the amendment was too much for my bill to carry, thereby killing it.

With increasing chances of a favorable committee report, some former opponents will become much more willing to accept amendments heretofore rejected. Other opponents will try to add *poison pill* amendments to make the bill so unattractive it can't get votes to pass. Or they will try to defeat it in other committees or on the floor, especially by inaction.

A bill going to conference, almost by definition, will be amended to resolve chamber differences. Because deal-making is foundational to resolving differences, closed conferences, that is, no public or media, may be most effective. Closed conferences, like caucus meetings, may be exempt from open meetings requirements. You'll want to check your state laws in this regard.

However, in states mandating open meetings, that is, open to the public or media, expect deal-making may be done outside the conference committee. "Instead, agreements are worked out (or not) in leaders' offices. 'Conference committees are not useful because they are public,' said a sympathetic lobbyist. 'It's better to resolve things in private in the leaders' offices.'"[140]

POST-CFR ACTIVITIES

Your favorable report from the committee of first referral is a huge step, especially in states with low enactment rates. While winning the race to the Governor's desk is hardly certain, nevertheless, the favorable report has skyrocketed probabilities of success. Improved chances of success bring challenges as, for example, leadership amending it onto an omnibus bill.

Presume other committees of referral and the floor will respect the CFR's favorable report, thereby reducing chances of it stumbling along the way. Further, at this point everyone who matters knows you and your bill, and you know them. With so much momentum on your side, opponents will be fighting a *rear-guard action*.[141]

Of course, chances of stumbling remain, however diminished. For example, a subsequent committee of referral may unfavorably amend or report your bill; or, a chair won't call up the bill; or the calendar committee refuses to send it to the floor.

It might not pass on second reading, and even less likely, on third reading (assuming sufficient time remains to finish the process). However, these kinds of negative actions undermine the committee process, perhaps leadership, and possibly and more importantly, majority caucus instructions. So while you must guard against them, your chances remain good.

As your bill continues along steps 10 – 25 of Chapter 6, you will work with subsequent committees of referral, the floor, receiving chamber, and perhaps a conference committee, Governor, and if you're successful, the Secretary of State.

THE WHOLLY UNEXPECTED

Lawmaking is a volatile process in which at times the expected falls in face of the wholly unexpected. A sudden crisis explodes such as the legislature and Governor vengefully killing each other's bills. Or a scandal breaks out such as indictments of important or several lawmakers that lead to lawmakers losing focus, as everyone awaits to see who is next to be led off in handcuffs. But most unexpected impacts, for good or ill, affect individual bills or people. For example, your bill suddenly is at the right place at the right time; or your main sponsor surprises even his own staff by quitting the legislature to become a lobbyist or an association executive director.

A lawmaker's promised vote evaporates with a startling outpouring of constituent opposition. Or you got a lawmaker's vote on a procedural matter only to lose it on a substantive matter, such as the roll call vote to approve your bill. Or you are looking at the chamber tally board with certainty, only to see your member vote opposite to what was promised to you 30 minutes earlier. You ask the lawmaker, "Why?" The answer is, "That's just where the momentum was going." Tommy Neal writes,

> Finally, there are times when there is simply no explanation at all for a legislative body's actions. That truth was best expressed years ago by Norris Cotton, a U.S. senator from New Hampshire. On one of those inexplicable days when nothing was proceeding along rational or predictable lines, Senator Cotton observed: "The members are in such a mood today that if somebody introduced the Ten Commandments, they would reduce them to eight." And so it goes in legislative bodies.[142]

Even after you've gotten the winning vote, chamber leadership can take it away by immediately forcing errant members to change their votes. Or as *sine die* approaches late at night you are sitting in the gallery when you heard your amendment pass, only to find the next morning that the engrossed bill doesn't contain it. Or the Governor conditionally vetoes your bill demanding amendments that take away everything you thought you got. You don't know what you really have until you read the law as signed by the Governor.

YOU HAVE TO BE THERE

You must be physically present at every committee meeting or chamber session considering your bill to protect it from stalling, shield it from burdensome amendments, and prevent unfavorable votes. You must relentlessly build momentum by lobbying for your bill at every opportunity. Lobby every committee through which your bill must pass by speaking to the chair or senior staff. A Wisconsin lobbyist said to me, "I once had a Legislator tell me, 'I didn't see you around so I thought you didn't care.' Needless to say, he voted the wrong way for me."

Gain a sense of how each committee will look upon its particular area of jurisdiction over your bill. While a gatekeeper committee isn't likely going to amend the work of a policy committee, it can kill the bill by inaction. If the chair or staff indicates your bill may not pass the committee or may be amended unfavorably, you will also need to lobby committee members. You can be pretty sure of negative committee action, if after all the time members have invested in your bill, they don't see you or your lobbyist in the committee room. Their conclusion will be that you don't care, so why should they care? I've flown as far as from Florida to California just to babysit my bills.

Once your bill is sent to the Governor, you may have to lobby the executive agency that would implement your bill to ask the Governor to approve your bill rather than veto it. Expect the Governor to do as the agency recommends. Or the Governor on his or her own may veto your bill. However, most Governors veto few bills. In most legislatures, the principle of *comity* still prevails, that is, the respect one branch of government has for its co-equal branch. Expect comity especially in the 36 states (of this writing) in which the legislatures and governors are of the same party. Legislatures seldom undo the work of the Governor. Only about five percent of their vetoes are overridden.[143]

You have to be there in person. While your lobbyist could accompany you, this is your lobbying campaign and only you can make the command-level decisions that affect your principal.

POST-SESSION ACTIONS

If you were successful and your bill was enacted into law, congratulations! However, if it was not enacted, then you should capitalize on the legislative momentum you built this year to carry your bill through the veto session, special session, or farther next year.

In politics as in life, expressing thanks with a grateful heart enhances and improves relationships. If your bill passed, thank those legislators who supported it. If the new law will accomplish a genuine public good, write letters to the editor or purchase advertisements in district newspapers and social media praising the bill and the legislators' contributions.

226

You may also send a press release explaining the good of the bill and a legislator's role in its enactment. Ask important persons, organizations, and companies to send letters of thanks to those lawmakers who helped. Praise key legislators in as many forums as possible, including organization newsletters and on social media, theirs, yours, and others.

If the Governor signed your bill, consider asking for a bill signing ceremony. A ceremony reenacting the signing of your bill into law could benefit both of you politically. Here, you can gather mementos, such as photographs with the Governor, copies of the signed bill, and pens bearing the Governor's name. Be aware that, due to constitutional requirements, your enactment already became an act before the ceremony could be scheduled.

Hold an awards ceremony to present your sponsor(s) with a plaque. Call the award the "Legislator of the Year" or something similar and present it at a state-wide meeting. Normally, but not always, plaques are exempt from limits on gift-giving – make sure your plaque does not exceed ethics law gift-value limits. These awards are more than nice looking on the walls. The recognition is valuable to election campaigns and in campaign literature.

Encourage your association members to remember the reelection campaigns of supportive legislators with financial and other contributions. Ask them to invite those legislators to visit their organizations or to attend social events. Invite lawmakers to visit employees or at least visit the facility to greet them going to, leaving, or at work.

Thank staff who were especially helpful and emphasize their contribution to their legislators. This includes committee, personal staff, and secretaries. Thank helpful associations for their support.

Consider giving your contract lobbyist a bonus if: you want to keep him or her working for you next year; or you want to fire your lobbyist and use a bonus to cushion the discharge. Before you take any actions with your contractor, please first read *Insiders Talk: Winning with Lobbyists, Professional edition*. Its guidance will help you ascertain:

- Were you a good client? If you didn't do your job as a client, then your lobbyist may have been unable to compensate for your failures. Were you where you needed to be when you needed to be there? It may be your fault, not the lobbyist's, the bill failed.

- Did the lobbyist do well in light of the probabilities of bill passage? Was the theme of the legislative session so contrary to your bill that enactment was already unlikely? Did that which seemed possible at the start of the session become impossible due to forces beyond your lobbyist's control?

- Do you want to work with your lobbyist next year? If you don't have a positive emotional connection with your lobbyist, then get a new one. If you had a great emotional connection but the lobbyist spent more time lobbying you to stay on the payroll than in the capital, then get a new one. If you feel you and your lobbyist can have a mutually beneficial relationship with some adjustments, then keep your lobbyist.

As emphasized in Chapter 4, firing your lobbyist is a drastic step that suggests you didn't hire well initially. Nevertheless, you cannot let yourself be captive to a contractor. If you have a relationship that is salvageable, then use advice from *Insiders Talk* to fix it. Finally, if you want to fire your lobbyist, *never do it during the session* because that will make you appear unstable to the legislature and your capitol players. The least controversial way to fire is to simply not to rehire the lobbyist next session.

JUST BECAUSE YOUR BILL DIDN'T PASS DOESN'T MEAN YOU FAILED

Failure to see bill enactment in a session does not mean you or your lobbyist failed. This is why *Insiders Talk: Winning with Lobbyists, Professional edition* includes job performance checklists for both you and your contract lobbyist that evaluate lobbying success by more than bill enactment. You may have done exceedingly well under the circumstances described in Chapter 2, section *Assessing Political Strength*.

Bills die much more frequently than they pass. For the first half of 2016, "19.3% of state Senate bills and 13.3% of state House bills are enacted on average compared with 3.6% and 1.9% of US Senate and House bills respectively."[144] Smaller states have higher enactment rates.[145] Larger states have lower enactment rates. For example, during Florida's 2018 session 1,654 general bills were filed, of which 166 passed both chambers, for a ten percent rate. As illustration for the infrequency of hard kills, the Florida House and Senate had 1 and 5 unfavorable reports, respectively.[146]

You have been successful if you generated momentum and interest in your bill. A bill often takes years of lobbying before it becomes law. Your efforts in the first year likely built a foundation of relationships and momentum that will move you forward in the next year or later sessions.

If your bill did not pass, send a short note of thanks to lawmakers, associations, and others that interacted with you. Tell your supporters that you will be back next year and that you hope they will again help you. To those lawmakers who did not support your bill, politely and briefly restate your case for adoption, why it's good for the lawmaker, district, and state, and make clear you hope to satisfy their concerns next year.

Whether your bill passed or not, thank the members of your association who participated in the lobbying effort. Recognize the accomplishments of key person(s) in your association who worked on behalf of the bill. If they served at their employers' directions, compliment them in a thank you note written to the employers.

EVALUATIONS

Next, complete internal and external evaluations of the effectiveness of your main sponsor and co-sponsors, consultants including contract lobbyists, and all persons inside and outside of your association who worked on the bill. Consider:

1. If your bill did not pass, do you still need the benefit the bill would have brought?

2. For an *ad hoc* association, should you keep it for another year or form a new one? For a permanent association, are you the best group to lobby or should you form a new association or internal sub-group? Do smaller members feel their interests were devalued because the association is more interested in those paying higher dues?

3. Should a different organization take the lead in lobbying the issue next year?

4. How did your association interact with your members, member companies, or member organizations? Did you coordinate efforts well or did their legislative activities conflict with yours?

5. Was your communication effective with your members, allies, lawmakers, staff, opponents, and media?

6. How well did you work with your supporters? Did each of you follow through on commitments to each other? Would you want an alliance with them again next year?

7. How well did you work with your opponents? Could you have handled their opposition better and, if so, how?

8. Could you develop a bill that you and your opponents might be able to support next session?

9. Did you make any new enemies? If you did, what is their significance? Did you amend your concepts onto someone else's bill that caused it to stall or be defeated? Did you anger one or more lawmakers or staffs? If so, try to heal relationships off-session.

10. Was your sponsor effective? Do you want to work with the same sponsor next year or should another legislator be approached for sponsorship? Would your sponsor want to sponsor the bill again? Would he or she release "ownership" of the bill to another lawmaker?

11. Which lawmakers surprised you as supporters or as opponents?

12. How did the Governor or executive agencies impact your effort? Can you obtain their support in the future?

13. How effective were your negotiations?

14. What additional help could you have used?

15. What would you have done differently? Does any single event

stand out as the turning point in the failure of your bill? How did you respond to this event and how could you have responded better?

16. What will your internal association politics be next year?
17. Will there be enough member consensus and commitment to try again?
18. Do next year's capitol politics look promising?
19. Is your management prepared to continue investing time, money, and political capital in your legislative project?

As to point 10 above, when pulling a bill from an ineffective sponsor try to gain his or her acquiescence. Your sponsor may have invested time, effort, ego, and political capital in your bill. That investment must both be acknowledged and *effusively* appreciated. To just jerk the bill away would be insulting and provoke the lawmaker's animosity. As mentioned earlier, a *Lobby School* participant told the story of her organization replacing an ineffective sponsor. The spurned sponsor turned into an enemy making sure the bill henceforth died each time it was subsequently introduced.

EXECUTIVE AGENCY RULEMAKING

In Chapter 1 we first mentioned the three venues in which an agency impacts you, the first two being before the legislature and with the Governor. Here we touch upon the third, that is, the agency in its role as sole implementer. This is because, for all practical purposes,

- You don't have a law until the regulatory agency charged with implementing your law tells you that you have a law.
- You don't know what your law means until the agency tells you what it means.

They do both by rulemaking and enforcement.

While constitutions authorize lawmakers to enact legislation and appropriate state money, they can implement nothing. Implementation of laws belongs solely to the executive branch and its agencies, of which the net result is, that agencies give and take away by rulemaking and enforcement.

Rulemaking. Expect that for every page of legislative law – which tends to be broad – agencies will make another ten pages of highly detailed agency law, that is, rules. And their rules are every bit as much law as are laws enacted by the legislature.

Agencies have great discretion in implementing legislation. At their pleasure, they can declare they have no intention of implementing your law and they are going to allow your hard-won appropriation to revert back to the general fund.

Or the agency can adopt rules that impose upon you demands that clearly go beyond the authority they have in the legislation authorizing them to regulate you. This is called an *ultra vires* action, that is, "beyond the powers."

Or they may enter into rulemaking to implement paragraph one of your law this year, and next year they will enter into rulemaking to implement paragraph two. Except in a clear recalcitrance of duty, it's all up to them and there is little anyone can do about what they choose to do, or not do.

Enforcement. They can also adopt rules and then not enforce those same rules. By doing this, the agency effectively vetoes the legislature because agency non-enforcement in effect nullifies the statute, making meaningless your legislative victory.

Because agencies can take away your legislative win, you have to defend your win. Opponents may lobby the agency to take away your legislative win by convincing the agency not to adopt implementing rules, or not enforce the rules they do adopt, or adopt rules that no one ever could have dreamed were authorized by your law. Or you may do the same thing to take away your opponent's win.

You may also lobby the agency to give you what the legislature would not give you. If you can show the agency that it has the legal authority to do more for you than the legislature authorized in the law it adopted or refused to adopt, then this becomes a possibility. For example, authority to do some of what you want may be found in another statute or in another existing agency rule.

Agency power to give and take away has been federal law since the 1984 U.S. Supreme Court in *Chevron USA v. Natural Resources Defense Council* established judicial deference to agency interpretations of law and by extension application thereof.[147]A number of U.S. states have adopted *Chevron's* guidance, although many more have not.[148] However, recent appeals court decisions may suggest a gradual thinning of *Chevron* judicial deference to agency interpretations.[149, 150]

SUMMARY CHAPTER 9

Getting a favorable report from the committee of first referral is an indispensable first step to getting your idea into law. However, further steps must be accomplished before *sine die*. Leadership's intentions toward your bill, how well it was written, concurrent legislation, and amendments will speed up or slow down your bill's race to the Governor's desk to be done before time expires. If your bill became law, begin a gratitude campaign thanking all those who played a part in your success, including giving your lobbyist a bonus. If you got an unfavorable committee report from the CFR then expect your bill is dead.

Evaluate how well you did, what your mistakes were, and what you will do next year. However, if you are at the end of the first year of the legislative session and your bill is still alive, you may have the advantage of *carry over*.[151] In either case, estimate the likelihood of moving your bill the second year and begin lobbying immediately after lawmakers have had time to rest after the first year. After completing the above evaluation ask yourself again, "Is a bill still necessary?" If the answer is, "Yes" then ask, "Do we want to try again?" If the answer to this second question is "Yes," then go to the beginning of this book and start the process again. This time, however, you will be an experienced lobbyist(s) who will know how to lobby your bill into law.

Finally, you don't have a law until the agency tells you that you have a law. You don't know what the law means until they tell you what it means. They do this through rulemaking and rule enforcement. Expect you must lobby one or more executive agencies to defend your legislative win, take away your opponent's win, and otherwise advance your interests.

IRS LOBBYING GUIDANCE TO 501(C)(3), IRC ORGANIZATIONS

Editor's Note: The following letter provides guidance to charitable organizations considering lobbying lawmakers, including your state legislators. The letter makes clear that 501(c)(3) organizations may advocate their issues before legislatures and executive agencies and still preserve their tax-exempt status. Contact your legal counsel for the applicability of this letter to your associations lobbying efforts.

DEPARTMENT OF THE TREASURY
INTERNAL REVENUE SERVICE
WASHINGTON, D.C. 20224

JUN 26 2000

Charity Lobbying in the Public Interest,
a Project of Independent Sector
2040 S Street, NW
Washington, DC 20009

Dear Sir or Madam:

This is in response to a letter, dated April 18, 2000, submitted on your behalf by your attorneys, in which you request information on questions related to lobbying by publicly supported charitable organizations recognized as exempt from federal income tax because they are described in section 501(c)(3) of the Internal Revenue Code. Your questions and our responses are set forth below.

1. **Is lobbying by section 501(c)(3) organizations permissible under federal tax laws?** Yes (except for private foundations under most circumstances).

2. **How much lobbying may a "public charity" (a section 501 (c) (3) organization other than a private foundation or an organization testing for public safety) conduct?** There are two sets of rules, and with the exception of churches, public charities can choose which set to follow. One rule is that no substantial part of the organization's activities can be lobbying. The alternative rule, that an organization must affirmatively elect, provides for sliding scales (up to $1,000,000 on total lobbying and up to $250,000 on grass roots lobbying) that can be spent on lobbying. (The scales are based on a percentage of the organization's exempt purpose expenditures.)

3. **What are the advantages and disadvantages of the two options?** Organizations covered by the "no substantial part" rule are not subject to any specific dollar-base limitation. However, few definitions exist under this standard as to what activities constitute lobbying, and difficult-to-value factors, such as volunteer time, are involved. Organizations seeking clear and more definite rules covering this area may wish to avail themselves of the election. By electing the optional sliding scale, an organization can take advantage of specific, narrow definitions of lobbying and clear dollar-based safe harbors that generally permit significantly more lobbying than the "no substantial part" rule. However, as noted above, there are ceilings (unadjusted for inflation) on the amount of funds that can be spent on lobbying. Thus, these dollar limits should be considered when making the election.

4. **How does a public charity elect? May an election be revoked?** The organization files a simple, one-page Form 5768 with the Internal Revenue Service. The election only needs to be made once. It can be revoked by filing a second Form 5768, noting the revocation.

5. **Does making the election expose the organization to an increased risk of an audit?** No. The Internal Revenue Manual specifically informs our examination personnel that making the election will not be a basis for initiating an examination.

6. **Does the Internal Revenue Code allow public charities that receive federal grant funds and contracts to lobby with their private funds?** Yes. However, while it is not a matter of federal tax law, it should be noted that charities should be careful not to use federal grant funds for lobbying except where authorized to do so.

7. **May private foundations make grants to public charities that lobby?** Yes, so long as the grants are not earmarked for lobbying and are either (1) general purpose grants, or (2) specific project grants that meet the requirements of section 53.4945- 2(a)(6) of the Foundation Excise Tax Regulations.

8. **May section 501(c)(3) organizations educate voters during a political campaign?** Yes. However, organizations should be careful that their voter education efforts do not constitute support or opposition to any candidate.

9. **May public charities continue to lobby incumbent legislators even though the legislators are running for reelection?** Yes. Charities should be careful, however, to avoid any reference to the reelection campaign in their lobbying efforts.

If you have any further questions, please feel free to contact me at (202) 283–9472, or John F. Reilly, Identification Number 50–05984, of my office at (202)283–8971.

Sincerely,
Thomas J. Miller
Manager, Exempt Organizations Technical
cc: Mr. Thomas A. Troyar
Caplin & Drysdale, Chartered
1 Thomas Cir., N.W.,
Washington, D.C. 20005

cc: Mr. Marcus S. Owens

Caplin & Drysdale, Chartered
2005 Thomas Cir., N.W.
Washington, D.C. 20005

SUGGESTED LOBBYING VISIT LEAVE-BEHIND

Leave-Behind Template: laminated and on colored paper. This facilitates an imme-diate staff generated cost-benefit calculation as to why supporting your request is good for lawmaker, district, and state overall.

XYZ Association Requests____ (lawmaker name) **Support**____ (bill name, number, sponsors' names, to accomplish specific action, e.g., *Fund Expansion of Hwy. #1 in district.*)

Presented by:
_____ (constituents' names, titles, entities in the district represented, contact info)
_____ (lobbyist's or association staff name, title, organization, contact info)

1. (XYZ or current law) benefited ____ (areas in district) **during** ____ (past 2–4 years) **by:**
_____ (what your group did specifically benefiting the district)
_____ (specific groups within district you benefited)
_____ (value in dollars of benefits to the district)

2. (XYZ or future law) will benefit ____ (lawmaker's district) _____ (next 2–4 years) **by:**
_____ (this wonderful thing for the lawmaker's constituents)
_____ (benefit to named groups or businesses within the district)

____ (putting this number of dollars into the district)
____ (implementing key promise lawmaker made last election)

3. Your support will benefit (state name, subdivisions in state) **by:**
_____ (dollars and services) _____

_____

4. (XYZ or bill) is supported by:
____ (names of groups on record as supporting the lawmaker)
____ (names of state groups that generally support the lawmaker)
____ (names of key supportive constituents or groups within the district)
____ (names of lawmaker(s) liked by your lawmaker)

5. (XYZ or bill) is opposed by:
____

____

**6. Estimated cost to state is: $_____ resulting in a net benefit: cost ratio
of ____:____.**

7. Please support _____ (action, bill number, sponsor's name)
For more information please contact ____ (name) ____ at (telephone &
email)

(Back page)

Name of Contact:
Name of Association:
Address:
Telephone:
Email:
Webpage:
(Purpose of association in two sentences or less.)
(Connection to lawmaker's district historically or prospectively.)
(2–3 sentence narrative explaining why your bill will benefit the district and
state.)

ABOUT THE AUTHOR

Robert L. Guyer has been involved in lobbying since 1990 working for a number of major corporations and industry associations. Since 2000 his *Lobby School* has trained thousands of advocates in effective lobbying skills. The *Lobby School* offers online, public and private seminars, as well as state of the art lobbying manuals and books. You may learn more about him, the *Lobby School*, and his writings at www.lobbyschool.com or contact him at rlguyer@lobbyschool.com.

ENDNOTES

1   Tommy Neal, "Learning the Game," *National Conference of State Legislatures* (June 26, 2018) http://www.ncsl.org/research/about-state-legislatures/learning-the-game.aspx.

2   "Idaho's Citizen Legislature," *Idaho Legislature* (accessed October 27, 2018) https://legislature.idaho.gov/resources/citizenlegislature.

3   "When the legislative and executive powers are united in the same person, or in the same body of magistrates, there can be no liberty; because apprehensions may arise, lest the same monarch or senate should enact tyrannical laws, to execute them in a tyrannical manner." "Modern History Sourcebook: Montesquieu: The Spirit of the Laws, 1748," *Fordham University* (accessed November 7, 2018) https://sourcebooks.fordham.edu/mod/montesquieu-spirit.asp.

4   "From Thomas Jefferson to Edward Carrington, 16 January 1787," *Founders Online* (accessed November 7, 2018) https://founders.archives.gov/documents/Jefferson/01-11-02-0047.

5   Hope Eastman, *Lobbying: A Constitutionally Protected Right* (Washington: American Enterprise Institute for Public Policy Research, 1977), quoting *Stromberg v. California*, 283 U.S. 359,

243

369 (1931), 1.

6   Edgar Lane, *Lobbying and the Law* (Berkley: University of California Press, 1964), 3.

7   Lane, 4.

8   Lane, 4.

9   Lane, 8.

10   Lane, 179.

11   Jack Davies, *Legislative Law and Process* (Thomson-West Publishing, Co., 1986), 4.

12   Davies, 5.

13   The Senate average includes Nebraska's entire 49-member legislature. The House average excludes New Hampshire's 400 House members.

14   John L. Zorack, *The Lobbying Handbook* (Washington, D.C.: Professional Lobbying and Consulting Center, 1990), 762.

15   "The 50 State Project," *CQ Roll Call* (March 2015), 5.

16   Mid-Atlantic lobbyist, email communication with author, July 10, 2019.

17   Doug Mann of Littlejohn and Mann, Tallahassee, Florida delineated these classes of lobbyists during his 2002 guest lecture to my graduate class at Florida State University.

18   Kleinheider, "A Republican In The Legislature Only: House GOP Votes To Keep Williams," *Nashville Post* (March 11 2009) https://www.nashvillepost.com/business/blog/20417669/a-republican-in-the-legislature-only-house-gop-votes-to-keep-williams.

19   Suzanne Weiss, "Birds of a Feather," *State Legislatures Magazine* (October 26, 2015) http://www.ncsl.org/legislators-staff/legis-

lators/legislative-leaders/birds-of-a-feather.aspx.

20   Robert L. Guyer, *Insiders Talk: Winning with Lobbyists, Professional edition* (Gainesville, Florida: Engineering THE LAW, Inc., 2018), 296.

21   "Legislative Caucuses in Texas," *The Texas Politics Project* (accessed October 18, 2019) https://texaspolitics.utexas.edu/archive/html/leg/features/0300_01/slide1.html.

22   Suzanne Weiss.

23   0 votes - "Lots of luck for Republican as Virginia election tie settled by random draw," *The Guardian* (January 4, 2018) https://www.theguardian.com/us-news/2018/jan/04/virginia-election-tie-drawing-lots-republican; Chris Mills Rodrigo, "Recount puts Republican ahead by 1 vote in Alaska state House race," *The Hill* (December 1, 2018) https://thehill.com/homenews/campaign/419260-recount-gives-gop-a-win-in-alaska-state-house-race-by-1-vote; 28 votes - Ramona Giwargis, "Recount confirms Pickard as winner of Nevada Senate race," *Las Vegas Review-Journal* (November 26, 2018) https://www.reviewjournal.com/news/politics-and-government/nevada/recount-confirms-pickard-as-winner-of-nevada-senate-race-1536022; 7 votes - Thomas Nelson, "Recount shows House District 55 race goes to Bergan," *The Courier* (November 28, 2018) https://wcfcourier.com/news/local/govt-and-politics/recount-shows-house-district-race-goes-to-bergan/article_c5ae48cc-191c-5180-86c5-0df846ebcf07.html.

24   "The Power of Associations," *American Society of Association Executives* (updated January 2015) https://www.thepowerofa.org/wp-content/uploads/2012/03/PowerofAssociations-2015.pdf.

25   "Types of Non-Profits," *Charity Navigator* (April 6, 2016) https://www.charitynavigator.org/index.cfm?bay=content.view&cpid=1559.

26   ASAE.

27   Jeremy Koulish, "There are a lot of 501(c)(4) nonprofit organizations. Most are not political," *The Urban Institute* (May 24, 2013)
https://www.urban.org/urban-wire/there-are-lot-501c4-non-
profit-organizations-most-are-not-political.

28   "501(c)(5)," *Ballotpedia* (accessed March 14, 2019) https://ballot-
pedia.org/501(c)(5).

29   "Frequently Asked Questions," *Small Business Administration
Office of Advocacy* (September 2012) https://www.sba.gov/sites/
default/files/FAQ_Sept_2012.pdf.

30   ASAE.

31   Aaron Martin, "How Cities Can Influence State Legislatures," *Connectivity, Congressional Quarterly* (November 27,
2015)   https://info.cq.com/resources/how-cities-can-influ-
ence-state-legislatures/.

32   Christian Britschgi, "Local Governments Spend Big on Lobbyists," *Reason* (August 8, 2017) https://reason.com/2017/08/08/
local-governments-spend-big-on-lobbyists/.

33   Chuck DeVore, "Government Spends Millions to Lobby Government," *Texas Public Policy Foundation* (September 29, 2018)
https://www.texaspolicy.com/government-spends-millions-to-
lobby-government-time-to-end-the-practice/.

34   "According to Madison and those whose progressive values he
reflected, the inculcation of virtue was too unreliable a foundation upon which to rest the new nation's governance. In fact,
according to the logic of Madison's plan for controlling the people through elite imposition, local moral majorities were to be
prevented from inculcating morality. Indeed, it was exactly such
actions that Madison hoped to control through extending the
size of the republic and national control over moral police. At
every structural level of his plan of government, be it the control
over the people or one branch of government over another, it was

self-interest that was to be in control, not the virtue of Christian or pagan apologists." Barry Shain, "Self-Interest Versus Virtue - Conservatism and America's Divided Inheritance," *The Philadelphia Society*, Regional Meeting, Williamsburg, Virginia, (October 4, 2003) https://phillysoc.org/shain-self-interest-versus-virtue-conservatism-and-americas-divided-inheritance/.

35   Professional: "Person formally certified by a professional body of belonging to a specific profession by virtue of having completed a required course of studies and/or practice. And whose competence can usually be measured against an established set of standards. "Professional," *Business Dictionary* (accessed August 21, 2019) http://www.businessdictionary.com/definition/professional.html.

36   Mid-Atlantic lobbyist.

37   "Types of Tax Exempt Organizations," *Internal Revenue Service* (June 22, 2018) https://www.irs.gov/charities-non-profits/types-of-tax-exempt-organizations.

38   Nayantara Mehta, "Nonprofits and Lobbying Yes, They Can!," *American Bar Association,* Volume 18, Number 4 March/April 2009, https://apps.americanbar.org/buslaw/blt/2009-03-04/mehta.shtml.

39   Marcia Avner, *The Lobbying and Advocacy Handbook for Nonprofit Organizations* (Amherst H. Wilder Foundation, 2002), 121. Ms. Avner was public policy director for the Minnesota Council of Nonprofits.

40   *Compliance Guide for 501(c)(3) Charities*, Publication 4221-PC (Rev. 3-2018) Catalog Number 49829R, Department of the Treasury Internal Revenue Service (accessed October 22, 2019) www.irs.gov.

41   This letter is still good guidance per David L. Thompson, National Council of Nonprofits, email to author, November 9, 2018. Other great information on charity lobbying can be found

through the National Council of Nonprofits (accessed October 26, 2018) https://www.councilofnonprofits.org/everyday-advocacy.

42   I was appointed the Bill Manager working 90 percent of my time on behalf of the association. My salary and travel expenses were trivial in comparison to the huge financial benefits that would accrue were we successful; and we were. Two other association members appointed their staffs to chair pretty much full-time the technical committee and the public relations committee, respectively.

43   "A handful of states have statutes that prohibit agencies from using public funds to retain a lobbyist. This could mean that agencies have no designated representative to communicate with the legislature, but often this means that an agency may only use full-time employees in dealing with the legislative branch." "50 State Chart: Limitations on Public Funds for Lobbying," *National Conference of State Legislatures*, (August 13, 2019) http://www.ncsl.org/research/ethics/50-state-chart-limits-on-public-funds-to-lobby.aspx.

44   "A Company's Basic Guide to Lobbying in Florida," *Carlton Fields Jorden Burt, P.A.* (July 24, 2012) https://www.carlton-fields.com/a-companys-basic-guide-to-lobbying-in-florida/.

45   Beth L.Leech, *Lobbyists at Work* (New York: Apress, 2013) Kindle edition.

46   "From wartime. Literally, 'Don't reveal even the location of a loved one on a ship, because the location could be communicated to the enemy by a spy.'" "Loose lips sink ships," *The Free Dictionary* (accessed January 10, 2018) https:// idioms.thefreedictionary.com/Loose+lips+sink+ships.

47   "'Isn't That the Trump Lawyer?': A Reporter's Accidental Scoop," *The New York Times* (September 19, 2017) https://www.nytimes.com/2017/09/19/us/politics/isnt-that-the-trump-lawyer-a-reporters-accidental-scoop.html.

48   This section is based primarily on a *Lobby School* survey of 31 lob-
      byists across the United States, with additional data from litera-
      ture, and Kevin Cate's poll of Florida legislative aides, "Florida
      Legislative Study 2018," *Catecomm* (accessed March 15, 2019)
      https://catecomm.com/legislativestudy/.

49   Cate. "Assuming a legislator doesn't have a firm opinion on an
      issue, how likely is he/she to be influenced by these methods?"

50   Ryan J. Foley, "Should public officials' private messages be a
      part of the public record?" *Christian Science Monitor* (AP) (July
      23, 2018) https://www.csmonitor.com/Technology/2018/0723/
      Should-public-officials-private-messages-be-a-part-of-the-pub-
      lic-record.

51   Jeb Ory, "How Social Media Has Changed Advocacy," *Phone-
      2Action* (June 27, 2017) https://goo.gl/Qn2NTd.

52   Nathan Sykes, "Weaponized social media is frightening and
      its happening more often," *TechTalks* (September 13, 2018)
      https://bdtechtalks.com/2018/09/13/weaponized-social-me-
      dia-how-protect-yourself/.

53   Lobby School participant, email to author RE: Social Media
      (October 31, 2017).

54   Joe Berkowitz, "Study confirms, Twitter is not real life," *Fast Com-
      pany* (April 24, 2019) https://www.fastcompany.com/90339526/
      study-confirms-twitter-is-not-real-life.

55   "To take a statement with 'a grain of salt' (or 'a pinch of salt')
      means to accept it while maintaining a degree of skepticism (sic)
      [ed. note - this is also a correct spelling] about its truth." *The
      Phrase Finder* (accessed March 27, 2019) https://www.phrases.
      org.uk/meanings/take-with-a-grain-of-salt.html.

56   Janet Burns, "How Many Social Media Users Are Real People?"
      Gizmodo (June 4, 2018) https://gizmodo.com/how-many-social-
      media-users-are-real-people-1826447042.

57   Burns.

58   Kurt Wagner and Rani Molla, "Facebook has disabled almost 1.3 billion fake accounts over the past six months," *Recode* (May 15, 2018) https://www.recode.net/2018/5/15/17349790/facebook-mark-zuckerberg-fake-accounts-content-policy-update.

59   Lobby School participant, email to author RE: Social Media (November 1, 2017).

60   Karl Kurtz, "Who We Elect: The Demographics of State Lawmakers," *National Conference of State Legislatures* (December 1, 2018) http://www.National Conference of State Legislatures.org/research/about-state-legislatures/who-we-elect.aspx.

61   Duncan L. Kennedy, *Bill Drafting,* (1958) apparently self-published.

62   Robert L. Guyer and Dean Griffith, "Succeeding in the State Legislature," *American Physical Therapy Association PT Magazine* Vol. 9 No. 3 (March 2001) quoting Jim Leahy, APTA Connecticut lobbyist, 46.

63   Chris Micheli, Principal, Aprea & Micheli, Inc., e-mail communication to author October 19, 2019.

64   Stateside Associates (accessed November 9, 2018) https://www.stateside.com/lobbyist-referrals.

65   MultiState Associations (accessed November 9, 2018) https://www.multistate.us/.

66   Donald E. deKieffer, *The Citizen's Guide to Lobbying Congress* (Chicago: Chicago Review Press, 1977), 68.

67   Alan Rosenthal, *The Third House: Lobbyists and Lobbying in the States* (Washington, D.C.: CQ Press, 2001), 241.

68   Guyer and Griffith, 46.

69   State and Federal Communications, Inc. (accessed May 28,

2019) https://www.stateandfed.com/.

70   CO Rev Stat § 24-6-308 (2016).

71   Joint Rule 36(b)(8), "Lobbying Practices, Lobbyist Laws and Rules Fiscal Year 2018-2019," *Colorado Secretary of State* https://www.sos.state.co.us/pubs/lobby/files/LobbyistLawsRules.pdf.

72   "CHART 2-A: CONTRIBUTION AND SOLICITATION LIMITATIONS, *Federal Elections Commission* (accessed October 22, 2019) https://transition.fec.gov/pubrec/cfl/cfl98/chart2a.html.

73   When capitol players label an advocate *ill-informed*, that is, an *amateur*, both the advocate and by extension his or her organization are henceforth disrespected, disparaged, or dismissed. *Disrespect for the ill-informed* is a fundamental rule in most professions.

74   Sadly, this state later became second in the Unites States in opioid addiction. Margaret Renkl, "We're all addicts here," *The New York Times* (May 28, 2018) https://www.nytimes.com/2018/05/28/opinion/opioid-addiction-tennessee.html.

75   Ken Sande, *The Peacemaker* (Grand Rapids: Baker Books, 2004 and updated 2018).

76   "The 50 State Project," *CQ Roll Call* (March 2015).

77   Chester Karrass, "Glossary, " *Karrass* (accessed November 10, 2018) https://www.karrass.com/glossary/.

78   I negotiated with a few Washington, D.C. attorney-lobbyists who employed the principle: *The greatest motivator of human kind is the avoidance of pain.* Their "death by a thousand cuts" tactics by design made working with them so unpleasant that just to stop the pain the unwary will surrender almost anything. Several of the negotiation tricks herein I learned from them. While I never saw such tactics applied at the state level, nevertheless review these tricks to prepare your negotiators for the worst.

79　　"There is only one generalization about the legislative process in the 50 states that requires no disclaimer—every state does things differently than every other state. The lawmaking procedure is never precisely the same in all 50 states or, for that matter, in the legislative chambers of the same state." Tommy Neal, "Learning the Game," *National Conference of State Legislatures* (June 26, 2018)　　http://www.ncsl.org/research/about-state-legislatures/learning-the-game.aspx. In this chapter we employ commonalities. For example, the commonality is the committee has a chair. Depending on state procedurally the chair may be appointed by the chamber leader, other chamber officer, committee on committees, committee itself, secret floor ballot, or by seniority.

80　　The appointment process differs markedly among states. "The Selection of Committee Chairs," *National Conference of State Legislatures* (May 27, 2009) http://www.ncsl.org/research/about-state-legislatures/the-selection-of-committee-chairs.aspx.

81　　Chris Micheli.

82　　Ballotpedia lists 108 legislative positions for elected lawmakers. "Leadership positions in State Legislatures," *Ballotpedia* (accessed July 15, 2019) https://ballotpedia.org/Leadership_positions_in_state_legislatures.

83　　"Table of Legislative Ethics Committees," *National Conference of State Legislatures* (February 1, 2018) http://www.National Conference of State Legislatures.org/research/ethics/table-of-legislative-ethics-committees.aspx.

84　　These rules are not laws; therefore the Governor does not and cannot approve them. Were the Governor's signature needed for the rules to become effective, a "separation of powers" constitutional problem would arise.

85　　"Vote requirements," *National Conference of State Legislatures* (accessed July 25, 2019) http://www.ncsl.org/documents/legismgt/ILP/96Tab5Pt2.pdf, 5-7.

86   "Using *Mason's Manual of Legislative Procedure*: The Advantages
      to Legislative Bodies," *National Conference of State Legislatures*
      (accessed November 13, 2018) http://www.National Confer-
      ence of State Legislatures.org/research/about-state-legislatures/
      masons-manual-for-legislative-bodies.aspx.

87   Jeremy B. White and Alexei Koseff, "How to Speak Like a Cap-
      itol Insider: Political Jargon Can Make State Politics Tough to
      Navigate," *Sacramento Bee* (August 16, 2015) http:// www.sacbee.
      com/news/politics-government/capitol-alert/   article31238789.
      html.

88   Jay Michael and Dan Walters with Dan Weintraub, *The Third
      House: Lobbyists, Money, and Power in Sacramento* (Berkeley, CA:
      Berkeley Public Policy Press, 2002), 141.

89   "Glossary of Legislative Terms," *National Conference of State
      Legislatures* (Feb. 26, 2016) http:// www.National Conference
      of State Legislatures.org/research/about-state-legislatures/glos-
      sary-of- legislative-terms.aspx.

90   Robert L. Guyer, *Insiders Talk: Glossary of Legislative Concepts
      and Representative Terms* (Gainesville: Engineering THE LAW
      Inc., 2019) www.lobbyschool.com.

91   In instances when the legality of a proposal is at issue, the state
      attorney general or the legislature's in-house legal counsel may
      have rendered an opinion on the legality of proposed legislation,
      which opinion may be reviewed by advocates in determining
      action to take on a bill.

92   Violet Baffour, "The Fiscal Note Process in State Legisla-
      tures," *North Carolina General Assembly, Fiscal Research Division*
      (accessed December 7, 2018) http://www.National Conference
      of State Legislatures.org/documents/fiscal/FiscalNoteProcess.
      pdf.

93   Conservation of legislative resources has created several ways to
      streamline compliance with the three-readings rule. For exam-

ple, in some jurisdictions bills placed on the consent calendar need not be read three times or publication in the chamber's journal may constitute first reading.

94 Any member may object to a bill on first reading by raising the question to the chamber of whether the bill should be rejected. A bill may be rejected if its subject matter is inappropriate for legislative consideration or for procedural error. If the question is rejected, then the bill is referred to committee(s) for detailed consideration.

95 The presiding officer, chamber clerk or secretary, or Rules or other committee refers bills to committees, called *committees of referral*. The first committee of referral is the committee with subject matter jurisdiction over the bill.

96 These are called "joint," "double," "multiple," or "split" referrals. In a joint referral, each committee is given jurisdiction over the same bill. In double or multiple referrals, one committee finishes with a bill and then sends it to another, and so on. The referral may be split, in which case, the bill is divided among two or more committees, each committee having jurisdiction over part of the bill. A split referral may require two or more committees to find time to meet together as a single group to consider the bill. This may be difficult to schedule. Referral to too many committees promises that time will surely expire before all of them can consider the bill.

97 As to whether your state's caucus is opened of closed, see: Legislative Organization, Table 99-2.11 "Openness of the Majority Caucus Meetings," *National Conference of State Legislatures* (accessed November 1, 2018) http://www.National Conference of State Legislatures.org/documents/legismgt/ILP/99Tab2Pt3.pdf, 2-43. *Lobby School* participants have reported to me that the NCSL table, which relied on chamber *self-reporting*, incorrectly lists open caucuses which are in fact closed.

98 Generally, a local bill, a bill reported unanimously by a committee without amendment, and non-controversial bills are eligi-

ble for entry onto the consent calendar. In practice, the consent calendar works because it is requested only for demonstrably non-controversial matters. The chamber's members are advised and polled to make sure that there will be no objection. Bills on consent may not be amended.

99   Committee recommendations for amendments are accepted almost all of the time. This is a major reason why your main lobbying goal will be to get a favorable recommendation out of the committee(s) of referral, especially the CFR.

100 Some chambers use the Committee of the Whole. Many states do not use it at all, or it may be an informal meeting of legislators who just show up. In a state, one chamber may use it while the sister chamber does not.

101 The bill goes to the Rules Committee before going to third reading. Various jurisdictions have different titles for the Rules Committee, such as Calendar Committee, Rules and Calendar Committee, Committee on the Third Reading, Committee on Rules, or Joint Rules and Resolutions. This committee ensures the constitutionality and legality of bills before the entire chamber considers the bill. It or leadership schedules bills for second and third readings.

102 The party whip ensures caucus members vote as instructed by the caucus. Leadership doesn't want the embarrassment and loss of chamber productivity that would come from calling up bills that polling shows are going to die. Both in committees and on second reading problems with the bill should have been identified and fixed.

103 As mentioned earlier, generally chambers can adjust procedural rules to facilitate progress.

104 This problem would be fixed in conference with either one bill's extraneous language stripped out or the other bill's extraneous language added to produce one bill.

105 "Conference Committees," *National Conference of State Legislatures* (accessed November 23, 2018) http://www.National Conference of State Legislatures.org/documents/legismgt/ ILP/96Tab4Pt3.pdf, 4-39.

106 The Governor *actively* approves the bill by signing it into law. *Passive* approval may occur in states where a bill becomes law when the Governor fails to act on the bill within a given time period. Of course for completeness sake, we recall he or she can veto the bill.

107 *Comity* is the mutual respect and deference given by one political branch to the lawful actions taken by another co-equal branch.

108 For example, the Florida Legislature, in part upset over Governor Charlie Crist leaving the Republican party to run for the U.S. Senate as an independent, had a veto spree and for the first time in 12 years overrode gubernatorial vetoes. Robin Marty, "Florida Legislature Does Massive Veto Override – Ultrasound Bill Untouched," *Rewire.News* (November 19, 2010) https:// rewire.news/article/2010/11/19/florida-legislator-does-massive-veto-override-ultrasound-bill-untouched/.

109 "Forty state constitutions contain a provision that requires a bill to address or contain a single subject. In Mississippi, germaneness is implied, but a single subject requirement is not specifically stated in the constitution. No specific single subject provision is set forth by the constitutions in Arkansas, Connecticut, Maine, Massachusetts, New Hampshire, North Carolina, Ohio, Rhode Island and Vermont." "Germaneness Requirements," *National Conference of State Legislatures* (accessed July25, 2019) http://www.ncsl.org/research/about-state-legislatures/germaneness-requirements.aspx.

110 "Press-gang, verb (used with object): 1) to force (a person) into military or naval service. 2) to coerce (a person) into taking a certain action, political stand, etc.: to be press- ganged into endorsing a candidate." *Dictionary.com* (accessed November 2, 2018) https://www.dictionary.com/browse/press-gang.

111   "We must, indeed, all hang together, or most assuredly we shall all hang separately." Benjamin Franklin, "Franklin's Contributions to the American Revolution as a Diplomat in France," *U.S. History.org* (accessed November 13, 2018) http://www.ushistory.org/valleyforge/history/franklin.html.

112   "Germaneness Requirements," *National Conference of State Legislatures.*

113   Harvey J. Tucker, "The Use of Consent Calendars on American State Legislatures," *Journal of the American Society of Legislative Clerks and Secretaries* Vol. 11, No. 1 Fall 2005, http://www.National Conference of State Legislatures.org/Portals/1/documents/aslcs/Jrn2005_Fall.pdf,19.

114   For example, in one state the first regular session may consider any topic, while the second regular session is limited to Governor's legislation, legislation submitted by citizen initiative, emergency legislation, and legislation flowing from legislatively authorized studies.

115   For the legislature to call itself into session, a supermajority of each house is required. During sessions called by the legislature, members may consider any matters they wish. During sessions called by the Governor the legislature may meet only to consider the items listed in the proclamation or those items added by a supermajority of the legislature. Generally, there is no legal limit to the number of special sessions that may be called.

116   "Inside the Legislative Process: Legislative party caucuses," *National Conference of State Legislatures* (accessed April 15, 2019) http://www.ncsl.org/documents/legismgt/ILP/99Tab2Pt3.pdf.

117   "How States Define Lobbying and Lobbyist," *National Conference of State Legislatures* (December 3, 2018) http://www.National Conference of State Legislatures.org/research/ethics/50-state-chart-lobby-definitions.aspx.

118   "Overview-Lobbyist Regulation," *National Conference of State*

Legislatures (accessed November 13, 2018) http://www.National Conference of State Legislatures.org/research/ethics/lobby-ist-regulation.aspx.

119   "A person who is listed by a principal or public body on a regis-tration form pursuant to section 41-1232 or 41-1232.01 as a lob-byist for compensation, designated lobbyist or designated public lobbyist shall... read a handbook containing statutes and rules governing lobbyists for compensation, designated lobbyists and designated public lobbyists, written guidelines and forms and samples for completing the lobbyist disclosure forms." *Lobbyist registration; handbook*, A.R.S. section 41-1232.05 (A).

120   Staffing levels vary among the states. These levels range from no personal staff to having several full-time personal staff; from having one part-time committee clerical staff to hav-ing several full-time clerical and professional staffs. "Size of Legislative Staff," *National Conference of State Legislatures* (October 2, 2018) http://www.National Conference of State Legislatures.org/research/about-state-legislatures/staff-change-chart-1979-1988-1996-2003-2009.aspx.

121   Chamber staffs: Chambers employ a Clerk or Secretary, Ser-geant at Arms, and their assistants. Chamber staffs perform clerical functions, maintain order in the chamber, and complete other related duties. Computer support services, bill room, and a host of other offices are managed to enable the chamber to operate smoothly. You will be in regular contact with chamber staff. However, you will not lobby them as they are charged with being non-partisan functionaries. LSA staffs: Unlike personal and committee staffs who in larger states are appointed as much for their politics as support skills, legislatures have non-partisan offices to assist members and the chamber in technical matters. For example, LSA-Bill Drafting Services assists lawmakers as they draft bills and LSA-Office of Legislative Counsel ensures all bills are procedurally and legally correct. Other non-partisan offices of the legislature report objectively on the likely economic, environmental, social, and other impacts of proposed legislation.

Although it is unlikely you will work with them, your sponsor could still request they allow you to explain your bill.

122 *By Request*, "Glossary of Hawai'i Legislative Terms," *Hawaii Legislative Reference Bureau* (accessed July 26, 2019) http://lrbhawaii.org/reports/lglos.html.

123 Mid-Atlantic lobbyist.

124 "You can tell within minutes of meeting someone which of those fates [friends, partners, or strangers] the new relationship will have. You can tell by the enthusiasm with which you converse, the degree to which you share an interest, the spark of an idea that you both share. You don't have to state it. You'll feel it right away, and every result is fine." Joel Comm, "The 5 Things You Learn Within 3 Minutes of Meeting Someone New," *Inc.* (January 15, 2016) https://www.inc.com/joel-comm/the-5-things-you-learn-within-3-minutes-of-meeting-someone-new.html.

125 "The 50 State Project," 78-80.

126 Brenda Erickson, "Limiting Bill Introductions," *National Conference of State Legislatures* (June 2017) http://www.ncsl.org/research/about-state-legislatures/limiting-bill-introductions.aspx.

127 "Legislative Guide," *Iowa Legal Services Division* (December 2006) https://www.legis.iowa.gov/DOCS/Resources/gaguide.pdf, 30.

128 "Bills and Bill Processing - Referral of Bills," *National Conference of State Legislatures* (accessed November 19, 2018) http://www.National Conference of State Legislatures.org/documents/legismgt/ILP/96Tab3Pt3.pdf.

129 As of this writing, only Minnesota has a divided legislature, that is, each chamber is controlled by the other political party. Historically, divided legislatures are few.

130 "Bills may not be withdrawn after reference to committee." "Rule

18, Introduction and Printing of Bills," *General Operating Rules of the* [Pennsylvania] *House of Representatives* (accessed November 20, 2018) http://www.house.state.pa.us/rules/2011HouRules.htm.

131 "A motion to withdraw allows the sponsor of a measure before the Chamber to remove that measure from consideration." "Maryland General Assembly Explanation of Floor Motions and Legislative Actions," *Maryland General Assembly* (accessed November 20, 2018) http://mgaleg.maryland.gov/pubs-current/current-motions.pdf.

132 "Hail Mary pass: a long forward pass in football thrown into or near the end zone in a last-ditch attempt to score as time runs out—often used figuratively." "Hail Mary," *Merriam Webster* (accessed November 5, 2018) https://www.merriam-webster.com/dictionary/Hail%20Mary.

133 Rule 3, "Access to Senate Chamber and Rules of Senate Decorum," *Iowa Senate* (January 28, 2016) https://www.legis.iowa.gov/docs/publications/SDR/1037370.pdf.

134 Gary Marbut, "Attending public hearings on bills before the Montana Legislature" (accessed August 7, 2019) http://progun-leaders.org/Legislative%20Process/hearing.html. This site has two additional pages of good advice applicable beyond Montana, including legislative process, and how to read a bill.

135 "When 25 members of the House shall have signed the resolution, it shall be entered in the Journal and the title of the bill or resolution and the name of the committee to be discharged shall be printed on the calendar." Rule 53 (2011-2012), *General Operating Rules of the House of Representatives* (House Resolution 1, adopted January 4, 2011) http://www.house.state.pa.us/rules/2011HouRules.htm#53.

136 "A motion to discharge a committee from consideration of a bill or resolution may be filed with the Principal Clerk if accompanied by a petition signed by two-thirds of the members of the

Senate asking that the committee be discharged from further consideration of the bill or resolution." Rule 47.(b) *Permanent Rules of The Regular Sessions of The Senate 2017 General Assembly of North Carolina* (January 11, 2017) https://www.ncleg.net/Sessions/2017/Bills/Senate/PDF/S1v2.pdf.

137   Sam Bradsch, "'Kill Committees' Are the Graveyards and Safeguards of Colorado Politics," *Colorado Public Radio* (March 9, 2018) http://www.cpr.org/news/story/kill-committees-are-the-graveyards-and-safeguards-of-colorado-politics.

138   "Table 4: Conference Committee on Appropriations Bill(s)," *Minnesota Senate* (accessed January 11, 2019) https://www.senate.mn/committees/2015-2016/1007_Committee_on_Finance/Conference%20Committees%20on%20Appropriations.pdf.

139   "A free-conference committee is authorized to consider any portion of a bill, may add or delete provisions and report out an entirely new bill." *Insiders Talk: Glossary of Legislative Concepts and Representative Terms* (Gainesville: Engineering THE LAW, Inc., 2019), 24.

140   "State Legislative Policymaking in an Age of Political Polarization," *National Conference of State Legislatures* (February 2018) http://www.National Conference of State Legislatures.org/Portals/1/Documents/About_State_Legislatures/Partisanship_030818.pdf, 17.

141   "[I]f someone is fighting a rearguard action or mounting a rearguard action, they are trying very hard to prevent something from happening, even though it is probably too late for them to succeed." *Collins English Dictionary* (accessed January 9, 2019) https://www.collinsdictionary.com/us/dictionary/english/to-fight-a-rearguard-action.

142   Tommy Neal, "Learning the Game," *National Conference of State Legislatures* (June 26, 2018) http://www.ncsl.org/research/about-state-legislatures/learning-the-game.aspx.

143   "Veto overrides in state legislatures," *Ballotpedia* (November 13, 2018) https://ballotpedia.org/Veto_overrides_in_state_legislatures.

144   "State Legislatures vs. Congress: Which Is More Productive?," *Quora* (accessed April 2, 2019) https://www.quorum.us/data-driven-insights/state-legislatures-versus-congress-which-is-more-productive/176/.

145   Quora.

146   "Florida Legislature Regular Session-2018," *Florida Legislature* (accessed April 2, 2019) http://www.leg.state.fl.us/data/session/2018/citator/Daily/stats.pdf.

147   *Chevron U.S.A., Inc. v. Natural Resources Defense Council, Inc.*, 467 U.S. 837 (1984).

148   Aaron Saiger, "CHEVRON AND DEFERENCE IN STATE ADMINISTRATIVE LAW," *54 Fordham L. Rev. 555*, 585 (2014).

149   "Absent statutory ambiguity, however, agencies do not have the authority to decide what the law shall be. So when an agency invokes Chevron deference where it does not belong (because the relevant statutory text is not ambiguous), it is not deferring to Congress's exercise of legislative authority, but rather doing exactly the opposite—here, claiming for itself the power to grant or deny collective bargaining rights at particular workplaces. This is no hypothetical concern." *Voices for International Business and Education, Inc. v. NLRB*, United States Fifth Circuit, No. 17-60364 (September 21, 2018), Ho concurring.

150   "The government's argument shows how far Auer has come and will go if left unchecked by the courts. Under Auer, agencies possess immense power. Rather than simply enacting rules with the force of law, agencies get to decide what those rules mean, too. But just as a pitcher cannot call his own balls and strikes, an agency cannot trespass upon the court's province to 'say

what the law is.' Marbury v. Madison, 5 U.S. (1 Cranch) 137, 177 (1803). Auer nevertheless invites agencies into that province, with courts standing by as agencies 'say what the law is' for themselves. Perez v. Mortg. Bankers Ass'n, 135 S. Ct. 1199, 1215–22 (2015) (Thomas, J., concurring in the judgment). Not only that, but Auer incentivizes agencies to regulate "broadly and vaguely" and later interpret those regulations self-servingly, all at the expense of the regulated. Id. at 1212–13 (Scalia, J., concurring in the judgment); see also Sessions v. Dimaya, 138 S. Ct. 1204, 1223 (2018) (Gorsuch, J., concurring in part and concurring in the judgment) No. 17-5772 United States v. Havis Page 16 ("Vague laws invite arbitrary power.")." U.S. v. Jeffery Havis, United States Court Of Appeals For The Sixth Circuit, No. 17-5772 (October 22, 2018), Thapar concurring.

151 *Carryover* means that a bill that has not completed its race to the Governor's desk by *sine die* can continue its progress in the following year of the same legislative session. For greater detail on implementation of carryover see, Brenda Erickson, "To carry over or not," *National Conference of State Legislatures* (accessed April 2, 2019) http://www.ncsl.org/blog/2017/07/24/to-carry-over-or-not.aspx.

Index

www.ingramcontent.com/pod-product-compliance
Lightning Source LLC
Chambersburg PA
CBHW021853020426
42334CB00013B/310